ROUTLEDGE LIBRARY EDITIONS: LITERARY THEORY

Volume 25

UNFOLDING THE MIND

UNFOLDING THE MIND
The Unconscious in American Romanticism and Literary Theory

JEFFREY STEELE

Routledge
Taylor & Francis Group
LONDON AND NEW YORK

First published in 1987 by Garland Publishing, Inc.

This edition first published in 2017
by Routledge
2 Park Square, Milton Park, Abingdon, Oxon OX14 4RN

and by Routledge
711 Third Avenue, New York, NY 10017

Routledge is an imprint of the Taylor & Francis Group, an informa business

© 1987 Jeffrey Steele

All rights reserved. No part of this book may be reprinted or reproduced or utilised in any form or by any electronic, mechanical, or other means, now known or hereafter invented, including photocopying and recording, or in any information storage or retrieval system, without permission in writing from the publishers.

Trademark notice: Product or corporate names may be trademarks or registered trademarks, and are used only for identification and explanation without intent to infringe.

British Library Cataloguing in Publication Data
A catalogue record for this book is available from the British Library

ISBN: 978-1-138-69377-7 (Set)
ISBN: 978-1-315-52921-9 (Set) (ebk)
ISBN: 978-1-138-69366-1 (Volume 25) (hbk)
ISBN: 978-1-138-69367-8 (Volume 25) (pbk)
ISBN: 978-1-315-52981-3 (Volume 25) (ebk)

Publisher's Note
The publisher has gone to great lengths to ensure the quality of this reprint but points out that some imperfections in the original copies may be apparent.

Disclaimer
The publisher has made every effort to trace copyright holders and would welcome correspondence from those they have been unable to trace.

UNFOLDING THE MIND

*The Unconscious in
American Romanticism
and Literary Theory*

JEFFREY STEELE

*Garland Publishing, Inc.
New York & London*
1987

Copyright © 1987 by Jeffrey Steele

All Rights Reserved

Library of Congress Cataloging-in-Publication Data

Steele, Jeffrey, 1947–
Unfolding the mind.

(Harvard dissertations in American and English literature)
Thesis (Ph. D.) — Harvard University, 1981.
Bibliography: p.
1. American literature — 19th century — History and criticism. 2. Subconsciousness in literature.
3. Psychology in literature. 4. Psychoanalysis and literature — United States. 5. Criticism — United States — History — 19th century. 6. Emerson, Ralph Waldo, 1803–1882 — Knowledge — Psychology. 7. Romanticism — United States. I. Title. II. Series.
PS217.S92S74   1987   810'.9'353   87-15013
ISBN 0-8240-0076-5

The volumes in this series are printed on acid-free, 250-year-life paper.

Printed in the United States of America

To Jocelyn and Doran

All our progress is an unfolding, like the vegetable bud. You have first an instinct, then an opinion, then a knowledge, as the plant has root, bud and fruit. Trust the instinct to the end, though you can render no reason. It is vain to hurry it. By trusting it to the end, it shall ripen into truth and you shall know why you believe.

    Emerson, "Intellect" (1841)

CONTENTS

	Abbreviations	vi
	Acknowledgements	vii
1	Discovering the Unconscious	1
2	Heart of Light or Heart of Darkness: Romantic Organicism and Psychic Energy	26
3	Projective and Interpretive Form	51
4	Sublimation: The Psychological Dialectic of <u>Nature</u>	83
5	Circumscribing the Mind	109
6	Emerson's "Philosophy of History" and Jungian Psychology	136
7	Interpreting the Self	162
8	Aspects of Power: Toward a Phenomenology of the Self	188
9	Masks of Dionysius: Enthusiasm and Inflation in the 19th Century	213
10	Deconstruction and Reconstruction	236
	Bibliography	268

ABBREVIATIONS

EMERSON

CW   The Collected Works of Ralph Waldo Emerson. Vol.1: Nature, Addresses, and Lectures. Ed. A.R. Ferguson, R.E. Spiller. Cambridge, Mass.: Harvard Univ. Press, 1971-

EL   The Early Lectures of Ralph Waldo Emerson, 1833-1842. Ed. S.E. Whicher, R.E. Spiller, W.E. Williams. Cambridge, Mass.: Harvard Univ. Press, 1959,1964,1972.

JMN   The Journals and Miscellaneous Notebooks of Ralph Waldo Emerson. Ed. W.H. Gilman, A.R. Ferguson, M.R. Davis, et. al. Cambridge, Mass.: Harvard Univ. Press, 1960-

W   The Complete Works of Ralph Waldo Emerson. Ed. Edward Waldo Emerson. The Centenary Edition. Boston: Houghton Mifflin Co., 1903-4.

FREUD

SE   The Standard Edition of the Complete Psychological Works of Sigmund Freud. Ed. James Strachey. London: The Hogarth Press, 1948-1974.

JUNG

CW   The Collected Works of C.G. Jung. Ed. Sir Herbert Read et. al. Trans. R.F.C. Hull. Princeton Univ. Press: Bollingen Series XX, 1957-1979. (Note: all references are to volume and paragraph number.)

PJ   The Portable Jung. Ed. Joseph Campbell. New York: Viking Press, 1971.

ACKNOWLEDGEMENTS

This essay was written under the direction of Joel Porte, who first suggested that I consider the topic of Emerson and the unconscious, and of Warner Berthoff.

In addition to Joel Porte's criticism of the American Renaissance, I am especially indebted to the ideas of Carl Jung and Paul Ricoeur.

I wish to thank the following teachers who have shaped my vision of literature: Herschel Baker, Ronald Bush, Wayne Carver, Owen Jenkins, David Perkins, and David Porter.

Finally, the largest debts: I thank my mother and my father, who taught me to love books, and Jocelyn Riley and Doran Riley Steele, who helped me keep everything in perspective.

CHAPTER ONE

DISCOVERING THE UNCONSCIOUS

"The more we examine the mechanism of thought," Oliver Wendell Holmes declared to the Phi Beta Kappa Society at Harvard in 1870, "the more we shall see that the automatic, unconscious action of the mind enters largely into all its processes."[1] Eighteen years later, Henry James, in his preface to the volume containing The Aspern Papers, commented upon the "unconscious cerebration of sleep";[2] while his brother William, in Principles of Psychology, published two years later, described "sleep, fainting, coma, epilepsy" as "'unconscious' conditions."[3] Clearly, the concept of the unconscious - as Freud himself admitted - had a long foreground, a foreground stretching back, in American literature, at least to Emerson's discussion in his lecture on "Literature" (January 5, 1837) of the "portion of ourselves" that "lies within the limits of the unconscious" (EL,II,56).[4] That same month, we see Francis Bowen complaining in The Christian Examiner of Germanic distortions of the English language represented by words like the "unconscious":

> As the object and method of philosophizing are altered, it is obvious that language also must be modified, and made to subserve other purposes than those for which it was originally designed. Transcendental philosophy took its rise in Germany, and the language of that country, from the unbounded power which it affords of composition and derivation from native roots, is well adapted to express results that are at once novel and vague....Our own tongue is more limited and inflexible. It must be enriched by copious importations from the German and Greek, before it can answer the ends of the modern school. And this has been done to such an extent, that could one of the worthies of old English literature rise from his grave, he would hardly be able to recognize his native tongue.
>   Among other innovations in speech made by writers of the Transcendental school, we may instance the formation of a large class of abstract nouns from adjectives, -- a peculiarity as consonant with the genius of the German language, as it is foreign to the nature of our own. Thus we now speak of the Infinite, the Beautiful, the Unconscious.[5]

While we are in a position to question Mr. Bowen's historical accuracy (since the "unconscious" was imported, not invented, by "the Transcendental school"), we must commend his philosophical insight. For American writers in the 1830's and 1840's *did* feel the need for a new terminology to express their awakening perception of "new" aspects of the mind. Without words like the "unconscious" (decidedly outside of the empiricist epistemology then prevailing in America), vast areas of the psyche would have remained unexpressed and thus unapproachable. This "discovery" of the unconscious in America constitutes my theme.

If by the 1870's in America and Europe, there was - as Lancelot Whyte observes in The Unconscious Before Freud - "a keen awareness of the importance of unconscious levels of the mind,"[6] one must go back to the seventeenth century of Rene Descartes and the Puritans to find the origins of such awareness. For, as Whyte explains,

> Until an attempt had been made (with apparent success) to choose awareness as the defining characteristic of an independent mode of being called mind, there was no occasion to invent the idea of unconscious mind as a provisional corrective. It is only after Descartes that we find, first the idea and then the term, "unconscious mind" entering European thought.[7]

In other words, perception of the unconscious entails a prior differentiation of consciousness -- an examination of "self-reflective awareness."[8] Or, to use the popular terminology of Geoffrey Hartman, a longing for "antiself-consciousness" necessitates an alienated self-consciousness[9]-- for example, a perception (like Carlyle's in "Characteristics") that self-conscious isolation from unconscious vitality and spontaneity had become a "disease." The human figure must stand out from the ground for reunion with and participation in the ground to become a desideratum. Differentiated identity longs for that unity which can reabsorb and transcend it -- a unity later to be imagined by Emerson as "One Mind," "One Man," and "Oversoul."

If the discovery of the unconscious can be seen to chart the progress of individualism, such individualism took on acute forms in Puritan America where institutionally-sanctoned "authenticity" (to use Lionel Trilling's term) reigned as a difficult ideal. Preparing the way - through their acute self-consciousness - for a discovery of the unconscious, Puritan divines outlawed any manifestation of the unconscious that originated within, rather than through the rigidly defined forms of dogma. The individual soul could accept God's grace, but only after clerical preparation, and only grace that originated without, from "on high." Roger Williams, Anne Hutchinson, and the Quakers all learned the severe fate of those who had the temerity to challenge such hierarchical assumptions by intimating that God might reside within.

Awareness that such emphasis upon external authority eventually did erode underlies most analyses of the rise of modern thought. Thus Trilling measures distance from external solidarity through charting the appearance of conceptions of "sincerity" and "authenticity." But schism without - we must remember - reflects a parallel schism within, as the psychic needs of the emerging individual fail to find fulfillment in norms which begin to be perceived as "exterior" and not as participatory vehicles. Indeed, incipient reflection upon such norms, upon the collective wholes that once defined one's being, marks the rise of a "problematic" of participation -- the growing intuition that identity must be sanctioned elsewhere. Consequently, the new focus upon "sincerity" - appearing with Renaissance individualism - is seen by Trilling as measuring a widening rift between mind and society. For this attention to the dramatic presentation of the self, arising "in the epoch that saw the sudden efflorescence of the theatre,"[10] signified a growing distance between the individual and the social whole which once might have defined his being. "The sixteenth century," Trilling observes, "was preoccupied to an extreme degree with dissimulation, feigning, and pretence."[11] Drama copiously "exploited the false presentation of the self."[12] Although inimical to the theatre, Puritan thought was equally obsessed with dissimulation and hypocrisy.[13]

Such obsession - an emblem for Trilling of a "new kind of personality"[14] - indicates a slippage of faith in collectivity as the ground of spiritual authority. For example, the intense political discussion arising after the English Civil War examined the grounds of membership in society and, ultimately, the conditions under which society could be acceptably dissolved. Such debate mirrored the growth of disturbing reflection upon the deracinated individual resulting from the withdrawal of once unquestioned allegiance to the state. Similarly, Milton's Satan, challenging the authority of God's polity (and, by analogy, the divine right of kings) cast the archetype for those who preferred even exile and torment over submission to spiritual authority outside of the self. (Gothic archetypes, emerging at the end of the eighteenth century, continue this line of thought.) The uneasy consciences of many Puritans, one suspects, measured the extent of unconscious dissimulation necessary to accept spiritual definitions that could not entirely satisfy the heart.

Michael Wigglesworth's revealing diary represents the self-lacerations of this type. The birth-pangs of individualism became an agony for Wigglesworth who, between 1653 and 1657, repeatedly castigated himself for pride, sloth, sensuality, and - most important - the "cooling" of his affections towards the Lord. "Caus thy face to shine upon me and I shall be saved," he beseeches God; "Put the spirit of a child into me and constantly maintain it."[15] Although he knows "the bottom support of my heart be in god," he is unable to "prize actuall communion with him at present."[16] Unwilling to relinquish adult awareness for childish dependence, he feels "no balm in Gilead" and only deadness inside: "I feel death creeping into and seizing my soul ever and anon."[17] Unprepared for grace, he cannot (like John Green whose spiritual account he copies into his diary) avow that "the Lord was pleased to break my heart...and let me see an infinite need of Christ to save me out of that estate."[18] Later, such anxious obsession over one's relationship to hostile spiritual authority will recur in Gothic romance -- Wigglesworth's image of death creeping into his heart is worthy of an Edgar Allan Poe. In both cases, consciousness resists submission to forces which transcend the ego and thus humble its pretensions to certainty and absolute knowledge.

To the extent that such brooding turns inward to focus

upon the mysterious motions of the heart - movements out of man's control - we observe that aspiration toward "authentic" being, toward consciousness reconciled with the unconscious, which Trilling found in isolated cells of awareness in the seventeenth century but epidemic by the time we reach the nineteenth century. In the interim, the power of external authority had to lapse to the extent that such freethinking was both safe and possible. For, as Perry Miller reminds us, in seventeenth-century America Puritan divines went only so far in their acceptance of inward movements of spirit. The antinomian assertion that God communicated directly through the heart (the unconscious) was rooted out and expelled from the community in the form of Anne Hutchinson. For such ideas threatened the stability of the clergy by questioning the absolute authority of their interpretation of scripture:

> If they exceeded these limits, then along with Lord Herbery [of Cherbury] they would find themselves so confident of an inward access to truth that they would relegate the Bible to a supernumerary; natural religion would thereupon suffice for salvation, original sin no longer be a serious blight, the criteria of religious truth become common notions and the consent of mankind.[19]

If these sound like the sins of Transcendentalism, Lord Herbert of Cherbury, along with the antinomian views of the Quakers, were among Emerson's sources.

For Emerson attempted to articulate that very awareness of the unconscious which the Puritans avoided. His vision of theology, to quote Perry Miller's description of the views anathemic to Puritanism, was "centered, not upon a transcendent God, but upon an all-sufficient, all-compelling natural instinct, possessing all the characteristics of divine grace, but feeding the reason not with visions of heaven but with an ecstasy of the earth."[20] That such an "ecstasy of the earth" might be ambiguous was the disturbing discovery of Emerson's generation, alternating in their visions of the psyche between the divine and the demonic. But first, Miller reminds us, they had to go outside of "the New England tradition" to "Swedenborg, Plotinus, and the wonders of Oriental philosophy" in order to express their sense of "innate ideas" and "direct intuitions."[21] If the "attributes" of God allowed accomodation of potentially unknowable Godhead to finite seventeenth-century consciousness, in the nineteenth century attention was displaced to the "attributes" or "manifestations" of the "God within" -- to archetypes and myths emerging from the unconscious.

Such manifestations were recognized by Romantic writers as images of "power" embodying sublime energies. In this regard, Thomas De Quincey opposes the "literature of power" to the "literature of knowledge." The function of a literature of power, he explains, is not to teach, but to move -- a movement which "must operate...on and through that _humid light_...of human passions."[22] What it communicates is not truth, but "_power_, or deep sympathy with truth." "What do you learn from _Paradise Lost_?" De Quincey asks,

> Nothing at all....What you owe Milton is not any knowledge...; what you owe is _power_, that is,

> exercise and expansion to your own latent capacity of sympathy with the infinite, where every pulse and each separate influx is a step upwards, a step ascending as upon a Jacob's ladder from earth to mysterious altitudes above the earth.[23]

Such concern with the vertical axis of imagination, with "what is highest in man,"[24] distinguishes Romantic literature; except that ascension is often matched by an equal but opposite imagination of powerful depths. Coleridge's apprehension of "A light in sound, a sound-like power in light"[25] finds its mirror-image in the demonic forces with which Byron's Manfred conjures:

> a power,
> Deeper than all yet urged, a tyrant-spell,
> Which had its birthplace in a star condemned,
> The burning wreck of a demolished world,
> A wandering hell in eternal space.[26]

Whether a gentle breeze coming unbidden and graciously to the poet or a stormy force which threatens to blast its vehicle, power - the motive force of poetic inspiration - becomes the central subject of a literature founded upon self-conscious examination of the organic fluctuations of creativity.

Given the problematic nature of this inspiration - the periodic alternations between access to power and loss of power leading to "dejection" - Romantic writers learned to structure their works as patterns of conscious relationship to founts intuited within the unconscious. Consistently, we find works centered upon images of power which, through symbolic reference, connect the known with the unknown, consciousness with the unconscious. By assimilating the unconscious energies embodied in such "sources," consciousness attempts to regain participation in a world of living myth, to reestablish secure roots giving access to the power of being. In such terms, the relationship to creative energy becomes an overt subject as Romantic writers examine their proximity to or distance from centers of power which are projected into their works.

Wordsworth's self-conscious evocation in <u>The Prelude</u> of "spots of time" epitomizes this pattern. Mythic childhood images are used by the adult poet to rejuvenate inspiration through the presentation to consciousness of symbols evoking unconscious energies. Similarly, in Coleridge's "Dejection: An Ode" symbols of the absent creative source are embedded like jewels within the poet's consciousness which surrounds them as a setting. (Compare T.S. Eliot's evocation of jewellike sources of inspiration -- the "sapphires in the mud" referred to in "Burnt Norton.") Attempting to resuscitate his imagination, Coleridge projects into his poem a series of archetypal images ("fountains...within," "fair and luminous cloud," "sweet and potent voice") which potentially embody enough energy to become a creative source. By naming the energy which he lacks (in a sense, <u>calling</u> the muse), the poet establishes a relationship between his alienated consciousness and designated symbols of power. Such a pattern of relationship, between consciousness and projected myth, is analogous to the psychic process which Carl Jung labels "individuation."

Referring thus to Jung reminds us of the <u>interpretive</u> aspect of this process. For Jung explicitly balances patterns of projection (the symbolization of dreams) against interpretive patterns of analysis. The point of Jungian analysis is that consciousness must learn how to relate to and interpret mythic energies projected from the unconscious. Accordingly, Jung defines individuation as the process through which an individual "becomes conscious of his invisible system of relations to the unconscious."[27] By uncovering these lines of relation, by consciously realizing one's projective coloration of image and persons, one gains access to psychological and spiritual powers hitherto buried. As a model of artistic creation, individuation emphasizes both the projection of archetypal symbols into literary works and the conscious confrontation and assimilation of the power embodied in those symbols. We focus, accordingly, not solely upon the dream or myth, but upon the <u>relationship between dreaming and analysis</u>, <u>between mythmaking and interpretation</u>. This critical stance allows us to analyze the <u>interpretive frames of reference</u> Romantic writers evolved to utilize the power of archetypes such as fountain, maelstrom, white whale, or dark lady. Our focus is upon the ways in which Romantic works are structured in order to allow consciousness to step back and examine its points of contact with unconscious sources. The recurrence of themes of fascination, possession, and mesmerism reveals a widespread tendency to examine the dynamics of the relationship between consciousness and compelling centers of power.[28]

Similarly, Friedrich Schlegel's concept of "Romantic irony" refers to the orientation of consciousness toward the unconscious. For Schlegel's theory involves not only the <u>projection of myth</u>, but at the same time the mind's <u>interpretation of the myth</u> it attempts to reveal. The quest for a psychic center firmly planted in the unconscious is balanced by the careful observation of the forces underlying psychic growth as they reveal themselves in literary form. On the one hand, Schlegel calls for a "new mythology...forged from the deepest depths of the spirit," for a "living center" within the self, for that "invisible primordial power" which he characterizes as "a spark of...creative spirit" that "lives in us and never ceases to glow with the secret force deep under the ashes of our self-induced unreason."[29] But on the other hand, Schlegel also focuses upon the need for self-conscious reflection examining the process of unfolding myth. Literature, he asserts, should portray "the producer along with the product"; it should combine "preliminary exercises for a poetic theory of the creative power with...artistic reflection and beautiful self-mirroring."[30] That is, myths recovered from the unconscious must be portrayed along with depictions of the mind's stance toward those myths.

But Romantic irony, for Schlegel, is more than mere literary self-consciousness. For it involves issues that foreshadow the crucial nineteenth-century debate between faith and skepticism. The sense of irony, Schlegel realizes, entails an awareness of self-division between the need to believe and the recognition of the limits of belief. Man, he writes, "is divided spirit"; his "self-restraint is consequently the result of self-creation and self-destruction."[31] Schlegel's translators, Ernst Behler and Roman Struc, draw out the full implications of such an assertion. They observe in their introduction that if Schlegel "like Nietzsche...derived the origins of Greek poetry from a Dionysian phenomenon," conversely he saw the need for "irony as a destructive reaction against the primordial Dionysian ecstasy of poetic enthusiasm."[32] Schlegel, they continue, saw the need for an "agility" that balanced "self-creation" and "self-destruction," "overflowing vitality" and a "limiting skepticism toward one's own productive capability."[33] Thus, Schlegel's call for a "universal mythology" revealing the depths of the mind coexists with self-conscious literary structures in which that mythology is embedded. Myth excavated from the unconscious is circumscribed by a skeptical consciousness that limits and focuses its energy.

Similarly, in the major works of the American Renaissance, one finds a formative impulse involving the attempt to establish stable relations between the unconscious and consciousness, to explore the precarious and shifting boundary between hidden powers of blackness and the light of common day. Earlier students of American literature have addressed this issue whenever they have explored the tendency of romance "to plunge into the underside of consciousness,"[34] or have linked frontier consciousness and depth psychology,[35] or have studied the archetypes and myths organizing much of American writing.[36] At this date, it need not be established that authors such as Poe, Hawthorne, and Melville were adepts at psychological analysis, like Roger Chillingworth able to sift the gold from the dross in their examinations of the human heart. For we now have Freudian studies of most of the major authors; and even a small minority who have begun to apply the insights of Jung.[37] "American Adam," "frontier," and "regenerative violence" have all had their day as central myths organizing the field of American literary study. Like Carl Jung's extensive catalogue of symbols and archetypes, each performs the useful function of illustrating manifold objectifications of psychic energy, of "spirit." However, the danger of myth criticism or Freudian analysis, as many have noticed, is reductionism. One identifies the myth or the hidden complex, describes its various guises, and commentary comes to an end. For what is left to say?

One thing left is to observe that Romantic literature involves more than the mere presentation of myth; it also involves the structuring of attitudes toward myth, patterns of relationship toward the depths of the mind that myth attempts to reveal. Thus our extensive commentaries upon American myths must be balanced by a criticism that sets myth in perspective by revealing American attitudes toward myth. So argues Robert Richardson, whose <u>Myth and Literature in the</u>

<u>American Renaissance</u> details the complex, often contradictory attitudes toward myth found in our major Romantic writers.[38] An earlier study which exploits a similar perspective is Joel Porte's <u>The Romance in America</u> which analyzes the ambivalence of American romance writers toward the psychic depths exploited by their art.[39] I see this study as extending the line of inquiry suggested by such works -- analyzing not only myth but the mind's attitude toward myth, not only archetypal images projected from the unconscious but also the varying conscious attitudes displayed in American Romantic literature toward the unconscious and the mysteries it was felt to contain.

Let me conclude this chapter with a few words upon my methodology. If this study focuses upon one episode in the "discovery" of the unconscious, the psychological emphasis of Modernist and post-Modernist writing reveals that this discovery is not yet complete. Whatever gods are emerging to replace the failing Christian <u>logos</u> have not yet been revealed. As the schismatic forces of the Reformation have eroded external ecclesiastical authority, man has been forced to turn inward to seek for divinity. For many, this quest has also involved a turning eastward, to the psychological wisdom of the Orient, back to the spiritual springs of Western tradition, in the hope of repairing the once grand avenues leading to the mysteries of the soul. Those "great highways north, south, east, and west to the centre of every province of the empire"[40] have crumbled into fragments shored against the ruins of psychic and spiritual disarray. And the voices of Eliot's gods, as well as Emerson's, speak in Eastern accents. If Friedrich Schlegel's and Schopenhauer's Orientalism was continued in the Hindu studies of Emerson and Thoreau, and Yeats' Hermeticism and his translation of the Upanishads paralleled the Confucianism of Ezra Pound, today we are witnessing an even more fervent assimilation of Eastern thought. The studies of Richard Wilhelm and Alan Watts, as well as current fascination with Transcendental Meditation and Zen Buddhism, all lend support to Jung's observation that "the East is at the bottom of the spiritual change we are passing through today."[41] Like our nineteenth-century forebears, we continue the search for effective terminologies which can hold open the channel between consciousness and the unconscious, between the isolated individual and what the Upanishads call "the sacred place of the heart."[42] The alternative is a sterile formalism.

In the face of devaluations of the psyche, Jung challenges us to connect the manifestations of culture with the deepest needs of the mind. In his own day, Emerson served a similar function. Many works of contemporary literary criticism, for example those of continental schools of thought such as Structuralism and Phenomenology, continue this enterprise. The current popularity of such theories reveals the psychological vacuum caused by critical attention that neglects the unconscious. For as the psychological insights of New Criticism, now forty years old, have been obscured by an exclusive formalism (by the failure to see literary structure as an index of deeper forces), the way has been open for theories that reconnect surface structure with deep structure, conscious pattern with unconscious archetype. (Despite Levi-Strauss's misreading of Jung, it is apparent that the unconscious "structural laws" discovered by Structuralism and Jungian "archetypes" are close kin.) Gaston Bachelard, Jacques Derrida, and Jacques Lacan all include a concept of the unconscious in their theories. Along with linguistics, theories of the unconscious have taken on a more and more central role in literary criticism. Usually theorists have turned to Freud for understanding of the psychic economy. In the above list, only Bachelard openly acknowledges the significance of Jung. In part, this seems due to an accident of chronology. For the forty years since Freud's death, as compared with the twenty since Jung's, have given us twice as long to assimilate his insights. By now, we have a surfeit of Freudian literary studies. What is needed today is an equal assimilation of Jung's thought and, more important, the creation of critical perspectives which can use both Freud and Jung, which can see the commonality - as well as the divergence - of their psychological projects. The syncretistic philosophy of Paul Ricoeur provides the best example I know of such an enterprise. For example, Ricoeur's relation in Freud and Philosophy, of a "hermeneutics of faith" to a "hermeneutics of suspicion" establishes the ground for a meeting of Freud and Jung. As I argue in the following pages, we see a similar dialectic in the competing psychological visions of Emerson and Melville, as well as within the vision of Emerson itself.

In summary, this is a study of the unfolding of the mind in American literature. Focusing upon American Romantic writers, I attempt to place their various psychologies into the context of Romantic psychology in general -- conceptions of mind which persist throughout the nineteenth century and which underlie the discoveries of Freud's psychoanalysis and Jung's depth psychology. For while Freud and Jung popularized the idea of the unconscious, this conception - as M.H. Abrams and others have shown - was essential to the Romantic view of psychic dynamics. Indeed, Coleridge and Emerson both talk explicitly about the "unconscious." The contribution of twentieth-century psychologists, it would seem, was to work out theories of psychic dynamics, articulating concepts such as "sublimation" and "projection." But again, when we turn back to Romantic writers, we see a profound understanding of psychic dynamics as well. As Freud himself admitted, the poets "were there" before him. And the reliance of Jung upon writers such as Goethe, Schiller, and Nietzsche is well-known.

Our task, then, becomes one of mapping one terminology onto another -- illustrating the points of contact and dissimilarity between, say, Emerson's "Reason" and Jung's "unconscious."[43] This is not to privilege either terminology over the other, but to illustrate the attempts of both Emerson and Jung - in periods of eroding faith - to secure consciousness to a transcendent ground located within the psyche. But at the same time, we cannot ignore the existence - at least since Nietzsche - of a healthy, not to say arrogantly vital, counter-tradition. For Nietzsche and his heirs (for example, Freud and Derrida), the search for a transcendent ground of being is an activity enmeshed in illusion, since - to their minds - consciousness is less a myth than a fiction which necessarily simplifies and hence falsifies its relationship to somatic roots which transcend articulation. At some point, an exploration of the physical background of libido passes into wordlessness. Consciousness, from this perspective, is vulnerable to demythologizing, "deconstructive" perspectives. Thus Freud wounds the ego in its pretensions toward transcendent meaning, illustrating the extent to which the edifice of faith is built upon the shifting sands of self-deception. In Emerson's own day, this role was filled by Herman Melville, who moves from Moby-Dick through Pierre and The Confidence Man toward a radical deconstruction of the self.

Before turning to a consideration of these two rival traditions, several words about the structure of this study are in order. For if my thesis began as a consideration of the theme of the unconscious in American Romantic literature, it has evolved into something else. I have discovered, the more I have become immersed in my subject, that the psychological problems confronted by Emerson and his contemporaries are still with us, but in a more extreme form. Today, consideration of the unconscious and its relationship to consciousness is as central as it was for Emerson's age. Like us, they saw themselves threading their way through rival schools of thought, importing ideas, searching for a terminology that might adequately communicate their conception of mind. Thus, attempting to examine the unconscious as a literary theme, I have realized the need for a comprehensive theory of the unconscious (if any such theory is possible) -- a theory in which the insights of Coleridge and Emerson, of Melville and Nietzsche, of Freud and Jung, each form one chapter. For the more one considers Emerson and the other American Romantic authors within the light of intellectual history, the more it becomes apparent that their ideas - specifically, their conceptions of the mind and its dynamics - form part of a development that continues up through current interest in the unconscious. We are talking about the appearance of modern psychology, which only came into being after theology started to erode as the locus of ultimate meaning. Clearly, we ourselves exist within the matrix of the problems we are attempting to analyze.

Furthermore, one finds that if Emerson's ideas are often best illuminated by later formulations within the same intellectual tradition (for example, Jung's), his ideas - embodying an earlier stage of Romantic psychology - also frequently shed light forward onto twentieth-century theoreticians. If one views _any_ psychology that treats the unconscious as a presentation of a _myth of the mind_, a figure of psychic dynamics, then the psychological myths of Coleridge, Carlyle, Emerson, and Nietzsche can be seen - in their own terms - to have as much validity as later, more "scientific" formulations. The unconscious, whatever its true nature, has always been with us. What has changed is the terminology used to describe its manifestations, terms shifting with our needs -- the modern preference being for psychological theories cleansed as much as possible of theological assumptions. (One sees the Transcendentalist generation, through their furtherance of the displacement from theology to psychology, unwittingly abetting this "cleansing.") But to the extent that even our modernized psychologies confront the problem of the unconscious, they implicate themselves in theological perspectives, advocating stances of either faith or suspicion toward the unknown, transcendent, psychic ground. Even Freud felt compelled to use myth (foe example, the myths of Oedipus and Eros) to communicate his insights. Significantly, his last works confront (albeit skeptically) the question of faith and religion.

NOTES: CHAPTER ONE

[1] Lancelot Law Whyte, *The Unconscious Before Freud* (London: Tavistock Publications, 1962), p.171.

[2] Whyte, p.155.

[3] *The Compact Edition of the Oxford English Dictionary* (New York: Oxford Univ. Press, 1971), p.3481.

[4] Ralph Waldo Emerson, *Early Lectures*, Vol. II, ed. S.E. Whicher, R.E. Spiller. W.E. Williams (Cambridge, Mass.: Harvard Univ. Press, 1964), p.56. (Subsequent references to this edition will be abbreviated *EL*. See "Abbreviations.")

[5] Francis Bowen, *The Christian Examiner*, XXI (Jan. 1837), pp.377-8. Rptd. in M. Sealts and A. Ferguson eds., *Emerson's Nature -- Origin, Growth, Meaning* (New York: Dodd, Mead, & Co., 1969), p.84.

[6] Whyte, pp.170-1.

[7] Whyte, pp.27-8.

[8] Whyte, p.25.

[9] Geoffrey Hartman, "Romanticism and Antiself-Consciousness," *Centennial Review*, 6, No.4 (Fall 1962), pp.553-65. Rptd. in R.F. Gleckner & G.E. Enscoe eds., *Romanticism: Points of View* (Englewood Cliffs, N.J.: Prentice Hall, 1970).

[10] Lionel Trilling, *Sincerity and Authenticity* (Cambridge, Mass.: Harvard Univ. Press, 1971), p.10.

[11] Trilling, p.13.

[12] *Ibid*.

[13] Trilling, p.23.

[14] Trilling, p.24.

[15] The Diary of Michael Wigglesworth 1653-1657: The Conscience of a Puritan, ed. E.S. Morgan (Gloucester, Mass.: Peter Smith, 1970), p.10.

[16] Wigglesworth, p.20.

[17] Wigglesworth, pp.42,41.

[18] Wigglesworth, p.115.

[19] Perry Miller, The New England Mind (1939; rptd. Boston: Beacon Press, 1961), I,277.

[20] Miller, I, 278.

[21] Ibid.

[22] Thomas De Quincey, "Literature of Knowledge and Literature of Power," rptd. in English Romantic Works, ed. D. Perkins (New York: Harcourt, Brace & World, 1967), p.743.

[23] Ibid.

[24] Ibid.

[25] Coleridge, "The Eolian Harp," ll.26-9.

[26] Byron, Manfred, I,i,42-9.

[27] Carl Jung, Two Essays on Analytical Psychology, trans. R.F.C. Hull (New York: Meridian Books, 1956), p.205.

[28] For a discussion of Mesmerism and spellbinding as literary themes, see Maria Tatar, Spellbound (Princeton, N.J.: Princeton Univ. Press, 1978).

[29] Friedrich Schlegel, Dialogue on Poetry and Literary Aphorisms, trans. E. Behler & R. Struc (Univ. Park & London: Penn. State Univ. Press, 1968). The passages cited are from "Talk on Mythology" in Dialogue on Poetry, p.82; Selected

Ideas, p.153; Dialogue on Poetry, p.54.

[30] Schlegel, Aphorisms from the Athenaeum, #238, Behler & Struc, p. 145.

[31] Schlegel, Aphorisms from the Lyceum, #28, Behler & Struc, p.123.

[32] Behler & Struc, "Introduction," p.39.

[33] Behler & Struc, p.40.

[34] Richard Chase, The American Novel and Its Tradition (Garden City, New York: Doubleday, Anchor Book, 1957), p.ix.

[35] Joel Porte, The Romance in America (Middletown, Conn.: Wesleyan Univ. Press, 1969), p.53.

[36] For example, R.W.B. Lewis, The American Adam: Innocence, Tragedy and Tradition in the Nineteenth Century (Chicago: Univ. of Chicago Press, 1959); and Daniel Hoffman, Form and Fable in American Fiction (New York, Norton, 1973).

[37] A prominent Freudian study: Frederick Crews, The Sins of the Fathers: Hawthorne's Psychological Themes (New York: Oxford Univ. Press, 1966). An important Jungian study: Edward Edinger, Melville's Moby-Dick: A Jungian Commentary (New York: New Directions, 1978).

[38] Robert D. Richardson Jr., Myth and Literature in the American Renaissance (Bloomington & London: Indiana Univ. Press, 1978).

[39] Joel Porte, The Romance in America (Middletown, Conn.: Wesleyan Univ. Press, 1969).

[40] Emerson, EL,II,17.

[41] Jung, PJ,476. (See "Abbreviations.")

[42] From the "Katha Upanishad" in The Upanishads, trans. Juan Mascaró (New York: Penguin, 1965), p.56.

[43] For a detailed comparison of Emerson and Jung, see Chapter Six: "Emerson's 'Philosophy of History' and Jungian Psychology."

CHAPTER TWO

HEART OF LIGHT OR HEART OF DARKNESS:

ROMANTIC ORGANICISM AND PSYCHIC ENERGY

In <u>The Order of Things</u>, the contemporary French philosopher, Michel Foucault, defines the shift from Classicism to Romanticism as a transformation of models of knowledge. Beginning in the late eighteenth century, Foucault argues, ideas were structured in a new way. In place of <u>representation</u> as the organizing principle of thought, one finds <u>growth</u>. The question of identity or non-identity with an ideal is replaced by concern with the historical unfolding of organic structures. "History" becomes "the unavoidable element in our thought" as focus shifts to the empirical realization of generative principles which unfold in time.[1] Consequently, attention shifts from visible surfaces to unseen functional laws which determine the "hierarchized organic structure" visible to the observer:

> To classify, therefore, will no longer mean to
> refer the visible back to itself, while allotting

> one of its elements the task of representing the others; it will mean, in a movement that makes analysis pivot on its axis, to relate the visible to the invisible, to its deeper cause, as it were, then to rise upwards once more from that hidden architecture towards the more obvious signs displayed on the surfaces of bodies....[2]

Thus, in the nineteenth century, one comes to search surface manifestations "as a visible sign directing us toward a buried depth" -- drawn toward the imagination of "a profound, interior, and essential space."[3] From this organic perspective, things

> turn in upon themselves, posit their own volumes, and define for themselves an _internal_ space.... It is from this starting-point of the architecture they conceal, of the cohesion that maintains its sovereign and secret sway over each one of their parts, it is from the depths of the force that brought them into being and remains in them, as though motionless yet still quivering, that things - in fragments, outlines, pieces, shards - offer themselves, though very partially, to representation.[4]

Let us focus here upon two aspects of Foucault's observations -- the new emphasis upon hidden principles of being, and the recognition that any attempt at representing those principles is doomed to a necessary partiality, to the limitations frequently spoken of as "Romantic irony." It is upon efforts to represent the unrepresentable - to portray the depths and the dynamics of the mind - that I focus in this study.

One approach to portraying the mind, available to Romantic writers, was to concentrate upon generative principles of psychic energy which effect the translation from unplumbed depths to the "surface" phenomena of consciousness. "Of our Thinking," Carlyle observes in "Characteristics,"

> ...it is but the mere upper surface that we shape into articulate Thoughts;--underneath the region of argument and conscious discourse, lies the region of meditation; here, in its quiet mysterious depths, dwells what vital force is in us; here, if aught is to be created, and not merely manufactured and communicated, must the work go on.[5]

Such wisdom dates back to the German philosophers whom Carlyle drew upon as sources, disseminating to the English-speaking world their new theories of the "unconscious" and its organic manifestation. For as M.H. Abrams reminds us, the modern discovery of the unconscious coincided with the elaboration in Germany of organic models of literary invention. Seizing upon "suggestions that a great work of literature grows out of the impenetrable depths of the mind of genius," writers like Herder and Goethe began to envision the unfolding mind "as an unconsciously growing plant."[6] Consciousness was seen to derive its power from "a process of nature within the realm of the mind."[7] Consequently, philosophy, for a dialectical thinker like Friedrich Schelling, originated from the opposition of "conscious" and "unconscious" principles.[8]

In fact, German philosophers and poets were so successful in elaborating and promulgating their theories of unconscious organic processes that by the 1830's, Abrams observes, "the notion of an unconscious element in the inventive process had already become almost a commonplace of English literary criticism."[9] Thus, by the time Emerson delivered his views of the unconscious in his lectures on "The Philosophy of History" (1836-7), he was able to draw upon a growing literature devoted to exploring unconscious sources of creativity. The recent works of Coleridge and Carlyle pointed the way. Confronted with the problem of grounding the mind - of establishing a spiritual authority that might compensate for the decay of exterior religious forms - both writers had located divinity within, in the depths of the psyche. Roles once performed by theology were falling by default to psychology. "God" was being transformed into the "unconscious"; while principles of divine "grace" metamorphosed into concepts of psychic energy expressed through the biological metaphors of Romantic organicism.

So long as psychic energy was viewed as Spirit, there was little difficulty in associating intuited depths of the mind with moral order. For if God resides within, in the unconscious, our most spontaneous impulses receive a divine sanction -- they partake of a divinely authorized ethical order backed by two thousand years of religious teaching. But within the context of nineteenth-century intellectual history, such idealism runs counter to a general movement toward materialistic conceptions of psychic energy. It is a major premise of this study that inner contradictions in the psychological terminology of Romantic organicism contributed to this advancing materialism. For the organic view of the mind, with its analogy between psychic dynamics

and physical growth, contained within its assumptions the
unsettling suggestion that psychic energy might be entirely
physical in its provenance. This possibility was there from
the earliest comparisons of the unfolding mind to a growing
plant. Thus, when writers such as Coleridge describe the
mind's "current," one wonders how literally to read such
images. Or let us consider Coleridge's description of his
reaction to the language of Wordsworth's "Descriptive Sketches" -- his sense of

> words and images all a-glow, which might recall
> those products of the vegetable world, where gorgeous blossoms rise out of the hard and thorny
> rind and shell....[10]

Dropping Coleridge's "might recall," later generations came
closer to identifying the mind literally with the growing
plant, rather than figuratively using growth as a metaphor
for essentially spiritual process.

To the extent that they conceived of psychic energy as
blind physical force, Schopenhauer and Nietzsche promoted
this materialization (which leads to Freud's _libido_). Along
these lines, Schopenhauer describes the underlying principle
of reality not as "One Mind" or a rational "Absolute," but
rather as "Will" which is "without knowledge and merely a
blind incessant impulse."[11] In the hands of thinkers like
Schopenhauer, idealism was moving toward materialism -- as
ultimate ptinciples were given a body, a physical aspect
which they had lacked. Accordingly, Frederick Coplestone
sees Schopenhauer's philosophy as "a bridge between rational-

istic idealism and the philosophy of Life in Germany and France":

> Both instinct and reason are described by Schopenhauer as biological instruments or tools.... Hence he provides the material, as it were, for a substitution of the idea of Life as the central idea in philosophy for that of Thought.[12]

Life and Thought, irrational energy and rational power, are weighed in the balance during the mid-nineteenth century -- a period which derives much of its interest from the increasingly open competition of opposing models of psychic energy.

By the end of the century, in the writings of Sigmund Freund, we see the culmination of this development. Rather than viewing natural process as a metaphor for spiritual unfolding, Freud leaves spirit out of the question altogether. What had once been figures of speech are now viewed literally. The mind is conceived as the product of a physical energy, <u>libido</u>, which is derived from the body and is transformed or sublimated into ideas. Rather than viewing Nature as a function of Spirit, Spirit is now a function of Nature -- the religious impulse being, for Freud, merely one of the manifold disguises of instinct. Completing the process of interiorization established years before by German Romantic philosophers, Freud envisions a universe in which the dynamic principle of causality has shrunk entirely to the human sphere. Impulses once found in Nature now exist entirely within man, who maintains an uneasy relationship with the body's volatile energy. This "dehumanization" effectively alienates man from Nature without and Nature within -- the unconscious. The only option open is an adversary relationship -- man must try to dominate Nature or be dominated in return. He must subordinate natural resources (including the "natural resources" of the mind) to imperialistic and exploitative programs. In such terms, Freud imagined the ego's spreading circle of domination: "Psycho-analysis is an instrument to enable the ego to achieve a progressive conquest of the id."[13]

Given their problematic relationship to creative energy, Romantic writers also focused upon the need of directing unconscious energies to the end of psychic expansion. Emerson's essay "Circles" merely represents the culmination of a long tradition advocating the expression of power encircling itself in larger and larger circumferences. This substitution of "an interminable pursuit of an unattainable goal, for that of a final rest of the soul in the contemplation of perfection," Arthur Lovejoy comments,

> ...was no invention of Goethe, nor of the German Romanticists, nor even of Lessing, but has been expressed repeatedly throughout the [eighteenth] century.[14]

But for Emerson and his predecessors, each expansive growth reflected "a new influx of the divinity into the mind" (CW, II,309), and not the subjugation and articulation of purely physical energy.

We see this emphasis in Coleridge, who viewed the unconscious as a divine source manifesting itself spiritually.

Accordingly, Coleridge's "Reason" (a concept eagerly adopted by Emerson) is an intuitive function sensitive to the promptings of a hidden spiritual source. For example, Shakespeare's genius is described by Coleridge as his ability to shape his works according to the impulses of "a power and an implicit <u>wisdom</u> deeper than consciousness."[15] This "implicit wisdom," a "living power" within, is seen to embody itself in "organic form"; for "it shapes as it develops itself from within, and the fullness of its developement is one and the same with the perfection of the outward form."[16] Thus Coleridge uses a biological metaphor to express his sense of a force which he believes to be divine in essence. This power, he emphasizes, "must of necessity circumscribe itself by rules" -- "it must embody in order to reveal itself."[17] In other words, spiritual energy is seen to <u>incarnate</u> itself through physical forms which objectify and express it. There is a clear distinction here between what Coleridge, in <u>The Statesman's Manual</u>, describes as a "reconciling and mediatory power" and the "images of sense" in which that power clothes itself, creating symbols which point toward its essence. Spiritual and natural processes are seen to <u>correspond</u>, but they are not equated. For example, when Keats enjoins us to "open our leaves like a flower" or to write a poetry which comes "as naturally as the leaves to a tree,"[18] images of growth are used to symbolize a spiritual unfolding. As we shall see, later writers like Emerson focus more explicitly upon the mind's symbolization of its own processes, upon the objective forms of spirit which offer themselves for analysis.

However, Romantic writers (Coleridge included) often tended to blur such fine distinctions. For the use of metaphors of natural energy to express theological ends competed with an awakening appreciation of natural energy for its own sake. Rather than reading Nature's face as a correspondent symbol of Spirit, writers frequently perceived one force running throughout creation -- "the one Life within us and abroad" as Coleridge calls it in "The Eolian Harp."[19] But by positing a world-soul or universal force running throughout the mind and Nature, Romantic pantheism obscured the fine line between natural energy and spiritual energy. Frequently, we find the tendency to view both mind and Nature as incarnations of the same energy. But is that energy spiritual or physical, rational or irrational? To the extent that nineteenth century thinkers inclined toward monism, they were forced to confront such issues -- making either "Reason" or physical life-force into an absolute principle of being.

It makes a great deal of difference whether the conscious self is seen as incarnating transcendent spiritual power or, by contrast, as embodying energy derived from physical forces. If God is found at the root of the psyche, one's attitude toward psychic energy can be one of faith, of subordination to a "higher" power. But if the unconscious is seen to contain only primitive physical urges, the ego gains dominance as a more advanced stage of civilization. From Freud's perspective, the ego brings light to the heart of darkness, spreading the illumination of advanced European culture, subduing the savagery within. Its goals are those of imperialism, as the line of the frontier is pushed further into the wilderness.[20] While we can recognize the appeal of such imperialistic psychological myth for Emerson's generation, which rode a cresting wave of enthusiasm at the untold natural resources now falling to their grasp in the heartland, we must recognize that its egocentrism was based upon materialistic premises which ran counter to much of their best psychology. For if one side of the Romantic self in America longed for the conquest of the wilderness, another side recognized that "the wild" (as Thoreau called it[21]) was essentially sacred. From this latter perspective, one subdued and cultivated the unconscious only at the expense of faith and creative inspiration. Without an openness to the unkown within and without, one foreclosed many of life's possibilities. Such, in various guises, was Emerson's message to his generation -- an age in danger of forgetting that human being promised more than a thin, advancing edge of egotism.

But if cultural conditions, such as the sudden access to new wealth in America, threatened to subvert faith in the wild as a sacred territory, other factors contributed to this deterioration as well. For philosophies of incarnation, with their necessary emphasis upon the carnal, maintained a precarious balance between apprehension of spirit through the flesh and immersion in the flesh so total that the lens of spiritual vision was permanently darkened: "every window of your Feeling, even of your intellect,...begrimed and mud-bespattered, so that no pure ray can enter."[22] This darkening impended as the result of internal contradictions within Romantic organicism and its vision of psychic energy. Adjudicating the claims of idealism <u>and</u> of an emerging materialism, thinkers like Carlyle and Emerson found it increasingly difficult to organize their thought under one head or the other -- for the claims of both positions beckoned. Thus, it makes less sense to discuss Emerson as an "idealist" than to recognize that he was a transitional figure, bridging the gap between Romantic idealism and Realistic materialism, struggling to maintain the old verities while new physical truths threatened. In his thought, as in that of many of his contemporaries, materialism struggles with idealism for supremacy. That is, the correspondence of Spirit and Nature is maintained against forces which threaten its dissolution.

Looking back, we see the emergence of this dialectic between idealism and materialism, between "Reason" and physical life-force, in the thought of Coleridge. Accordingly, Walter Jackson Bate sees Coleridge's criticism as an effort "to combine the concreteness and the organic vitalism that the romantic movement prized, with the traditional values of classical rationalism and idealism," especially as those values were expressed in "the Platonic doctrine that universal forms or 'ideas' have an absolute existence of their own and can be known by man through reason."[23] Nature, from this perspective, is "regarded as concrete activity, organically evolving in accordance with universal forms."[24] What we have here, as Charles Feidelson reminds us, is a definition of thinking as a process of symbolism.[25] The advantage of this insight is that it places Coleridge's thought within a hermeneutic tradition extending to the present. For if Coleridge, and later Emerson, evolve theories of symbolic form, they define problems of value and meaning that we have yet to emerge from. Their <u>awareness</u> of symbolic participation as problematic defines the crisis of meaning characteristic of the modern spirit.

Stopping short of the heights of Coleridge's idealism, we still must see that such idealism exists not alone but in dialogue with an implicit realism. In Emerson's case, this realism is made explicit -- for in his life and thought the purest insights of "Reason" run smack against unmovable physical verities. One can believe in the divine potential of the mind -- and then one's wife, one's brother, one's son, all die. What good is self-reliance then? By weighing the openness of self-reliance against the closure of physical necessity, Emerson's thought adumbrates the more austere self-questionings of the modern age. As our precursor, he defines faith as a question which must be lived and kept open against the continuous pressure of non-being.

During the American Renaissance, then, we see the

development of two competing concepts of psychic energy. By some the psyche was seen to be motivated by a potentially divine energy intuited through "Reason" -- so runs a strain which Emerson inherited from Coleridge. But the unsettling truth which Emerson and his age learned was that the fusion of theological ends with biological metaphors formed an unstable compound. For concepts of psychic energy lay open to increasingly materialistic interpretations. As Emerson begins to describe psychic energy as an abstract "power" (instead of as the theological "spirit"), he presents a dynamic which is easily materialized. One merely needs to conceive of this power as a fluid, a kind of sap running through the mind and body. Then, psychological laws can be imagined in terms of a fluid dynamics. It was one thing to identify with Coleridge the force driving the psyche as spirit expressing itself through natural forms. But what about the disturbing suggestion that this polarity might be reversed, that spirit might be a function of natural energy -- one of the disguises of the body's power?

One encounters this possibility in Hawthorne's and Melville's romances. If Hawthorne hints in The Scarlet Letter that the energy driving Arthur Dimmesdale's election sermon resulted at least in part from his sexual excitement at meeting Hester in the woods,[26] Melville in Pierre openly examines the self-delusions of a character who mistakes incestuous sexual attraction for spiritual illumination. The commentary upon Transcendentalist intuition is clear, as

Melville ruthlessly questions the sincerity of a philosophy founded upon spontaneous impulse. For how does one know, he asks, what forces are being released by faith in the unconscious? Isn't it all too easy to mistake the message of instinct as that of "reason"? Freud's position is adumbrated here -- the view that faith in a spiritual energy motivating the psyche is an illusion masking more primitive urges.

Friedrich Nietzsche, in The Birth of Tragedy, continues this de-idealization of psychic energy. For Nietzsche sees individuated Apollonian consciousness as "a veil" hiding the "Dionysian world" of the unconscious from man's vision.[27] Unconscious energy - initially non-verbal and non-visual - is seen to project itself into bright images of order, such as "the Olympian world which the Hellenic 'will' made use of as a transfiguring mirror."[28] Through this act of projection (which objectifies previously unconscious forces), "the 'will'" is able "to contemplate itself in the transfiguration of genius and the world of art."[29] But artistic genius, Nietzsche continues, is more than this bright consciousness of spiritual order. For the artist transforms more primitive energies, the "primordial artist of the world,"[30] into shining images. The mistake of earlier thinkers was to mistake the projected ideal for the darker reality motivating it -- to accept at face value "the Apollonian appearances in which Dionysius objectifies himself."[31] In a sense, these bright images, for example "the bright image projections of the Sophoclean hero," are compensations -- "necessary effects of a glance into the inside and terrors of nature; as it were, luminous spots to cure eyes damaged by gruesome night."[32] They are a "bright image which healing nature projects before us after a glance into the abyss"[33]-- into the heart of darkness.

Nietzsche's formulations give us the tools to define more clearly the spiritual and psychological crisis confronting Emerson's age. Is the unconscious a heart of light or a heart of darkness? Is it the locus of rational spirit or irrational passion? The problem for Emerson, as well as for Melville, is that neither light nor darkness can exist in a pure form. The Apollonian and the Dionysian are blended in various proportions. But during the American Renaissance, we observe a darkening of this blend as the irrational takes on an increasingly important role in visions of the psyche. There is a movement from pantheistic visions of the world akin to that of the Neoplatonist Thomas Taylor - of a cosmos "not heaving and throbbing with animal life or Dionysian rage but shining and awake with a life of mind or spirit"[34]- toward an acceptance of Dionysian animal urge. Through this darkening, the body reenters the mind, and the mind is firmly placed again back in the body -- as abstract psychologies inherited from the eighteenth century give way to visions of mental phenomena as modes of incarnation, of symbolic form. But the dilemma confronting psychologies of incarnation is to maintain a creative balance between light and darkness, rational spirit and irrational energy. If this balance is upset, there is the danger of fragmenting the vision of the mind into partial views in which spirit or passion is given supremacy. But spirit divided from matter degenerates into lifeless and bodiless moralism -- into "spectral" preachers delivering spectral sermons, to paraphrase Emerson's "Divinity School Address" (CW,I,85). At the other extreme, passion isolated from rational control turns into destructive and violent energy. The goal is somewhere between -- for example, in Emerson's vision of Christ who "saw that God incarnates himself in man, and evermore goes forth anew to take possession of his World" (CW,I,81).

That extremes of inhuman abstraction and immoral passion confronted Emerson's age we know from Hawthorne's portraits -- from the contrast between Priscilla's repression or Hollingsworth"s chilling monomania and Zenobia's luxuriant vitality in The Blithedale Romance, or between Hilda's ethereal spirituality and Miriam's guilty passion in The Marble Faun. In The Romance in America, Joel Porte clarifies the sexual polarities involved in the contrast between "Fair" and "Dark" ladies such as Hilda and Miriam. In Hawthorne's vision of women, Porte observes, a "desperate flight...from sexuality" stands opposed to "sexual knowledge and attractiveness," to a "nexus of violence, sexuality, and artistic power associated with the femme fatale of romance."[35] In such terms, we see Hawthorne imagining extremes of repression and expression of sexual energy. Rarely do we find a balanced character, embodying a moderately restrained and normal sexuality.

But it is important that we see such imbalance as more than just a sexual issue. For, as Porte observes,

> Hilda's refusal to accept her own sexuality - in effect, to admit that her 'pure' self harbors 'impurity' and is therefore a mixed, or human, nature - turns her into a rigid dualist, an absolutist in morals and the sworn enemy of ambiguity.[36]

We encounter a similar plea for "mixture" in Nietzsche's rejection of a "true world" which is not lived on earth, but rather aspired toward as an other-worldly ideal.[37] The goal of morality Hawthorne implies and Nietzsche explicitly argues, must not be an abstract realm of ethereal notions which turns mankind into a spectre, but rather a philosophy of incarnation and embodiment which maintains a vision of ideality fixed and potentially attainable in this world. This emphasis upon incarnation and embodiment leads toward twentieth-century existential phenomenology with its vision of "thrownness," "facticity," and "being-in-the-world." In the mid-nineteenth century, we see stirrings of this concrete vision in the realization that life must regain depth, density, solidity, weight -- and not float off towards an unreal ideal.

From this perspective, we see the "spiritual" crisis which impends throughout the Romantic period not merely as the decline of religion or the loss of contact with unconscious forces of inspiration. A more useful scheme is to see both that spiritual and that psychological loss as symptomatic of a dissociation which threatened to fragment the self into extremes of bodiless spirit and spiritless body. In America, the lines of cleavage were there, waiting for sufficient force to divide the mind against the body. Many among the clergy were growing increasingly abstract and immaterial in their speculations; while much of the populace succumbed to the materialistic lure of the land's potential. On the one hand, there was the threat of that loss of the "sense of solidity and substantiality of existence" which Hegel had seen as the desiccated fruit of self-consciousness -- the product of a state of mind that has moved beyond even the "extreme of insubstantial reflection of self into self."[38] From this pole, man desperately seeks to regain "the substantial fullness of life" and to "restore the feeling of existence"[39] -- motives that we find in both Coleridge and Emerson. But on the other hand, there is the threat of a materialism so complete that man is "sunken in what is sensuous, vulgar, and of fleeting importance" -- his "mind and interest...so deeply rooted in the earthly that we require a...power to have them raised above that level."[40] Bodiless religion or atheistic materialism (Barzillai Frost or State Street) were the Scylla and Charybdis that confronted the age of Emerson.

Existing studies of Romanticism reveal, in their implicit critical assumptions, the ambivalent nature of psychic energy. As we have seen, the Romantic model of the psyche - articulating the flow and patterning of energy - expresses both a sense of physical energy, the growing organic body, but also unfolding spiritual potential. Not surprisingly, the two major studies of M.H. Abrams reflect these two perspectives.

For if one stops to consider, a contradiction emerges between
Abrams' examination in <u>Natural Supernaturalism</u> of the Romantic vision of the unconscious in theological terms and his
earlier analysis, in <u>The Mirror and the Lamp</u>, of the unconscious in terms of organic models derived from biology. In
<u>Natural Supernaturalism</u>, Abrams analyzes the displacement
of theological conceptions which made a psychology of the
unconscious possible. As he amply illustrates, in the 1790's
the nature of the psyche became problematic for German and,
eventually, English writers. Sensing a decline of faith,
these early Romantics began to foreground their problematic
relationship to what threatened to become an inaccessible
ground of being. (See, for example, Holderlin's laments at
the disappearance of the gods). Accordingly, Abrams documents the adaptation of religious terminology to what was
increasingly viewed as a psychological problem. It is clear
from his discussion that the "lost home" quested for on
those many "circuitous journeys from alienation to reintegration" represents what Carl Jung (as well as Coleridge
and Emerson) calls the "unconscious." As Abrams observes
of Wordsworth's "Prospectus" to <u>The Excursion</u>, "the heights
and depths of the mind are to replace heaven and hell, and
the powers of the mind are to replace the divine protagonists."[41]

But the "powers of the mind," as we have seen, can be
viewed either spiritually or naturalistically. Abrams' earlier study adopts the latter perspective. For in <u>The Mirror</u>

and the Lamp, Prof. Abrams relates the Romantic concern with the unconscious to biological models of growth in an enlightening chapter entitled "The Psychology of Literary Invention: Unconscious Genesis and Organic Growth." The contrast between Abrams' two studies of the Romantic vision of the unconscious centers on the question whether the unconscious should be viewed as spiritual energy or natural force. The tension between these two views, between spiritual "topology" (heights-depths) versus natural "economy" (transformations of energy), runs throughout the nineteenth and well into the twentieth century. Indeed, this tension structures contemporary critical debate. For the question remains open whether one should view the psyche as a theological field or as the product of an economy of physical forces. As Paul Ricoeur observes, even Freud wavered between topology and economy in his analyses of the mind.[42]

Does one find "God" or "Nature" at the bottom (or should I say "root") of the psyche? The most interesting discussions of the mind - for example, those of Wordsworth, Coleridge, Emerson, and Nietzsche - equivocate between these two poles. But at the same time, we can identify the outlines of two rival traditions. On the one hand, there is the tradition of psychological discourse stretching from Friedrich Schlegel, Schelling, and Hegel through Coleridge and Emerson to Jung and Ernst Cassirer. This view subordinates Nature to Spirit and envisions the unconscious as a teleological force embodying itself in creative activity. But in contrast, there is the counter-tradition, emerging fully in Nietzsche, and gaining great momentum with Freud, that subordinates Spirit to Nature, viewing the unconscious as physical energy sublimating and disguising itself in cultural manifestations. But even Freud was forced to use myth (for example, the myth of Oedipus) to articulate his theories. For despite extremes of emphasis, neither Spirit nor Nature, as Emerson so often reminds us with his theory of "correspondence," can exist in a vacuum. The mind perceives its own activity through images derived from nature, while natural law is disclosed through thought. Philosophy and poetry, the play of spirit and the theatre of desire, intersect -- they illuminate each other. Neither can exist in a pure form.

Ultimately, Spirit and Nature must be seen as two facets of the same force. If thought is driven by psychic energy derived from the body, ultimately that energy is transformed into patterns which transcend its roots. Power projected from the unconscious takes on spiritual forms. Traditionally, the term "sublimation" has been used to describe this process. But it is necessary to see sublimation neither as an unconscious function nor as a conscious patterning, but rather as <u>the region where unconscious and consciousness meet</u>, where energy derived from the body is made available to the will. Paul Ricoeur's conception of sublimation underscores this dynamic by focusing upon what I shall call its "projective" and "interpretive" aspects.

Significantly, Ricoeur sees "sublimation" as "the symbolic

function itself" because "revealing and disguising coincide in it."[43] If an "economics [of desire] isolates the element of disguise in the symbolic function" (Freud's position), this view "must be counterbalanced by a phenomenology of mind or spirit in order...to show that symbols involve a development of the self that opens up what the symbols disclose." This latter perspective coincides with the view of Jung, who opposed his perspective of "finality" against Freud's "causality."[44] But these two aspects do not alternate in the symbolic process. They coincide. The opacity of the symbol, the disguise of "forbidden desires," forms part of a movement of meaning in which the symbol opens out into a new context that unfolds what had been unconscious. The "second function of symbols (the phenomenology of spirit) takes into itself the projective function in order to raise it up and the proper sense of the term, sublimate it." Projection calls for interpretation. Objectifications of spirit, as they ripen and fall from experience into reflection (to use Emerson's metaphor), are detached from their original patterns in order to be framed by new, "elevating" interpretive contexts. They become symbolic and, through such symbolism, connect alienated self-consciousness with the living power of unconscious energy. In the following chapter, we shall examine in greater detail this dialectical relationship between projection and interpretation.

NOTES: CHAPTER TWO

[1] Michel Foucault, The Order of Things: An Anthology of the Human Sciences (New York: Random House, Vintage Book, 1973), p.219.

[2] Foucault, p.229.

[3] Foucault, pp.229,231.

[4] Foucault, p.239.

[5] Thomas Carlyle, "Characteristics" in Critical and Miscellaneous Essays (New York: Charles Scribner's Sons, 1899), III,4-5.

[6] M.H. Abrams, The Mirror and the Lamp: Romantic Theory and the Critical Tradition (New York: Norton, 1958), pp.202,205.

[7] Abrams, p.206.

[8] Abrams, p.209.

[9] Abrams, p.214.

[10] Coleridge, Biographia Literaria, ed. J. Shawcross (London: Oxford Univ. Press, 1965), I,56.

[11] Frederick Coplestone Jr., Modern Philosophy: Schopenhauer to Nietzsche, Vol. 7, Part II, A History of Philosophy (Garden City, N.Y.: Doubleday, Image Book, 1965), p.37.

[12] Coplestone, p.55.

[13] Freud, SE 19:56.

[14] Arthur Lovejoy, The Great Chain of Being: A Study of the History of an Idea (1933; rptd. Cambridge, Mass.: Harvard Univ. Press, 1976), p.250.

[15] Coleridge, "Shakespeare's Judgment Equal To His Genius," in D. Perkins ed. *English Romantic Works* (New York: Harcourt, Brace & World, 1967), p.500.

[16] *Ibid*.

[17] *Ibid*.

[18] Keats, Letter to J.H. Reynolds, 19 Feb. 1818, D. Perkins ed., *English Romantic Works*, p.1211; Letter to John Taylor, 27 Feb. 1818, D. Perkins ed., *English Romantic Works*, p.1212.

[19] Coleridge, "The Eolian Harp," 1.26.

[20] For a discussion of psychic imperialism in the American Renaissance, see Quentin Anderson, *The Imperial Self* (New York: Alfred A. Knopf, 1971).

[21] "Walking" in *The Portable Thoreau*, ed. Carl Bode (New York: Viking Press, 1964), pp.609,611.

[22] Carlyle, *Sartor Resartus: The Life and Opinions of Herr Teufelsdrockh*, ed. C.F. Harrold (New York: Odyssey Press, 1937), p.164.

[23] Walter Jackson Bate, *Criticism: The Major Texts* (New York: Harcourt Brace Jovanovich, 1970), pp.359,360.

[24] Bate, p.360.

[25] For a general discussion of literary symbolism in the mid-nineteenth century, see Charles Feidelson Jr., *Symbolism and American Literature* (Chicago & London: Univ. of Chicago Press, 1953).

[26] Joel Porte, *The Romance in America* (Middletown, Conn.: Wesleyan Univ. Press, 1969), p.109.

[27] Nietzsche, *The Birth of Tragedy & The Case of Wagner*, ed. & trans. Walter Kaufmann (New York: Random House, Vintage

Book, 1967), p.41.

[28] Nietzsche, p.43.

[29] Nietzsche, p.44.

[30] Nietzsche, p.52.

[31] Nietzsche, p.66.

[32] Nietzsche, p.67.

[33] Nietzsche, p.68.

[34] Robert D. Richardson Jr., *Myth and Literature in the American Renaissance* (Bloomington & London: Indiana Univ. Press, 1978), p.56.

[35] Porte, *The Romance in America*, pp.147,135,141.

[36] Porte, p.148.

[37] *The Portable Nietzsche*, ed. & trans. Walter Kaufmann (New York: Viking Press, 1954), p.485.

[38] Hegel, *The Phenomenology of Mind*, trans. J.B. Baillie (New York: Harper & Row, 1967), p.72.

[39] Hegel, p.71.

[40] Hegel, p.73.

[41] M.H. Abrams, *Natural Supernaturalism: Tradition and Revolution in Romantic Literature* (New York: Norton, 1973), p.25.

[42] See Paul Ricoeur, *Freud and Philosophy: An Essay on Interpretation*, trans. D. Savage (New Haven & London: Yale Univ. Press, 1970), Book II, Part I: "Energetics and Hermeneutics," p.65ff.

[43] Ricoeur, p.497.

[44] Jung, *CW*,8,par.462.

CHAPTER THREE

PROJECTIVE AND INTERPRETIVE FORM

The major premise of this study is that <u>a literature predicated upon contact with unconscious sources of energy cannot operate without conscious patterns designed to uncover and assimilate that energy</u>. In other words, the unconscious energies embodied in myth entail what Kenneth Burke calls a "machinery of transcendence" -- literary forms whose function is to transform unconscious energy into conscious creation.[1] If plot, as Northrop Frye asserts in <u>The Anatomy of Criticism</u>, is displaced myth,[2] what we need to analyze is the mechanism of displacement. That is what I propose to do in this study, taking Emerson as my primary example of literary self-consciousness dedicated to regrounding thought in the hidden energy of the unconscious. It is one of my aims to see Emerson as the great psychologist of his age, portraying in his addresses and essays many of the themes which take on more concrete form in the romances and poems of his contemporaries.

A major focus will be on Emerson's vision of psychic dynamics, for example the reception of the "Ideas of the Reason" (JMN,V,270) by the "Understanding," a process which unfolds the mind and reveals its previously-hidden powers. As we shall see, striking similarities exist between Emerson's vision of the mind and the depth psychologies of Freud and especially Jung. Indeed, the unwary reader might be startled by the apparent modernity of Emerson's terminology in a passage such as the following, written in 1837:

> & so the great word Comparative Anatomy has now leaped out of the womb of the Unconscious. I feel a cabinet in my mind unlocked by each of these new interests. Wherever I go, the related objects crowd on my Sense & I explore backward & wonder how the same things looked to me before my attention had been aroused (JMN,V,427).

While he usually calls it by other names, the "Unconscious" - I hope to show - is one of Emerson's ruling concepts. As Lancelot Whyte has amply illustrated[3] and Freud himself acknowledged, there was a long foreground to modern depth psychology. Indeed, the "discovery" of the unconscious during the eighteenth and nineteenth centuries necessarily preceded twentieth-century systematizations of its dynamics. If Schelling, Coleridge, Carlyle, and Nietzsche represent important chapters in this growing psychological awareness, we can see that Emerson also contributed to this reinterpretation of the mind, this shift from theological to psychological perspectives. While M.H. Abrams focuses upon the antecedents of nineteenth-century psychological insights, their displacement from theology, I shall look ahead to their succession in modern psychology and philosophy. As a bridge between religious myth and psychoanalytical practice, writers such as Emerson hold a special interest.

As Charles Feidelson suggests in Symbolism and American Literature, the emergence of psychological perspectives coincided with a "sense of the inherent power of language," its potential for symbolic expression.[4] Symbolism for Emerson and his contemporaries became a method of revealing the undiscovered self through the equation of being and vision.[5] Unfolding the mind through the process of literary creation, American Romantics learned to manipulate literary form as a means of self-discovery. As an early and influential analysis of symbolic form in mid-century America, Feidelson's study deserves its acclaim. However, one aspect of his argument needs to be refined. For example, let us consider the following account of Emerson's symbolic method:

> Thus Emerson gave the poet a role by transforming man and the universe out of all recognition. In his effort to shake off any links with the rational world view, he projected a world in which only symbols exist. We ourselves, from his standpoint, "are symbols," and we "inhabit symbols."[6]

In a similar vein, Feidelson later asserts that "Emerson had a theory of poetry which eliminated the particular poem, since it provided no means of halting the proliferation of metaphor and synecdoche."[7] Finally, in a statement revealing his prejudice in favor of Melville, Feidelson comments, "Emerson could never feel the potential disunity of thought, word, and object as a tragic dilemma; this was Melville's discovery."[8] These are serious charges -- for, if true, they weaken our vision of Emerson's strength as a thinker. More to the point, Feidelson's commentary here obscures one of the most important aspects of Emerson's symbolic method.

Admittedly, Feidelson is quoting Emerson. But we must be wary of taking Emerson's more expansive affirmations (especially those made later in his career) at face value. For to do so leads to absurdities such as the conclusion that Emerson's "theory of poetry...provided no means of halting the proliferation of metaphor and synecdoche." This is perhaps true if we define "theory of poetry" very narrowly and divorce it from Emerson's theory as it is revealed in his poetic practice. For Emerson obviously did halt the proliferation of metaphor; indeed, we know from comparing his finished works with earlier versions in his journals that his essays and poems were carefully crafted and not uncritical profusions. Even in essays such as "The Poet," Emerson can make his points only by limiting the proliferation of metaphors and making them subserve specific rhetorical ends. More importantly, we must see Emerson's acute apprehension of "the potential disunity of thought, word, and object." For his sense of possible meaninglessness informs many of his most profound statements about "correspondence" and meaning. What I am saying is that Emerson knew very well the tragic limitations of action and the limitations of symbolic action, in particular. Furthermore, his literary practice (as all literary practice must be) is based upon such self-limitation. What I propose to do in this chapter is to look more closely at one aspect of such limitation -- Emerson's structuring of what I call "interpretive form." At the same time, our earlier glance at Paul Ricoeur should remind us that such interpretive form stands as a prototype of later "hermeneutic" perspectives. For Emerson, as well as Ricoeur, was aware of the self-referentiality of symbolic form and of the way language must be limited in order to attain meaning.

This is a study, then, of some of the ways the mind expresses itself and its processes through the limitation of symbolic form. Such self-awareness involves examination of projected psychic processes as objects of analysis. In Romantic literature, symbolism performs this function by drawing our attention to the <u>relation between figure and ground</u>. Images are seen to stand for, to emerge from, a defining context which gives them meaning. This context evades less concrete expression. In terms of the psyche, it can be described as the "unconscious" -- that is, as a psychic field transcending the limited scope of particular awareness, a field which stretches out from the center of vision embedded within it in the form of symbolic images. As Romantic (and later, Symbolist) writers learned, it is possible to manipulate these symbols through explorative forms such as the <u>quest</u> in order to map the hidden psychic ground.

The occult meditative practices of Yeats present a revealing example of this process. I am thinking of Yeats' discussions of the magical center as gate to the dream-world. The poet, Yeats believed, must fan this vulnerable spark of subjectivity until it flames into illumination. Yeats' letter of 1 January 1898 to the seer Dorothea Hunter explicitly describes a meditation in which he attempted to expand such a symbolic center through careful exploration. Yeats had been meditating upon a vision of the well of the druid Connla:

> I have had a number of visions on the way home, greatly extending the symbolism we got tonight. The souls of ordinary people remain after death in the waters and these waters become an organized world if you gather up the flames that come from the waters of the well when the berries fall upon it, and make them into a flaming heart, and explore the waters with this as a lamp.[9]

This letter gives us some idea of how Yeats, during his early days as an active student of the occult, structured his meditations upon mystical symbols. But important to our argument here is that Yeats himself saw such meditative practice as analogous to the symbolic method of Romantic literature. For example, Yeats finds in Shelley's poetry a similar use of the well or cave as an entry point into the unconscious:

> Cythna...speaks of the 'cave' of her mind which gave its secrets to her...and then passing more completely under the power of the symbol, she speaks of growing wise through contemplation of the images that rise out of the fountain at the call of her will.[10]

Throughout Romantic literature, we encounter similar centers which function as points of contact between consciousness and the hidden powers of the unconscious. If Shelley writes of fountains, Poe and Melville describe maelstroms and whales.

Without going into detail as to the vexing question of the meaning of such symbols, we can see that much of their significance resides in their function as centers which require encircling contexts of <u>interpretation</u>. Indeed, it frequently becomes the specific function of certain fictional characters to provide the needed commentary. Thus, the narrator of "The Fall of the House of Usher" leads us self-consciously into and out of the Gothic world he encounters; while Ishmael in <u>Moby-Dick</u> provides ample commentary upon Ahab's process of symbolization and its index of error. We notice here that our own function as readers and critics has been anticipated by those aspects of the literary work which are self-reflective and self-interpretive. We find such reflexivity in Hawthorne's "Rappaccini's Daughter," in which Giovanni embodies a process of interpretation as he ponders the enigmatic meaning of Beatrice Rappaccini and her garden. Similarly, Melville's Pierre broods obsessively upon the psychological claims of his mysterious half-sister.

One of the classic formulations of such self-interpretation is Coleridge's <u>The Rime of the Ancient Mariner</u>. We notice that Coleridge's Ancient Mariner needs the presence of the Wedding Guest as an audience. In this respect, the Wedding Guest serves as a representative of interpretive consciousness (Coleridge's and the reader's) listening to the tales the psyche offers it. For the Ancient Mariner as a figure of the psychic explorer serves up images of the mind, maps of its geography, to which the Wedding Guest responds. Thus, while The Rime of the Ancient Mariner ostensibly analyzes religious questions of guilt and redemption, at the same time it depicts questions of motivation and psychological dynamics which deeply concerned Coleridge's own creative activity. It is an essential part of my argument that for such a literary work to involve questions of depth psychology (the relation of consciousness to the unconscious) it must portray both a figuration of critical, self-conscious awareness (the Wedding Guest) and a projective process of symbolism revealing the hidden depths of the mind (the Ancient Mariner). In fact, neither can exist without the other -- projection and interpretation are two facets of the same process of psychological exploration.

Carl Jung places himself in this critical position when he observes, in Two Essays on Analytical Psychology, that Freud's emphasis upon unconscious instinct necessitated the development of a compensatory psychology -- Alfred Adler's theory of consciousness, of the ego's "will to power."[11] The relation between these two poles - unconscious and consciousness, libido and ego - forms the central dialectic of Jung's own theorizing. Taking our cue from Jung, we can observe the ways in which the differentiation and relation of conscious and unconscious functions serve the analysis of the mind. For example, Schiller differentiates the unconscious "naive" from the self-conscious "sentimental"; while Nietzsche opposes "Dionysian" power against the conscious differentiations of the "Apollonian" ego.[12]

To suggest a more general scheme which can encompass these different visions of the psychic economy, I propose that we organize our examination under the opposition of projective and interpretive functions. For if the unconscious was seen by Romantic writers to express itself through symbolic projection, such projection takes on value as a map of the dark side of the mind to the extent that consciousness draws out and interprets its implications. What one sees throughout Romantic literature is the dramatization of confrontations between consciousness and the unconscious, between "wedding guests" and the psychic depths toward which "ancient mariners" point. The contours of the modern concept of the mind, as a field with conscious and unconscious aspects, emerges from such patterns of analysis.

But Romantic writers structured literary quests in relation to powers they were losing hold of. In a sense, the interpretive structures developed to explore the depths of the mind signify the potential collapse of Romanticism. For projection and interpretation maintain a delicate balance which can easily veer off into profound but inexplicable myth on the one hand (an excess of projection), or, on the other hand, become an excess of self-conscious interpretation which inhibits the expression of unconscious forces. Ambiguity or smug certainty, at either extreme, signals the dissolution of "negative capability" into uncontrolled doubt or dogmatism -- that is, a breaking apart of myth and interpretation into opposed camps.

We know from The Birth of Tragedy that Friedrich Nietzsche witnessed such a development during his own period. For he argues that the development of nineteenth-century theorizing was fatal to mythmaking:

> He who recalls the immediate consequences of this restlessly progressing spirit of science will realize at once that myth was annihilated by it.[13]

Nietzsche saw that the tendency to allegorize myth by assigning abstract meaning to it can overpower apprehension of the symbolic power embodied in myth itself -- we forget the myth in favor of our interpretations of it. The danger of such analogizing is that it destroys symbolic patterns of relationship to the mythical ground (as we remember, Emerson's complaint against the attitude of the clergy of his own day). As Nietzsche explains the process:

> if our understanding is to content itself with the perception of these analogies; we are reduced to a frame of mind which makes impossible any reception of the mythical; for the myth wants to be experienced vividly as a unique example of a universality and truth that gazes into the infinite.[14]

Nietzsche saw this destructive tension between the mythical and the theoretical at work in his own society. Contact with myth, openness to the unconscious, was becoming more and more difficult. This demythologizing, which Nietzsche later characterizes as the "death" of God, became one of the targets of The Birth of Tragedy. By recovering a sense of the Dionysian, of ecstatic depths of the psyche, Nietzsche hoped to reestablish and strengthen contact with the unconscious. The sense of myth he saw, was in danger of being entirely lost to the objective spirit of late nineteenth-century science and philosophy.

In America, this sense of disappearing myth, of the possibility of entirely losing the doorway to the unconscious, was expressed by Nietzsche's contemporary, Henry James, especially in his series of prefaces to the New York edition of his fiction. Writing of the figures who had inspired "The Pupil," James observes that they, like him, "were, all together, of a better romantic age and faith." The dilemma today, James continues, is that "every key to interpretation" of that age of romance "has been lost":

> The comparatively brief but infinitely rich "cycle" of romance embedded in the earlier, the very early reactions and returns..., what does it resemble today but a goldmine overgrown and smothered, dislocated, and no longer workable? -- all for want of the right indications for sounding, the right implements for digging, doubtless even of the right workmen, those with the right tradition and "feeling" for the job.[15]

Given this sense of impending loss, one readily appreciates James' valuation - in his next preface - of the strangeness and obscurity of the "air of the old-time Italy" which helps to invest the romantic atmosphere of "The Aspern Papers."[16] Explicitly commenting upon his attraction to the "romance-value" of the fable which formed the germ of his plot, James explains that his effort "to tap" the creative "fount" involved his ability to appreciate "the mere essential charm ...of a final scene of the rich dim Shelley drama played out in the very theatre of our own 'modernity.'"[17] What that drama held for James was an example of a "palpable imaginable visitable past"-- one of the isolated outcroppings of the rich vein of romance that had not yet been "overgrown" and buried.[18] James' task thus becomes one of relating the lingering charm of romance, with its orientation toward the unconscious, to the brisk consciousness of the modern world.

James shows his audience that such Romanticism is still possible, must still possible, if one is to hold out "against certain general brutalities."[19] In this regard, we remember that Spencer Brydon's "haunted" house in "The Jolly Corner" represents a last refuge of romance amidst the urban brutalities of twentieth-century New York -- a final corner where the imagination with its spectral visitants can be nourished, where - as James puts it in an earlier preface - characters can

> revive...by a force or a whim of their own and "walk" round his house of art like haunting ghosts, feeling for the old doors they knew, fumbling at stiff latches and pressing their pale faces, in the outer dark, to lighted windows.[20]

Confronted with the possibility that one's fantasies might not find again the "old doors they knew," a refuge for such spirits must be established. In James' case, this "neutral territory" is imagined as a house where consciousness and unconscious forces can intermingle and enrich each other. But we notice the narrowing of the sphere of fantasy. If all of nature constituted a field of projection for Emerson, by the time of Henry James only a very few territories maintained the ambiance where one could nourish the dream of "correspondence" between inner and outer worlds. The old doors of romance were being closed.

One of James' great contributions to fiction was to demonstrate how the windows of the house of fiction could be "lighted." He does this by emphasizing one aspect of Romantic fiction -- the development of self-interpretive patterns of consciousness. By focusing upon the movement of a central consciousness, James posits a "lighted figure" whose drama of apprehension and "appreciation" organizes the ongoing tale. In this way, Christopher Newman is the lighted figure of The American, while "the others...were to be the obscured":

> If Newman was attaching enough,...his tangle would be sensible enough; for the interest of everything is all that is his vision, his conception, his interpretation: at the window of his wide, quite sufficiently wide, consciousness we are seated, from that admirable position we "assist."[21]

Similarly, Isabel Archer, the central consciousness of The Portrait of a Lady, represents "the posted presence of the watcher" at the window of the "house of fiction."[22] She is the delegate of the author's (and the reader's) process of vision. As James recounts in that famous catalogue of personae in the preface to The Princess Casamassima, the "interest" of nearly all of his fiction resides "in placing advantageously, placing right in the middle of the light, the most polished of possible mirrors of the subject."[23]

But if James structures his fiction around the "light" of a central consciousness, that consciousness can move and develop only in relation to a surrounding "obscurity." For there can be no story, he observes, without "bewilderment."[24]

"The picture of the exposed and tangled state is what is required."[25] The novelist must guard against "making his characters too <u>interpretative</u> of the muddle of fate, or in other words too divinely, too priggishly clever."[26] Thus, opposed to Rowland Mallet's striving after the "intelligible" in <u>Roderick Hudson</u>, there stands the "bedimmed and befooled and bewildered."[27] Opposed to Fleda Vetch's "interpretation and criticism," there is "the surrounding tangle."[28] Opposed to the "effort really to see," the "vivacity of intelligence" of Maisie, there is "muddlement" and "infected air."[29] Surrounding the "central light" of the Jamesian story, one always finds "the full thick wash of the penumbra."[30] While it is certainly not news that mystery and ambiguity and suspense reside at the heart of fiction, what is of interest here is the extent to which James focused and controlled such mystery through the use of <u>interpretive form</u> -- his central characters' interpretations of their ambiguous situations.

Joel Porte suggests in <u>The Romance in America</u> that the object of such interpretation in the Jamesian universe is frequently romance itself. If we observe James' characters attempting to cut their way through social "mystification" (for example, Isabel Archer's unraveling of the mystification of Gilbert Osmond and Mme. Merle), at the same time James frequently uses the interpretive structures of his fiction to interpret the psychological mystery embedded in romance. Thus, Porte observes of <u>The American</u>:

Newman's experience with the Bellegardes might be

> considered an introductory journey along precisely that dark circuit and subterfuge of thought and desire which James, in his Preface, associates generally with romance.[31]

Such criticism suggests that among the seeds lying at the heart of James' vision was Romanticism itself, that Realism made its way in America by carefully framing and assimilating the energies of that earlier fiction, and that an integral part of that assimilation was the self-conscious exploitation of the unconscious energies embodied in earlier Romantic archetypes. In other words, as Romantic avenues to the unconscious became overgrown and problematic, it was the burden of later literature to attempt to uncover such contacts with creative energy.

Moving back in time from the self-conscious interpretive structures of Henry James to the previous literary generation, we find a similar concern with the relationship of consciousness to unconscious energies embodied in the archetypal figures of romance. Again, the concern is with literary structures that allow the assimilation of creative energy. Perry Miller observes that the works of Hawthorne and Melville, falling "at the conclusion of three decades during which a host of American writers had cultivated, perfected, formalized the Romance," were themselves partly commentaries upon the Romantic conventions which constituted their reality.[32] Accordingly, Miller reads _Pierre_ not as "a regular romance," but as "a vicious perversion of a formula so universally worshipped as to be in effect sacrosanct."[33] Similarly, he argues that "The secret of Moby-Dick - or rather the innermost secret behind the myriad lesser secrets - is that it pushes the Romance to extremities which exhaust the form."[34] These are suggestive comments, pointing the way to studies such as those of Joel Porte and Robert Richardson which illustrate the reflexive quality of major American romances -- the ways in which writers such as Hawthorne and Melville used their fiction to comment upon its literary and psychological genesis.

Such reflexiveness was characteristic of the age. As Emerson remarked in retrospect:

> The key to the period appeared to be that the mind had become aware of itself. Men grew reflective and intellectual. There was a new consciousness (W,X,326).

This "predominance of the intellect in the balance of powers" (W,X,329) manifested itself as "a certain sharpness of criticism, an eagerness for reform, which showed itself in every quarter" (W,X,337). The human mind, society, religious attitudes, all became fuel for the consuming power of reform and analysis, that "holocaust" satirized by Hawthorne in "Earth's Holocaust." But the danger of such a critical spirit, this "tendency to introversion, self-dissection, anatomizing of motives" (W,X,329), was that it had the capacity to destroy myth. In a page foreshadowing Nietzsche's more astringent observations, Emerson wrote:

> The warm swart Earth-spirit which made the strength of past ages, mightier than it knew, with instincts instead of science, like a mother yielding food

> from her breast instead of preparing it through
> chemic and culinary skill,-- warm negro ages of
> sentiment and vegetation,-- all gone; another
> hour had struck and other forms arose (W,X,329).

As "instinct" yielded to "science," and mythmaking fell to the dissection of motives, men came to feel isolated from society and even from themselves. To become regenerated, man was forced to find both "society and deity within himself" (W,X,329) -- to return to the "Mother."

Symptomatic of such critical reflexiveness, according to Porte, was an acute sense of what Emerson called "double consciousness":

> it was precisely the problem of reconciling the
> soul with Nature, the "Not-Me"..., that plagued
> the Transcendentalists. Like Faust, torn be-
> tween his earthly lusts and his spiritual striv-
> ings, they were dualists; yet they yearned for
> unity.[35]

It is important to see that this cleavage extends between two mental functions -- between the capacity to exist in a world of living myth and existence through analysis and criticism. Or, in Emerson's familar terms, we see a tension between "Reason" and "Understanding." But what does it mean to recognize with "the best of the Transcendentalists" that one is "divided between Reason and Understanding"?[36]

It is tempting to stop with this dual classification, satisfied that - by labelling it - we have solved the problem. But at this very point, this sense of self-division, of alienation, we touch upon one of the central dilemmas of the nineteenth century. For as the age became secularized, as belief in divine power slowly atrophied and died, the very analysis of that loss - by positing divinity as distant or absent - facilitated the process of spiritual decay that it had hoped to retard by defining. By attempting to name the unnameable, by viewing it as an object, one places it in a position in which it is conditioned by the demands of the ego. One reads myth literally, instead as a symbol -- such was Emerson's recurrent complaint. The trick, instead, is to affirm one's connection to centers of spiritual power without severing that connection through the use of terminologies or perspectives that vitiate the vitality of those centers. At the same time, one must consciously and willfully place oneself in a position of relationship to energies which, ultimately, can compel unconscious adoration and will-less compliance. How can consciousness enter into the unconscious, secular "Understanding" comprehend inspired "Reason"? This was the dilemma confronting Emerson and his age.

This dilemma existed in Romantic thought from the beginning. For to the extent that Romantic writers were obsessed with reaffirming the mythical origins of consciousness, they were forced to examine those origins within the context of perspectives that potentially threatened mythologization. While Romantic symbols might plumb the depths of the unconscious, no work of literature can consist of symbols alone. Such symbols must be embedded within an interpretive context which presents them to consciousness. Another way of stating this is that one cannot live myth and observe it at the same time. Thus, the positing of mythical reality as a psychological goal (an image of power) is only possible <u>after</u> one has emerged from mythical process. As Ernst Cassirer explains:

> if we examine myth itself, what it is and what it <u>knows</u> itself to be, we see that this separation of the ideal from the real, this distinction between a world of immediate reality and a world of mediate signification, this opposition of "image" and "object," is alien to it. Only observers who no longer live in it but reflect on it read such distinctions into myth. Where we see mere "representation," myth, insofar as it has not yet deviated from its fundamental and original form, sees real identity. The "image" does not represent the "thing"; it <u>is</u> the thing; it does not merely stand for the object, but has the same actuality, so that it replaces the thing's immediate presence. Consequently, mythical thinking lacks the category of the ideal.[37]

In this light, Romantic writers, even though "they strove to replace the allegorical view of myth" and "to understand the basic phenomena of mythology in themselves and not through their relation to something else, did not <u>fundamentally</u> overcome 'allegoresis.'"[38] Even when myth is seen as the function of unconscious forces and one aspires to participate symbolically in the field of such energies, the literary treatment of myth necessarily involves the self-conscious presentation of myth to consciousness. Thus, as we shall see, the monistic intention of Emerson's <u>Nature</u> necessitates a dualistic terminology -- a creative balance between projection and interpretation, between Friedrich Schlegel's "overflowing vitality" and his "limiting scepticism." Accordingly, Robert Richardson sees in Emerson's writing the capacity to temper the Neoplatonic excesses of a Bronson Alcott with a healthy skepticism toward such myth. Balanced against Emerson's "attempt to fashion a new mythology out of new materials," he finds a "streak of cool skepticism."[39]

Careful readers of Emerson, of course, have always been aware of these two sides to his literary personality -- what Frederic Carpenter characterizes as the "strong Yankee realism and the ethereal transcendental idealism."[40] However, it is impossible to agree with Carpenter's interpretation of this phenomenon -- that these two strains "cohabited" in Emerson's mind, "but never formally joined."[41] For it is the <u>joining</u> of these two strands - the conflict <u>between</u> the real and the ideal, between skepticism and faith - that provides the source of Emerson's creative energy, as well as his strength as a thinker. Central to Emerson's project is the mind's examination of its relationship to its own unconscious origins through self-conscious presentation of mythic images to consciousness. For example, the psychological myths of Emerson's "Orphic" poet at the end of <u>Nature</u> are embedded within an interpretive context which transposes the lessons of "Reason" into the language of the "Understanding." Emerson's development of such psychological perspectives underlies his attempt to formulate what he came to call a "natural history of the intellect."

Kenneth Marc Harris comes very close to describing this process when he explains how both Carlyle and Emerson, "imprisoned in their self-awareness," attempted to resolve their dilemma by "a dual mode of thought, both 'conscious' and 'unconscious' at the same time." For "they hoped," he continues,

> to assimilate the supernatural truths that their parents accepted without reflection through the unreflective portion of the mind, all the while retaining the critical, self-dissecting qualities of intellect which would render such beliefs incredible.[42]

This comes very close, but it stops just at the crucial juncture. For Emerson did hope to assimilate supernatural truth, but not by withering it under the cold stare of critical skepticism. He hoped to secure "supernatural truths" through the <u>reflective</u> portion of the mind, translating the insights of "Reason" into the language of the "Understanding." In this way, such truth could be rendered <u>credible</u> -- as an object of faith, not dissected by skeptical intellection. It is a mistake to see the unconscious and consciousness as separated by an impermeable wall of skepticism and disbelief. In Emerson's case, this wall was very permeable. Dream and event, piety and criticism, illuminated each other.

In order to assimilate unconscious energy to consciousness, Emerson distinguishes between the "Me" and the "Not-Me," between "Spirit" and "Nature." The advantage of this dualistic terminology is that it allows him to differentiate and project a spiritual goal -- to posit <u>for</u> <u>consciousness</u> an image of power. Thus, Emerson's analysis contains within it images of transcendent power, what Jung calls "symbols of transformation."[43] Significantly, the penultimate song of Emerson's poet in <u>Nature</u> focuses upon the very processes we are considering:

> "Man is the dwarf of himself. Once he was
> permeated and dissolved by spirit. He filled
> nature with his overflowing currents. Out from
> him sprang the sun and moon; from man, the sun;
> from woman, the moon. The laws of his mind, the
> periods of his actions externized themselves in-
> to day and night, into the year and the seasons.
> But, having made for himself this huge shell,
> his waters retired; he no longer fills the veins
> and veinlets; he is shrunk to a drop. He sees,
> that the structure still fits him, but fits him
> colossally. Say, rather, once it fitted him,
> now it corresponds to him from far and on high.
> He adores timidly his own work. Now is man the
> follower of the sun, and woman the follower of
> the moon. Yet sometimes he starts in his slum-
> ber, and wonders at himself and his house, and
> muses strangely at the resemblance betwixt him
> and it. He perceives that if his law is still
> paramount, if still he have elemental power, 'if
> his word is sterling yet in nature,' it is not
> conscious power, it is not inferior but superi-
> or to his will. It is Instinct." Thus my Or-
> phic poet sang (CW,I,42).

If man once existed within a mythic world, peopling the cosmos with gods that were his unconscious projections, those myths - emblems of "elemental power" - have become nearly lifeless objects. Because man, as Emerson goes on to say, "works on the world with his understanding alone" (CW,I,42-3), he is cut off from the world of myth.

The original process of mythmaking seems to lead inexorably to the diminution of myth:

> The laws of his mind, the periods of his actions
> externized themselves into day and night, into
> the year and the seasons. But having made for
> himself this huge shell, his waters retired.

Here, the process of "externization" - the objectification of spirit (as Hegel would call it) - distances man from myth. By creating an image of spirit, a representation of god, man projects psychic energy into an external object which then becomes alienated from him. In the same way, an artist's creation is cast out, can no longer be a part of him, after it is given life. From this perspective, a process of secularization seems to be an unavoidable consequence of mythological projection. For the very act of worship, by setting up external images of god, signifies an increased distance from divinity. Sooner or later, man becomes aware of this distance and feels "shrunk to a drop" compared to the magnificence of his gods -- he sees "that the structure still fits him, but fits him colossally." Divinity becomes an analogue of human aspiration, exists in an allegorical relationship to man, as he slips from participation in its qualities. So runs Emerson's myth of the origin of consciousness -- awareness taking rise from a sense of difference and distance.

Attempting to recover that lost mythic power, man must focus upon symptoms of divinity, manifestations of unconscious activity, which can be presented to the understanding as centers for faith. At moments, for example, impressions of "strangeness" half suggest what has been lost:

> Yet sometimes he starts in his slumber, and wonders at himself and his house, and muses strangely at the resemblance betwixt him and it.

This sense of strangeness is akin to that "supernatural" impression which Wordsworth (according to Coleridge) attempted to capture in the poems composed for <u>Lyrical</u> <u>Ballads</u>:

> to give the charm of novelty to things of every day, and to excite a feeling analogous to the supernatural by awakening the mind's attention from the lethargy of custom and directing it to the loveliness and the wonders of the world before

> us; an inexhaustible treasure, but for which, in consequence of the film of familiarity and selfish solicitude, we have eyes yet see not, ears that hear not, and hearts that neither feel nor understand.[44]

We can equate the "lethargy of custom" and "the film of familiarity and selfish solicitude" with everyday understanding, the level of phenomenal consciousness. But beneath everyday consciousness is the intuited realm of "Instinct," of an "elemental power" which "is not conscious power" and which "is not inferior but superior to [man's] will." If myths exist in the nineteenth century, they exist in the unconscious.

In order to communicate his awareness of this elusive power, Emerson resorts, in the next paragraph, to cataloguing "examples of Reason's momentary grasp of the sceptre": "the traditions of miracles," "the history of Jesus Christ," "miracles of enthusiasm, as those reported of Swedenborg, Hohenlohe, and the Shakers" (CW,I,43). This catalogue, plus Emerson's earlier presentation of the intuitions of his "poet," embody the characteristic literary strategy which enables him to talk about myth and the unconscious. Symbols of power are posited within his discourse as representations which he then analyzes; a process of imaginative projection is framed by commentary and interpretation. Like moral exempla or Biblical texts embedded within a sermon, representative images are brought before us as models or ideals. We are given the song of Emerson's poet or a tradition of illumination, representations of "Reason." In a similar fashion,

Emerson - by publishing his essays and delivering his lectures and addresses (all models of thought in action) - presents his own experience as representative. In excellent pedagogical or ministerial fashion, we are invited to follow the movement of his discourse as a model of contemplation, his images becoming nodes for our reflection. (Like Coleridge, Emerson presents "aids to reflection.") Finally, Emerson's method of composition - cutting and polishing passages from his journals - involves his selection of representative situations which are isolated from the flow of experience and thought and set within his discourse as gems of insight.

But the point I wish to emphasize here is that this process of representation - the selection and arrangement of the representative - entails a reciprocal process of interpretation. Images of power are embedded within a matrix of commentary; the brief epiphanies of Reason are <u>presented</u> <u>to</u> the Understanding. Initially divided, Reason and Understanding are brought together in a process of <u>relation</u> in which representative images derived from the unconscious are assimilated by consciousness. This process of relation varied greatly among Emerson's contemporaries, according to their various attitudes toward mythmaking, their stances toward the power of the unconscious. On the one hand, mythic images emerging from the unconscious are presented as emblems of a desirable power, a sought-after illumination. On the other, they are presented as emblems of a feared and overpowering energy. Relations of love contrast with those of fear; images of life and psychological integration, with those of death and disintegration. Patterns of pursuit contrast with patterns of flight and defense. Symbols of transformation take on positive or negative valences.

I would like to suggest, at this point, that the interpretive process epitomized by Emerson's self-representation in Nature constitutes a reflective field analogous to that opened up in phenomenology. By subordinating Romantic archetypes to processes of psychological "allegory," Emerson and his contemporaries create what can be described as a phenomenology of fantasy. As we shall see, Carl Jung's depth psychology continues this contextualization of projected unconscious material. In such terms, one can understand Martin Bickman's observation that "Jungian psychology completes the movement of American Romanticism to turn metaphysics into a phenomenology of consciousness."[45] Similarly, one could argue that the Romantic "willing suspension of disbelief" anticipates the non-judgmental openness promoted within the psychoanalytic context (for example, through techniques of "free association"). In both cases, ordinary standards of judgment are "bracketed" (to use Husserl's term) in order to allow repressed unconscious material to appear. Consequently, the romance or essay, like the analytic session, becomes a phenomenological field revealing the free play of consciousness and the unconscious.

Paul Ricoeur's "hermeneutic" philosophy gives us an account

of the processes involved. For one of Ricoeur's projects has been to analyze the necessary dependence of philosophical discourse upon poetic symbolism. According to Ricoeur, our <u>awareness</u> of symbolism reveals the poverty of consciousness in danger of being cut off from its roots:

> The historical moment of the philosophy of the symbol is both the moment of forgetting and the moment of restoring: forgetting hierophanies, forgetting the signs of the Sacred, losing hold of man hismelf as belonging to the Sacred.[46]

In response to this alienation, "we wish to recharge language, start again from the <u>fullness</u> of language."[47] One route to this recovery of lost values, Ricoeur argues, is for consciousness to restore its link to the symbol, as a type of what Cassirer would call "mythical" thought: "a meditation on symbols starts from the fullness of language and of meaning already there."[48] By returning to the symbol, we return to the language of "profundity" and "inexhaustible depth."[49] We restore weight to consciousness and hence to things by anchoring abstraction in a sense of being transcending conscious thought.

This restoration is partly an interpretive process: "every symbol gives birth to understanding by means of an interpretation." But in order to interpret, one "must quit the position, or better, the exile, of the remote and disinterested spectator."[50] One enters the "hermeneutic circle" in which faith in the potential fullness of meaning necessarily precedes comprehension of the symbol:

> hermeneutics starts out from the comprehension of the very thing it is trying to understand. But thanks to this hermeneutic circle, I can today still communicate with the Sacred by explicitating [sic] the pre-comprehension which animates the interpretation.[51]

This process, Ricoeur emphasizes, situates itself <u>between</u> mythmaking and refelction. It neither surrenders to the illusion that one can "<u>know</u> the origin,"[52] nor does it rationalize myth by turning it into allegory.[53] Between these two poles, stands that discourse which acknowledges "the inscrutable and the unfathomable"[54] at the same time it attempts to reground consciousness in a sense of mystery. The smug self-certitude of consciousness is replaced by faith in the unknown, in the <u>un</u>conscious. In this manner, for Emerson and his age, interpretation nourishes projection. An unfathomable core of mystery defines the limits of expanding (or contracting) spheres of consciousness.

NOTES: CHAPTER THREE

[1] Kenneth Burke, "I, Eye, Aye -- Emerson's Early Essay on 'Nature': Thoughts on the Machinery of Transcendence" in M. Simon & T.H. Parson eds., *Transcendentalism and Its Legacy* (Ann Arbor: Univ. of Mich. Press, 1966).

[2] Northrop Frye, *The Anatomy of Criticism* (1957; rptd. New York: Atheneum, 1969), p.33ff.

[3] Lancelot Law Whyte, *The Unconscious Before Freud* (London: Tavistock Pub., 1962).

[4] Charles Feidelson Jr., *Symbolism and American Literature* (Chicago & London: Univ. of Chicago Press, 1953), p.151.

[5] Feidelson, p.143.

[6] Feidelson, p.145.

[7] Feidelson, p.149.

[8] Feidelson, p.160.

[9] Quoted in Reg Skene, *The Cuchulain Plays of W.B. Yeats* (New York: Columbia Univ. Press, 1974), p.9.

[10] Yeats, *Essays and Introductions* (New York: Collier Books, 1968), p.86.

[11] Jung, *Two Essays on Analytical Psychology*, trans. R.F.C. Hull (New York: Meridian Books, 1956), p.63.

[12] Friedrich von Schiller, *Naive & Sentimental Poetry*, trans. J.A. Elias (New York: Frederick Unger Pub. Co., 1966); Friedrich Nietzsche, *The Birth of Tragedy*, ed. & trans. Walter Kaufmann (New York: Random House, Vintage Book, 1967).

[13] Nietzsche, *The Birth of Tragedy*, p.106.

[14] Nietzsche, p.107.

[15] James' prefaces are conveniently reprinted in The Art of the Novel: Critical Prefaces by Henry James, ed. R.P. Blackmur (New York: Charles Scribner's Sons, 1934), pp.152-3.

[16] James, p.151.

[17] James, pp.161,162,163.

[18] James, p.164.

[19] James, p.245.

[20] James, p.73.

[21] James, p.37.

[22] James, p.46.

[23] James, p.70.

[24] James, p.63.

[25] James, p.65.

[26] James, p.64.

[27] James, p.16.

[28] James, p.129.

[29] James, p.149.

[30] James, p.130.

[31] Joel Porte, The Romance in America (Middletown, Conn.: Wesleyan Univ. Press, 1969), p.207.

[32] Perry Miller, Nature's Nation (Cambridge, Mass.: Harvard Univ. Press, 1967), p.255.

[33] Miller, p.243.

[34] Miller, p.246.

[35] Joel Porte, "Emerson, Thoreau, and the Double-Consciousness," New England Quarterly 41 (March 1968), p.42.

[36] Ibid.

[37] Ernst Cassirer, <u>The Philosophy of Symbolic Forms</u>, trans. R. Manheim (New Haven & London: Yale Univ. Press, 1955-7), II,38.

[38] <u>Ibid</u>.

[39] Robert D. Richardson Jr., <u>Myth and Literature in the American Renaissance</u> (Bloomington & London: Indiana Univ. Press, 1978), pp.65,70.

[40] Frederic Carpenter, <u>Emerson Handbook</u> (New York: Hendricks House, 1953), p.109.

[41] <u>Ibid</u>.

[42] Kenneth Marc Harris, <u>Carlyle and Emerson: Their Long Debate</u> (Cambridge, Mass.: Harvard Univ. Press, 1978), p.2.

[43] See Jung, <u>Symbols of Transformation</u>, vol. 5 of the <u>Collected Works</u>.

[44] Coleridge, <u>Biographia Literaria</u>, ed. J. Shawcross (London: Oxford Univ. Press, 1965), II,6.

[45] Martin Bickman, <u>The Unsounded Centre: Jungian Studies in American Romanticism</u> (Chapel Hill, N.C.: Univ. of North Carolina Press, 1980), p.39.

[46] <u>The Philosophy of Paul Ricoeur: An Anthology of His Work</u>, ed. C.E. Reagan & D. Stewart (Boston: Beacon Press, 1978), p.37.

[47] <u>Ibid</u>.

[48] Ricoeur, p.36.

[49] Ricoeur, p.38.

[50] Ricoeur, p.45.

[51] Ricoeur, p.46.

[52] Ricoeur, p.54.
[53] Ricoeur, p.46.
[54] Ricoeur, p.54.

CHAPTER FOUR

SUBLIMATION: THE PSYCHOLOGICAL DIALECTIC OF <u>NATURE</u>

The cultural crisis to which Emerson and his generation responded was more than the mere erosion of faith and the concomitant movement toward materialism. For this erosion involved the real danger of psychological atrophy, the possibility of losing contact with profound aspects of the mind for lack of a terminology, a language, to express them. Because of its rationalism and its emphasis upon empirical understanding at the expense of intuition and feeling, the Unitarian establishment against which Transcendentalism emerged was perceived as having diminished the vision of the psyche and its potential. Both the heights of spirit and the depths of the unconscious were slipping beyond the pale -- outside of the narrowing circle of circumscribed cognition. Only a massive reorientation of the mind, it was felt, could counteract the tendency of this restrictive rationalism. But first, before these vanishing facts of the psyche could be recovered and secured, new languages were necessary for their expression. Psychological terminologies as diverse as those provided by Swedenborgianism, German Idealism, and Hindu scripture fulfilled this need.

As an opening, Coleridge's distinction between "Reason" and "Understanding" was readily seen by Emerson to be the vocabulary of just such a language. For it expressed the first and foremost distinction of Transcendentalist psychology -- the assertion of the existence of a mental function ("Reason") outside of empirically-oriented cognition, a function that included what we have come to call the "unconscious.' But it is a mistake to see this "transcendental impulse" (as Jung would describe it) as negating sensuous, physical existence. Not only did Romantic organicism suggest the physical roots of spiritual sublimations; its terminology readily served a re-imagining of the "real" as well as an assertion of the "ideal." Indeed, this "sense of the concrete" cannot be divorced from the counter process of interiorization. Mastery over the outer world, Emerson asserts in Nature, corresponds to and facilitates mastery over the inner. The separation from what Thoreau in "Walking" would come to call the "wild" was perceived as an alienation from a wild within as well as the wild without. One was seen to need a sense of mystery, of unexplored wilderness, grounding the faith of self-directed activity. Thus, as Joel Porte explains, "the theme of 'life in the wilderness' and that of the deeper psychology are ultimately one."[1]

The interrelation of inner and outer worlds was articulated through concepts of psychological process. Like his contemporaries, Emerson epitomizes the nineteenth-century quest for organic principles. In Germany, philosophers such as Hegel had developed dialectical models to account for patterns of differentiation and growth. Narrowed to the sphere of psychology, we see the psyche viewed as an evolving process which involves the destruction of old patterns at the same time continuity of character is maintained. Accordingly, in the Hegelian conception of <u>aufhebung</u>, negation, continuity, and elevation are all taken into account. For historical change, Hegel realized, entails a reciprocal process of affirmation and negation, construction and deconstruction. We see, in Nietzsche's remodeling of <u>aufhebung</u> into <u>sublimieren</u> ("sublimation"), the analysis of change being moved from the arena of universal history to the individual psyche. Both Hegel's and Nietzsche's concepts of dialectic help to illuminate Emerson's vision of psychological process.

According to M.H. Abrams, Romantic quests for unity of being assume a dialectical form. Originating in an intuition of unity from which the poet is alienated by a "fall" into the world of time and becoming, these quests oscillate between moments of inspiration and dejection in a spiral of spiritual ascension leading toward possible reintegration with that lost "home":

        The poet or philosopher, as the avant-garde of

> the general human consciousness, possesses the
> vision of an imminent culmination of history
> which will be equivalent to a recovered paradise
> or golden age. The movement toward this goal is
> a circuitous journey and quest, ending in the
> attainment of self-knowledge, wisdom, and power.
> This educational process is a fall from primal
> unity into self-division, self-contradiction,
> and self-conflict, but the fall is in turn re-
> garded as an indispensable first step along the
> way toward a higher unity which will justify the
> sufferings undergone en route. The dynamic of
> the process is the tension toward closure of the
> divisions, contraries, or "contradictions" them-
> selves. The beginning and end of the journey is
> man's ancestral home....[2]

More succinctly, we can observe that the essential structure of Romantic literary quests (including Emerson's) mirrors the pattern articulated in the Hegelian dialectic. (Hegel's _Phenomenology_ _of_ _Mind_ is one of Abrams' major examples.) A vision of potential spiritual unity is purchased through the conquest - and not merely the denial - of non-being and death. Spiritual elevation is linked with organic sources of power which are "cancelled" and yet "preserved." To clarify this process, let us turn to Emerson's _Nature_.

Since the nineteenth century, critics and commentators have drawn our attention to the dialectical structure of this essay. For example, in 1898 William T. Harris uses a Hegelian model to illuminate Emerson's vision of psychological process:

> we find everywhere in this remarkable essay what
> may be called a dialectic, whereby one part joins
> to the next by a sort of natural growth. Thus
> commodity becomes beauty through the idea of all
> society existing for the well-being of each member
> of it,-- the whole existing in the part manifests
> beauty. So, too, beauty becomes language in its
> phase of presenting self-knowledge. Language in
> its highest form, wherein Nature as a whole reflects

> spirit as a whole, reveals the end of Nature as
> a discipline, and we reach an untimate unity.[3]

Since then, numerous critics have commented upon the rhetoric of ascension in Nature -- the way in which the essay starts with the material world of sensation and commodity and progresses by degrees to the heights of spirit. But while Nature movies from the concrete to the universal, from matter to ideas, focus upon this "ascension" alone overemphasizes one aspect of Emerson's thought - his "idealism" - at the expense of his imagination of psychic depth.

For if the end of Nature is the attainment of illumination, it is clear from Emerson's comments that this illumination is intimately connected with the unconscious. How else does one account for statements such as the following, which anticipates modern theories of psychic projection?:

> That which was unconscious truth, becomes, when
> interpreted and defined in an object, a part of
> the domain of knowledge,-- a new weapon in the
> magazine of power (CW,I,23).

Similarly, in a passage which sounds like Carl Jung's discussion of personified archetypes,[4] Emerson defends the human form as the preferred entrance to the depths of the psyche:

> In fact, the eye, - the mind, - is always accompanied by these forms, male and female; and these
> are incomparably the richest informations of the
> power and order that lie at the heart of things
> ....these all rest like fountain pipes on the unfathomed sea of thought and virtue whereto they
> alone, of all organizations, are the entrances
> (CW,I,28).

Finally, when we hear that "many truths arise to us out of the recesses of consciousness" (CW,I,38), there can be no question but that Emerson is concidering the unconscious as the origin of "the highest...present to the soul of man" (CW,I,38). At this point, it becomes evident that an interpretation focusing only upon ascension in Nature runs into trouble. Clearly, we need a way of talking about both the "ideal" and the "unconscious" in Emerson's thought, a way of accounting for the unconscious gestation in the spiritual formation. For, in many respects, Emerson saw the "heights" of idealism and the "depths" of the unconscious as the same thing.

We can begin resolving this dilemma by examining more closely what we refer to as Emerson's "dialectic" in Nature. Kenneth Burke, for example, considers Emerson's doctrine of "compensation" to be a dialectical principle:

> Though the Hegeliam dialectic lays much greater stress than Emerson's upon the cooperative competition (as with Hegel's pattern whereby antitheses become resolved in a synthesis that is the thesis out of which will arise a new antithesis, etc.), Emerson had his variant in his doctrine of "Compensation"....[5]

But while Burke's view opens up a perspective upon the important role of negation in Emerson's thought, his emphasis is upon Nature as "an idealistic exercise in transcendence up."[6] Thus, he does not amplify what he calls the "down implicit in such a pattern."[7] But heightening and deepening, Rollo May reminds us, are two sides of the same face: "human beings...grow 'down' at the same time as they 'grow up,' deeper while they grow higher."[8] By making this "down" explicit, we can clarify the dialectic between consciousness and the unconscious in Emerson's thought. In order to do so, let us examine more closely the Hegelian conception of dialectic and how it applies to Emerson's psychological argument.

Hegel's dialectic, as he reminds us in his "Preface" to the Phenomenology of Mind, emphasizes the role of negation and loss in growth. The "self-enclosed" circle of thought, he asserts, must be "cut loose from its containing circumference," a process effected by "the portentous power of the negative."[9] But this negative, Hegel is quick to remind us, is much more than a mere logical principle (as Kenneth Burke's comments might lead us to believe) -- for it involves an entire attitude of being, an acceptance of death:

> Death, as we may call that unreality, is the most terrible thing, and to keep and hold fast what is dead demands the greatest force of all....But the life of the mind is not one that shuns death, and keeps clear of destruction; it endures death and in death maintains its being. It only wins to its truth when it finds itself utterly torn asunder... mind is this power only by looking the negative in the face, and dwelling with it.[10]

We must live close to death, <u>dwell</u> <u>with</u> <u>death</u>, accepting the loss within us. Only in this way, Hegel asserts, can one progress to the next stage of spirit.

Of all our great American writers, Emerson may have dwelt most fully with death. While Hawthorne and Melville also lost their fathers during their childhood, Emerson lost not only his father, but as an adult his first wife, two brothers, and his first child. The importance of these deaths to Emerson's life and work cannot be overestimated. His life was punctuated by death, and each death became a significant turning point in his unfolding career, which is one of successive losses and recoveries. After the death of his first wife Ellen Tucker in 1831, Emerson resigned his pulpit and commenced a significant voyage of intellectual discovery in Europe. His first major written work, <u>Nature</u>, was composed the summer after the death of his brother Charles. And the death of his son Waldo six years later, as Joel Porte powerfully expresses it, "permanently darkened" his thought.[11] Thus, one should not be surprised to find along with Newton Arvin that even during Emerson's period of greatest optimism, "there is another tone, an undertone...which we should listen to if we wish to sensitize ourselves to the complex harmony of his total thought." Opposed to "the celebration of the powers of the human will," Arvin observes, we encounter "an insistence on its limitations -- on the forces in nature that are not friendly but hostile and even destructive to human wishes."[12] In this light, one finds Emerson in <u>Nature</u> attempting to arrive at a dialectical principle of personal growth which could account for his most recent loss and the reawakened memories of earlier griefs.

Perhaps the <u>locus classicus</u> of this principle of compensation is that apparently callous passage at the end of "Discipline" where Emerson writes:

> When much intercourse with a friend has supplied us with a standard of excellence, and has increased our respect for the resources of God who thus sends a real person to outdo our ideal; when he has, moreover, become an object of thought, and, whilst his character retains all its unconscious effect, is converted in the mind into solid and sweet wisdom,--

>it is a sign to us that his office is closing,
>and he is commonly withdrawn from our sight in
>a short time (CW,I,28-9).

"Is not this passage a euphemism for the death, or near-death, of a close friend?" Kenneth Burke asks.[13] Rather, it seems a thinly-veiled, and not wholly successful, attempt to compensate for the death of Charles. The emotional significance of this death is underlined by the seven pauses between the opening phrase (ending with "excellence") and the main clause of the sentence which Emerson takes up again fortynine (!) words later. Clearly, this is no ordinary death which he is working himself up to consider, by overcoming successive layers of repression. We note here, in Emerson's response to this death, a dialectical maneuver quite close to Hegel's principle of aufhebung: negation, preservation, and elevation. The removal of a friend by death (negation) is countered by transforming that friend into an idea (elevation) in an attempt to maintain psychological equilibrium (preservation).

We can compare our reading of this passage with that of James M. Cox who comments that "the clear despair which [Emerson] records on the loss of his brother Charles is but a prelude to the strong assertion of Nature."[14] But Cox goes on to interpret the above passage as the "conversion of life into thought," as "a taking of life."[15] While agreeing in principle with this observation, I would reverse the terms -- and see death, the acceptance of non-being, as the occasion of this compensatory reaction. Death converts life into thought by showing us life's limitations.

Once we are attuned to it, Nature resonates with death: "Then, there is a kind of contempt of the landscape felt by him who has just lost by death a dear friend" (CW,I,10-11). Or notice that three out of four of Emerson's examples of the natural beauty of virtuous action involve martyrdom: "when Leonidas and his three hundred martyrs consume one day in dying," "when Arnold Winkelried gathers in his side a sheaf of Austrian spears," "when Sir Harry Vane was dragged up the Tower-hill, sitting on a sled, to suffer death" (CW, I,15). Only Columbus' discovery of America escapes from this morbidity. Indeed, even the imagery of Emerson's descriptions of the landscape involves the compensatory transfiguration of death into beauty: "The leafless trees become spires of flame,...and the stars of the dead calices of flowers, and every withered stem and stubble rimed with frost, contribute something to the mute music" (CW,I,14, italics mine).

Similarly, the following - with its echo of Wordsworth's elegy, "A slumber did my spirit seal" - expresses Emerson's psychological need in this essay:

> The seed of a plant, - to what affecting analogies in the nature of man, is that little fruit made use of, in all discourse, up to the voice of Paul, who calls the human corpse a seed, - "It is sown a natural body; it is raised a spiritual body." The motion of the earth round its axis, and round the sun, makes the day, and the year (CW,I,19).

Compare the final sentence with Wordsworth's famous lines: "No motion has she now, no force;/ She neither hears nor sees,/

Roll'd round in earth's diurnal course/ With rocks and stones and trees!" As for Wordsworth, it is Emerson's compelling need to provide a compensatory context for death -- to prove that the dead _are_ transformed (into "music" and "flame"), that the spirit _is_ resurrected. However, the focus of this transformation and resurrection, for Emerson, is not upon the soul of the departed, but rather upon the spirits of those who remain. The dead who are transformed are the dead which we carry within us -- the grief in which we, as finite beings, necessarily dwell.

Thus, we must see Emersonian compensation, from the beginning, not - as Jonathan Bishop asserts - as a sidestepping of the problem of evil.[16] It is instead the affirmation of a dialectical principle of growth in which death is not forgotten or repressed, but preserved and elevated to a consoling spiritual context. This elevation does not eliminate death, but rather "frames" it in wider terms. More generally, we see that Emerson does not reject the life of the body, but that physical facts are retained at the same time they are transfigured. This transfiguration does not eliminate those earlier facts - things do not disappear - they become translucent.[17] We see the operation of spirit _through_ physical reality: "the universe becomes transparent, and the light of higher laws than its own, shines through it" (_CW_, I,22). If physical facts disappeared, if the problem of evil were dismissed, then language and thought - in Emerson's terms - would become impossible. For spirit would lose the means of its expression:

> The use of the outer creation is to give us a language for the beings and changes of the inward creation (CW,I,18).
> There seems to be a necessity in spirit to manifest itself in natural forms (CW,I,22).

This "objectification of spirit" is similar to that expressed in Ernst Cassirer's philosophy of "symbolic form."[18] Indeed, it is difficult to imagine a theory of creative expression that would not use such terms.

We can deepen our understanding of Emerson's sense of expression through the physical by turning to what is perhaps the crux of the entire essay -- to that difficult passage at the end of "Idealism" where Emerson caps a long proof that "motion, poetry, physical and intellectual science, and religion, all tend to affect our conviction of the reality of the external world" by a seemingly willful affirmation of the physical life of the body:

> I own there is something ungrateful in expanding too curiously the particulars of the general proposition, that all culture tends to imbue us with idealism. I have no hostility to nature, but a child's love to it. I expand and live in the warm day like corn and melons (CW,I,35).

Although one cannot escape the impression here that Emerson looks up, sees where his argument is going, and stops himself just short of a solipsistic abyss, it is also clear that Emerson attempts to preserve the phenomenal world in his thought at the same time he elevates it to be a symbol of spirit. Thus, this passage is not a denial of idealism or a wavering between idealism and materialism. For such interpretation invokes an either/or dualistic epistemology which Emerson has been attempting to sidestep.

Although his dualistic terminology partially obscures his purpose, we can see that Emerson attempts to assert <u>both</u> nature and spirit -- to lift nature up to the level of spirit, while retaining a grasp of physical qualities. As he states his intention: "I only wish to indicate the true position of nature in regard to man...<u>as the ground which to attain is the object of human life, that is, of man's connexion with nature</u>" (<u>CW</u>,I,36, italics mine). The problem, for Emerson, is that man does not see nature clearly enough -- his connection to it has become abstract and hence too loose, neither "high" nor "deep." What Emerson's Unitarian contemporaries failed to do was to retain a sense of concrete physical phenomena at the same time they were seen under the aspect of a higher meaning. In other words, they lost a sense of symbolism, treating nature instead as a sign. It is <u>they</u> who would rest content with what Emerson calls "idealism," but who would not make the transition to "spirit" -- a transition which entails an "original <u>relation to</u> the universe." It is this sense of relationship which is missing.

Central to Emerson's meaning, then, is the assertion that "the mind is part of the nature of things," that it is neither wholly spiritual nor wholly physical in its provenance, but a mixture of both spiritual and physical energies. Thus, Emerson must bypass the "hypothesis" of "idealism" because "the demands of the spirit" include "the existence of matter" -- that is, a sense of what he calls "substantive being" and "consanguinity" (CW,I,37). In twentieth-century terms, what Emerson strives toward here is an "incarnate philosophy" -- he attempts to put the mind "back into" the body. This is the task, for example, of Maurice Merleau-Ponty who wrote the following which serves as an excellent explication of Emerson's text:

> once man is defined as consciousness, he becomes cut off from all things, from his body and from effective existence. He must therefore be defined as a relation to instruments and objects -- a relation which is not simply one of thought but which involves him in the world in such a way as to give him an external aspect, an outside, to make him "objective" at the same time he is "subjective." This can be accomplished by defining him as a being who "suffers" or "senses," that is, as a being with a natural and social situation but one who is also open, active, and able to establish his autonomy on the very ground of his dependence.[19]

In this light, we see Emerson in Nature attempting to avoid a definition of man solely as consciousness. Instead, he defines a being with a physical, "objective" aspect -- one who is inextricably related to the world and others. More telling still, we see in Emerson's "compensation" an attempt to establish man's "autonomy on the very ground of his dependence." Emerson accepts and overcomes physical limitation and death. He assents to and transcends man's "thrownness."

Again, a comparison between Emerson's position and Hegel's underlines the urgency of this need for incarnation. The sickness of the time, Hegel observes, is its over-abstraction, its lost sense of the concrete:

>   self-consciousness has got beyond the substantial
>   fullness of life, which it used to carry on in
>   the element of thought -- beyond the state of im-
>   mediacy of belief, beyond the satisfaction and
>   security arising from the assurance which con-
>   sciousness possessed of being reconciled with ul-
>   timate reality and with its all-pervading pres-
>   ence, within as well as without. Self-conscious
>   mind has not merely passed beyond that to the op-
>   posite extreme of insubstantial reflection of self
>   into self, but beyond this too.[20]

What is needed, Hegel counters, is "to obtain once again through philosophy the restoration of that sense of solidity and substantiality of existence it has lost."[21] The solution, for Hegel, is to recover a sense of process -- to have an awareness both of the idea and of the history of its unfolding. In this way, he hopes, one can "run together what thought has divided asunder...and restore the feeling of existence."[22] It is a large part of my argument that Transcendenalist writers in America felt a similar need, that they too were acutely aware of the dangers of self-consciousness (those young men with "knives in their brains"), and that they diagnosed this self-consciousness as separating them from nature, from instinct, from the "unconscious." Like Hegel, they, also, asserted the conviction that "because the form is as necessary to the essence as the essence to itself, absolute reality must not be conceived of and expressed as essence alone."[23] As Emerson discovered in Nature, "essence alone" could not be expressed -- for our language and our actions are forms of "substantive being."

Although there is a dualistic side to Nature which is inescapable, the force of his argument is to bend that dualism toward a unified conception of being. He does this by focusing upon the incarnation of psychic energy through the body, energy which needs physical form for its articulation. In this way, spiritual energy is linked with the physical origins of the unconscious; "the highest" is connected with the "recesses of consciousness." This connection is evident in Emerson's use of the familiar terminology of Romantic organicism:

> spirit does not act upon us from without, that is, in space and time, but spiritually, or through ourselves. Therefore, that spirit...does not build up nature around us, but puts it forth through us, as the life of the tree puts forth new branches and leaves through the pores of the old. As a plant upon the earth, so a man rests upon the bosom of God; he is nourished by unfailing fountains, and draws, at his need, inexhaustible power (CW,I,38).

As we have seen, this sense of "inexhaustible power" nourishing spiritual growth was to receive further definition in Freud's and Jung's competing conceptions of "libido."

If one of Emerson's difficulties in Nature is to communicate his vision of the connection between the way up (spirit) and the way down (unconscious), our problem as critics is to find a terminology which can account for this complex idea. So far, we have used a dialectical model of psychic growth in order to analyze how instinct is preserved as energy, at the same time it is cancelled and elevated to spirit. If this sounds close to what we have learned to call "sublimation," Walter Kaufmann's analysis of Nietzsche's concept of sublimieren (the forebear of Freud's) makes the connection with dialectical thought which we need. Kaufman's analysis is worth quoting at some length:

> Nietzsche's position is best elucidated by comparing it...with Hegel's. Each of the two men found a single word that epitomizes his entire dialectic; and the two words, though not identical, have literally the same meaning and can be analyzed into the same three distinct connotations.
>
> Hegel's '<u>aufheben</u>' has been the despair of his translators. He was satisfied to remark that this word means both preserving and canceling; his translators, however, were grieved to discover that it also means lifting up....
>
> Nietzsche's '<u>sublimieren</u>' has imposed no similar hardship on his translators, who could use the English 'sublimating,' which goes back to the same Latin root. The Latin word in question, <u>sublimare</u>, however, means - in German - <u>aufheben</u>, and Nietzsche's sublimation actually involves, no less than does Hegel's <u>aufheben</u>, a simultaneous preserving, canceling, and lifting up.[24]

These remarks suggest that the dialectical development of <u>Nature</u> can be interpreted in terms of sublimation.

Professor Kaufman's expansion of Nietzsche's conception of sublimation strengthens this tie with Emerson. For this principle of sublimation, according to Kaufmann, embodies Nietzsche's view of the will-to-power as a "self-overcoming" which involves the harmonization and elevation of competing impulses, not their repression.[25] The goal of sublimation is "to 'organize the chaos'" of our impulses and to achieve "an organic harmony" which "leads to that culture which is truly a 'transfigured physis.'"[26] (<u>Physis</u> is the organic principle itself -- the natural life force which grows or becomes.) Sublimation is a principle of "rationality" which "gives man mastery over himself" and thus leads to freedom.[27] But, Kaufmann insists, this rationality is not to be seen as abstraction, but rather as a union of physical impulse and formal activity. To return to Nietzsche's well-known terms, Kaufmann interprets his view of sublimation as a synthesis between "Dionysian passionate striving" and the Apollonian desire of the mind "to give itself form."[28]

The similarities between this position and Emerson's are striking. This synthesis between Dionysian and Apollonian principles is analogous to Emerson's vision of the interrelationship between "nature" and "spirit" (which he will come to term "power" and "form"). Furthermore, when Kaufmann describes the sublimating "will to power" as a metamorphic principle which is "a ceaseless striving" with "an inherent capacity to give form to itself,"[29] the kinship with Emerson's vision of "metamorphosis" and "abandonment" is unmistakable.[30] Kaufmann, for example, discusses Nietzsche's conviction of the utility of suffering and of the need to abandon what one loves most,[31] an articulation to the level of self-conscious principle what for Emerson was a matter of psychological necessity. Both Emerson and Nietzsche saw moral growth as a strengthening through successful encounters with negation and death.

Turning to Freud's concept of sublimation, we find striking similarities to Hegel's and Nietzsche's principles, but also a narrowing of focus. Freud defines sublimation as:

> the sexual trend <u>abandoning</u> its aim of obtaining a component or a reproductive pleasure and taking on another which is <u>related</u> <u>generically</u> to the abandoned one but is <u>itself</u> no longer sexual and must be described as social. We call this process 'sublimation,' in accordance with the general estimate that places social aims <u>higher</u> than the sexual ones, which are at bottom <u>self-interested</u>.[32]

We see here an unmistakable emphasis upon abandonment, preservation, and elevation. However, Freud's psychology - with its naturalistic basis (the sublimated energy seen as a "sexual trend") - seems too narrow to fit Emerson's thought. For its restricted definition of psychic energy draws attention away from the religious questions which most concerned Emerson. This, basically, is Jung's critique of Freud, and Jung's conception of psychic dynamics can help us here. For example, Jung envisions psychological change in terms of a "transcendent function" which aims toward spiritual unfolding and not merely the "cleansing" of sexual energy.[33] Thus, the permutations of psychic energy are seen, not as disguises, but as figures defining the direction of spiritual growth.

Jan Cohn's and Thomas H. Miles' study of "The Sublime: In Alchemy, Aesthetics, and Psychoanalysis" clarifies the efficacy of this term as a bridge connecting body and spirit, the unconscious and transfigured consciousness. Tracing the etymologies of the terms "sublime," "sublimation," and "subliminal," Cohn and Miles observe that

> The American Heritage Dictionary...gives līmen for the source of sublime and līmin (an alternative spelling for līmen) for the source of subliminal. Līmen is defined as "threshold" and is said to be akin to līmes, "boundary" or "limit," particularly a boundary between fields.[34]

Cohn's and Miles' examination of these terms suggests that all three refer to the dynamic relationship between consciousness and the unconscious. For example, they define "subliminal" as referring to what lies "below the threshold (of consciousness)."[35]

By extension, "sublime" and "sublimation" both refer to the appearance of previously-unconscious energies within the field of consciousness -- to a "lifting up" above the threshold of consciousness. In support of this view, Cohn and Miles quote Partridge who offers the following etymological readings of "sublime": "to come up from under the threshold" and "to climb a steep slope."[36] From this perspective, the "sublime" and "sublimation" are seen as referring to psychological states of "elevation" which involve the release of hitherto unconscious energies. Acknowledgeing the historical divergence of these two terms, Cohn and Miles examine their fundamental relationship. Thomas Hardy, they observe, used "sublimation" in a manner similar to that usually associated with "sublime" -- "to indicate an ecstatic state of mind."[37] Emerson seems to make a similar connection between the "sublime" and "sublimation" when he writes of a dispirited friend, "It seems to me as if what we mainly need, is the power of recurring to the sublime at pleasure" (JMN,V,489). Here, "recurring to the sublime" entails a process of sublimation.

If "sublimation" involves the appearance of unconscious energies, this process includes more than the mere "elevation" or "purification" of thought. For it places thought in contact with unconscious roots stretching back into the body's _physical_ energy. Consequently, awareness of sublimation helps to "incarnate" the mind by placing it back within the body. Each in his own way, Emerson and his contemporaries "ground" sublimation by positing images of the "wild" toward which they aspire. This grounding establishes a relationship of faith aimed toward a transcendent realm of being, the "unconscious." Within the fiction of Poe and Melville, this relationship was portrayed as disastrous in its consequences. For their temperaments inclined them toward a Gothic terminology which incorporated death and dismemberment as the price of Promethean aspiration. For others, such as Emerson, death was an antagonist which seemed to offer the possibility of victory through the self-overcoming of grief, fear, and anxiety.

But, in either case, self-consciousness - as the motive initiating the literary quest - measures the mind's distance from unconscious sources of power. As Carlyle told the age in "Characteristics," this beginning was a kind of "disease" -- for the very articulation of the unconscious as a psychic locale measures the distance of consciousness from unconscious vitality and spontaneity.[38] We see this sickness in Hawthorne's portrayals of Chillingworth and Coverdale (in The Scarlet Letter and The Blithedale Romance, resepctively). Both characters become voyeurs of the spontaneous, like Milton's Satan gaping at Adam and Eve in their bower. But Hawthorne's 'Adams' and 'Eves' - as well as Melville's - exist in a world of fallen impulses. They, too, yearn for the innocence of unselfconscious, spontaneous activity in a world responsive to the desires of the spirit. The Scarlet Letter vividly depicts the expense of repression as a way out of this dilemma. For when Hester Prynne and Arthur Dimmesdale meet in the forest, the reader is shocked by the extent to which they have sacrificed vital energy:

> So strangely did they meet, in the dim wood, that it was like the first encounter, in the world beyond the grave, of two spirits who had been intimately connected in their former life, but now stood coldly shuddering, in mutual dread; as not yet familiar with their state, nor wonted to the companionship of disembodied beings.[39]

Such disembodiment erodes the basis of both self-knowledge and action. Cut off from his best powers, the individual stands on a diminished ground which has fallen away on all sides from him.

But the counter position, Emerson's "original relation to the universe," can only be achieved at the expense of a painful sublimation of failure and death in an ascending dialectic of spiritual aspiration. In a significant echoing of Emerson's major terms, Paul Tillich defines this process as the achievement of "power" through the dialectical incorporation of non-being:

> The power of being is its possibility to affirm itself against the non-being within it and against it. The power of a being is greater the more non-being is taken into its self-affirmation. The power of being is not dead identity but the dynamic process in which it separates itself and returns to itself. The more conquered separation there is the more power there is.[40]

In the career of Ralph Waldo Emerson, we observe this process of separation and assimilation in the composition of his lectures, addresses, and essays -- each one an attempt to comprehend his spiritual position and the position of man in his age. By abandoning each hard-won position in an ongoing dialectic of compensation, Emerson achieves that victory over necessity and loss which Tillich calls the "courage to be." For an appreciation of this accomplishment, one need only contrast the writings of Emerson's contemporary, Poe. They are equally profound; but Poe's fiction dramatizes successive and futile attempts to escape from an obsessive fixation upon death and the terrors of mortality.

NOTES: CHAPTER FOUR

[1] Joel Porte, *The Romance in America* (Middletown, Conn.: Wesleyan Univ. Press, 1969), p.53.

[2] M.H. Abrams, *Natural Supernaturalism: Tradition and Revolution in Romantic Literature* (New York: Norton, 1973), p.255.

[3] William T. Harris, *The Genius and Character of Emerson*, ed. F. Sanborn (Boston & New York: Houghton Mifflin, 1898), pp.349-350. Rptd. in M. Sealts & A. Ferguson eds., *Emerson's Nature -- Origin, Growth, Meaning* (New York: Dodd, Mead & Co., 1969), p.125.

[4] Jung discusses the *anima* and *shadow* in *Aion*, vol. 9, part 2 of the *Collected Works*.

[5] Kenneth Burke, "I, Eye, Aye -- Emerson's Early Essay on 'Nature': Thoughts on the Machinery of Transcendence," rptd. in M. Simon & T. Parson eds., *Transcendentalism and Its Legacy* (Ann Arbor: Univ. of Mich. Press, 1968), p.6.

[6] Burke, p.7.

[7] Burke, pp.6-7.

[8] Rollo May, *Power and Innocence: A Search for the Sources of Violence* (New York: Norton, 1972), p.226.

[9] Hegel, *The Phenomenology of Mind*, trans. J.B. Baillie (New York: Harper & Row, 1967), p.93.

[10] Ibid.

[11] Joel Porte, *Representative Man: Ralph Waldo Emerson in His Time* (New York: Oxford Univ. Press, 1979), p.163.

[12] Newton Arvin, "The House of Pain" in *Emerson: A Collection of Critical Essays*, ed. M.R. Konvitz & S.E. Whicher (Englewood Cliffs, N.J.: Prentice Hall, 1962), p.51.

[13] Burke, p.21.

[14] James M. Cox, "R.W. Emerson: The Circles of the Eye" in D. Levin ed., *Emerson: Prophecy, Metamorphosis, Influence* (New York: Columbia Univ. Press, 1975), p.72.

[15] Cox, p.74.

[16] Jonathan Bishop, *Emerson on the Soul* (Cambridge, Mass.: Harvard Univ. Press, 1964), p.72.

[17] Harold Bloom discusses Emerson's "transparency" in "Emerson: The Glory and Sorrows of American Romanticism" in D. Thorburn & G. Hartman eds., *Romanticism: Vistas, Instances, Continuities* (Ithaca, N.Y.: Cornell Univ. Press, 1973), p.173.

[18] Ernst Cassirer, *The Philosophy of Symbolic Forms*, trans. R. Manheim (New Haven & London: Yale Univ. Press, 1955-7).

[19] Maurice Merleau-Ponty, *Sense and Non-Sense*, trans. H.L. Dreyfus & P.A. Dreyfus (Evanston, Ill.: Northwestern Univ. Press, 1964), p.130.

[20] Hegel, pp.71-2.

[21] Hegel, p.72.

[22] *Ibid*.

[23] Hegel, p.81.

[24] Walter Kaufmann, *Nietzsche: Philosopher, Psychologist, Antichrist* (Princeton, N.J.: Princeton Univ. Press, 1974), p.236.

[25] Kaufmann, pp.218,224.

[26] Kaufmann, p.227.

[27] Kaufmann, p.230.

[28] Kaufmann, p.235.

[29] Kaufmann, pp.236,238.

[30] Stanley Cavell discusses Emerson's "abandonment" in "Thinking of Emerson," New Literary History 11 (1979), pp.167-176. Daniel Shea discusses Emerson's "metamorphosis" in "Emerson and the American Metapmorphosis" in D. Levin ed., Emerson: Prophecy, Metamorphosis, and Influence (New York: Columbia Univ. Press, 1975).

[31] Kaufmann, p.244.

[32] Freud, SE 16:345. Quoted in J. Cohn & T.H. Miles, "The Sublime: In Alchemy, Aesthetics and Psychoanalysis," Modern Philology 74 (Feb. 1977), pp.296-7.

[33] Jung, PJ,273 (CW 8,par.131).

[34] Cohn & Miles, p.289.

[35] Ibid.

[36] Cohn & Miles, p.290.

[37] Cohn & Miles, p.296.

[38] Carlyle, "Characteristics" in Critical and Miscellaneous Essays (New York: Charles Scribner's Sons, 1899), III,2.

[39] Hawthorne, The Scarlet Letter, vol. 1 of The Centenary Edition of the Works of Nathaniel Hawthorne, ed. W. Charvat, R.H. Pearce, C.M. Simpson (Columbus, Ohio: Ohio State Univ. Press, 1962-   ), p.190.

[40] Paul Tillich, Love, Power, and Justice (New York & London: Oxford Univ. Press, 1954), p.48.

CHAPTER FIVE
CIRCUMSCRIBING THE MIND

In *Nature* and his later works, Emerson examines the process whereby the mind circumscribes and limits itself as part of its dialectic of growth -- limits itself through the acceptance of non-being and death as boundary. In this regard, the principle Emerson came to call "compensation" is central to his dialectic of psychological expansion. For without this sense of limitation as formative, a philosophy of growth is impossible. Thus, we need to see that even Emerson's earliest affirmations of the self's expansion entail a keen perception of circumscription. The quest for creative affirmation is defined against the potentially tragic limitation of the human condition. As Stephen Whicher has shown us, an awareness of "fate" structures Emerson's thought from the beginning. Without this sense of limitation, thought cannot define itself and its aims.

In his analysis of "Language" in Nature, Emerson articulates his sense of the process through which spirit objectifies itself. Natural forms become "the vehicle of thought" (CW,I,17). According to Charles Feidelson, such a focus upon the medium of expression lies at the heart of symbolism as literary method. The "field of vision" becomes the center of attention; "the act of perception and the act of speech" are seen as the "locus" of an unfolding in which "the exercise of vision" is seen as "a mode of being."[1] But while Feidelson leads us this far into Emerson's symbolic method, we cannot agree with his conclusion that Emerson's symbolism is plagued with the threat of formlessness.[2] From the beginning, Emerson exhibits a self-conscious control of his materials -- a sense of form born out of a keen awareness of loss. Furthermore, among Emerson's most anguished apprehensions was the recognition that inspiration is variable and not wholly under the control of the will: "I am Defeated all the time; yet to victory I am born" (JMN,VIII,228). It is this recognition of the possibility of defeat which leads to the "means of control, evaluation, or limitation" that Feidelson cannot find in Emerson's thought.[3]

Consequently, Emerson's efforts to hypostatize himself into rhapsody[4] were chastened by "the realization that his kind of truth was to come through inaction and hope, through waiting for moments of illumination."[5] From the first, Emerson knew that "the forces of nature are not friendly but hostile and even destructive to human wishes."[6] The most pressing facts pounded home for Emerson the limitation of aspiration and hope. Despite the Swedenborgian excesses of his discussion of "Language," Emerson was no Swedenborgian. He quickly learned to differentiate the dream of correspondence in which "every appearance in nature corresponds to some state of mind" (CW,I,18) from the realities of composition which involved the painstaking accumulation and fusing together of isolated insights.

We see this clearly in Emerson's aphoristic style. His penchant for aphorism reflects what Roland Barthes describes as a pleasure of "the edge" -- a keen perception of discontinuity and limits.[7] For Emerson, a great deal of literary interest resides in the aphoristic drawing of boundaries, in a process of definition and self-circumscription. If one aphorism, in Emerson's texts, gives way to another, it is the very succession of aphorisms which makes us aware of each partial perspective. As Stanley Cavell observes, in Emerson's writing the mind draws a circle, posits a belief, and then abandons it for another one in an "onwardness" which imitates the process of thinking itself.[8] Each moment of "reception," of poetic "inhabitation," is revealed by an "abandonment" which uncovers the contours of earlier belief.[9] Thus, the mind gains awareness of itself by positing boundaries and then reflecting upon this creation of areas of discourse and belief. Or, in the terminology of Paul Ricoeur, reflection proceeds through the counterpoint of faith and skepticism, a sense of limits tempering and thus defining the contours of faith.[10] To define, we remember, is derived from de + finire: to end or limit, to draw a boundary.

Such an awareness of the mind's quest for self-definition is essential to Coleridge's view of the imagination, which he describes as

> that reconciling and mediatory power...incorporating the reason in images of the sense, and organizing...the flux of the sense by the permanence and self-encircling energies of the reason.[11]

Elsewhere, Coleridge asserts, "The spirit of poetry...must of necessity circumscribe itself by rules."[12] For this energy "must embody itself in order to reveal itself," thereby manifesting "the power of acting creatively under laws of its own organization."[13] Eventually, Emerson's twin concepts of "power" and "form" account for a similar insight. But more to the point here, the style of Emerson's essays exemplifies this process of self-definition. In Emerson's writing (as well as in Coleridge's), we observe the mind clearing a space for itself, circumscribing an object of reflection, through the use of an aphoristic method. Material is "raised up" to consciousness and then bounded in Emerson's style of journal entry and composition. Isolated moments of intuition are gathered, each one accepted as it comes as a self-contained perspective.

Significantly, it is exactly this process of circumscription which Coleridge focuses upon in his definition of "aphorism" in Aids to Reflection: "Aphorism, determinate position, from ἀφορίζειν, to bound, or limit; whence our horizon."

Then, in a homely but telling example which cements the concept forever in our minds, Coleridge expands his definition:

> In order to get the full sense of the word, we should first present to our minds the visual image that forms its primary meaning. Draw lines of different colors around the different counties of England, and then cut out each accurately, as in the common play-maps that children take to pieces and put together -- so that each district can be contemplated apart from the rest, as a whole in itself. This twofold act of circumscribing, and detaching, when it is exerted by the mind on subjects of reflection and reason, is to aphorize, and the result an aphorism.[14]

We see aphorizing, then, as a process in which thinking clears a space for itself by defining an area of concern and reflection.

Emerson, too, clears an opening for thought by focusing upon its boundaries, its limits. By defining an area of concern, he provides a form, a forum, for the mind's expansion into self-recognition -- a space which is "cleared and free, namely, within a boundary." Like Heidegger (to whom we have just been listening), Emerson recognizes that "A boundary is not that at which something stops but...that from which something <u>begins its essential unfolding</u>."[15] As we shall see, "unfolding" is one of the central metaphors in Emerson's lecture series "The Philosophy of History," in which he begins to consolidate the gains of <u>Nature</u> and to articulate even more openly his conception of the unconscious.

If Emerson's essays proceed from insight to insight, it is because the awareness of circumscription necessitates the abandonment of vision to the flow of argument. Acutely aware of the "partiality" and incompleteness of each individual articulation (as well as of each individual), Emerson can only hope to embody unconscious creative energy through the approximation of successive moments of writing. Each moment approaches but can never reach the intuited unity of unconscious origin (Emerson's vision of "One Mind"). The burden for Emerson and all those who attempt to portray the depths of the psyche is, as Coleridge remarks, to pursue the ineffable which transcends speech and thought itself. Attempting, for example, to comprehend the origins of our will, we find that

> the farthest distance our recollection can follow back the traces never leads us to the first footmark; the lowest depth that the light of our consciousness can visit even with a doubtful glimmering is still at an unknown distance from the ground.
> 16

It makes one pause for a moment to consider that an awareness of consciousness as "trace" similar to that which serves the cause of skepticism in thinkers such as Jacques Lacan and Jacques Derrida can equally function as an occasion for faith. If many intellectuals today have lost faith in the creative potential of the mind as an agent which <u>structures</u> belief, as well as being <u>structured by</u> the unconscious and linguistic context, perhaps it is through an inability to see thinking as a symbolic process which entails both freedom and limitation, both articulation and determination. It is this sense of dialectic which Emerson can still teach us -- his impulse toward self-mastery, as opposed to mastery by the other.

Let us examine more closely the opening which Emerson's *Nature* provides. This essay sets up a world that allows the earth to disclose itself in its beauty, moral tutelage, and mystery. Ultimately, what it opens is a space in which the Orphic poet of the conclusion can speak and dwell. By defining a space which gives meaning to his words, *Nature* gives those words the ring of authenticity and spiritual authority. Conversely, the poet's prophetic language extends and clarifies the nature revealed before. Thus, Emerson's essay defines a setting in which a new vision and a new poetry can unfold. It creates the context for its own meaning as it is most strikingly displayed -- in the Orphic poet's characterization of man's lapse from the highest meaning of nature and humanity. Emerson's text opens a clearing for the unfolding of his vision by defining its own difference from itself, a difference which allows speech to emerge by creating a rift in consciousness. Such a gap, which can be described as a sense of alienation, defines the original space in which Emersonian man dwells.[17]

In other terms, we can say that Emerson's sense of being is communicated through a rift or tear in traditional modes of perception. One cause of such a rift is an acute sense of loss or suffering that focuses attention upon the contingency of existence. That such a motive functioned for Emerson we have already seen in his sublimation of death. A sense of non-being provides him with an opening into which creative thought can grow. Life's vicissitudes, as nature's "discipline," teach him the laws of change. As we have seen, a remembrance of martyrdom underlies the glorious uncovering of a new world. A sense of alienation, of self-division or lapse, defines the distance which must be traversed to recover a whole being and a whole world:

> The ruin or the blank, that we see when we look at nature, is in our own eye. The axis of vision is not coincident with the axis of things, and so they appear not translucent but opake. The reason why the world lacks unity, and lies broken and in heaps, is, because man is disunited with himself (CW,I,43).

Significantly, James Hillman, a revisionary Jungian analyst, bases an entire psychology on just this insight - the sense of rift - arguing that essential psychological growth arises from "pathologizing," the imagining through of pain and loss.[18]

Besides the rip in consciousness that pain or death provides, there is the opening enacted by the radical clearing away of what are seen to be outmoded thoughts. Such an intention (which Paul DeMan sees as characteristic of *every* literary movement that announces its modernity[19]) Emerson asserts when he calls for "an original relation to the universe," asking us to reject the poetry and philosophy of tradition as a "faded wardrobe." This sense of clearing involves the radical deconstruction preceding construction, the cutting down and dragging away of old conceptions that no longer fit the demands of one's spirit. As Wallace Stevens asserts, one must "become an ignorant man again/ And see the sun again with an ignorant eye/ And see it clearly in the idea of it."[20] Suspending ordinary patterns of perception, one sees nature with new eyes, in a new perspective. Emerson, in the section of Nature entitled "Idealism," gives us a charming example to reinforce this point, describing how a ride through town in a coach, for "a man who seldom rides," "gives the whole world a pictorial air" (CW,I,31). Old patterns of vision are suspended and replaced by the enchantment of the new. Habit gives way to that wonder which Wordsworth took as his object in the planning of the Lyrical Ballads: "a feeling analogous to the supernatural...awakening the mind's attention from the lethargy of custom." A new stance toward nature and toward the mind is established.

One notices, throughout Emerson's writing, this stress upon stance as relationship -- as in that call to create an "original relationship to the universe." This phrase is usually interpreted as an injunction to break the mold of tradition and establish new modes of perception and being, new ties to the world. So far so good. But in American discourse especially, this call to revolutionary relationship has become such a cliché that its full meaning is too easily passed over. For we need to complement our understanding of the destructive aspect of this relation (the breaking of old forms) with a comprehension of its other side -- the construction of new modes of being and vision. Usually, the word "original" does not receive its full stress here. For the word means not just "new," but implies a mode of relation which goes back to a sense of origins -- back to the brute facticity of experience and our complex reaction to this given texture of the world.

One needs "to reach the primeval," as Albert Hofstadter says of a similar intention in Heidegger.[21] Like Heidegger, who exhorts us to open ourselves to the full being of things and of our own experience, Emerson in <u>Nature</u> begins to define his sense that we are in danger of losing our hold -- of slipping off into the shadowy world of abstraction. To view Emerson in this way relates him to the main current of a philosophical tradition stretching from Hegel to Heidegger -- a tradition in which the accelerating erosion of man's concrete experience as a being <u>in</u> <u>the</u> <u>world</u> and <u>in</u> <u>himself</u> is countered. The psychology of Carl Jung approaches a similar problem (the status of our being in the inner world) through its analysis of man's alienation from the "unconscious." What all these thinkers attempt is to establish a firmer ground on which being can be revealed.

On this firmer ground, spirit and nature "correspond" -- that is, they illuminate each other. The natural world becomes free to present itself to the human spirit as the arena of that spirit's unfolding. For it provides the physical forms which allow creative play -- whether it be in the construction of cities, clipper ships, or poetic language. Conversely, spirit illuminates nature by perceiving within it the order of law. This law - as Emerson's interest in natural history and geology reveals - can be scientific, as well as moral and spiritual. The important thing is that mind - through the process of its appropriation of nature - discovers at the same time its own power of construction.

Heidegger expresses this mutual interdependence as a tension between what he terms "world" (world-view) and "earth" (nature):

> The earth cannot dispense with the Open of the world if it itself is to appear as earth in the liberated surge of its self-seclusion. The world, again, cannot soar out of the earth's sight if, as the governing breadth and path of all essential destiny, it is to ground itself on a resolute foundation.[22]

Like Emerson, Heidegger asserts the mutual implication of thought and the perceived world, an awareness of the "resolute foundation" of language in experience. Both of them reject the excesses of idealism by recognizing that man's world cannot "soar out of the earth's sight," but must remain incarnate. Emerson, we must remember, does not give undue emphasis to subjectivity at the expense of creative action _in the world_. The two are seen as interdependent. It is noteworthy, for example, that he uses Columbus' discovery of America as a metaphor for the beauty of virtuous action, and that, throughout his career, he admires the physical mastery of Napoleon. As <u>Representative Men</u> was explicitly to reveal, Plato and Napoleon represent a duality which Emerson holds _in creative tension_. He does not succumb to the lure of the Platonic vision of the world. We see this dual purpose in Emerson's concept of "power," which connotes both visionary elevation and physical mastery. This concept - like the Freudian symbol - is "overdetermined" in its meaning. It looks forward and backward, inward and outward at the same time. Physical and spiritual energies are balanced on a pivot which includes both.[23]

Thus, Emerson's exhortations to expansive vision cannot be considered as disembodied movements of some ethereal being. His presentation in <u>Nature</u> of his epiphany as a "transparent eyeball" makes this very clear. Emerson's quasi-mystical ecstasy is related to his <u>physical</u> posture -- he is "<u>standing</u> on the bare ground," his "head...uplifted into infinite space." Furthermore, Emerson is careful to define his attitude <u>toward</u> such moments of vision -- he is the "<u>lover</u> of uncontained and immortal beauty" (<u>CW</u>,I,10). He himself is not as uncontained as much as criticism makes him sound. True, Emerson describes a moment of ecstasy, a standing "outside" of himself, but this epiphany is portrayed as happening in a perfectly real setting to a perfectly real persona. Emerson could have presented this vision without the dramatic context -- <u>that</u> would have been disembodied. But as it stands, there is a vast difference between Emerson's portrayal of a vivid moment of insight (a passage which, to use Paul Sheats' term, is "epistemologically critical"[24]) and that which presents a disembodied prophetic voice, such as the following, the opening of Bronson Alcott's "Orphic Sayings":

> Thou art, my heart, a soul-flower, facing ever and following the motions of thy sun, opening thyself to her vivifying ray, and pleading thy affinity with the celestial orbs.[25]

For while Alcott pronounces his utterance into a vacuum (we

<u>overhear</u> him amusing himself with his own profundity), Emerson implicates his audience, drawing us into his text through our sympathy for him as a real being who takes walks and stands still in entranced wonder at the beauty of the heavens. His concrete, dramatic style does not let us forget he has a body. Emerson, with his frail health (a tendency toward consumption, which had killed his brother) must have been acutely aware of the physical. As far as vision is concerned, we must not forget (as I am sure Emerson didn't) the irony that in 1825 he lost the use of one eye for six months (this for an avid reader), until his full vision was restored by an operation. This is the human, physical side of that longing for "transparency" which Emerson later exalted.

It would astound credulity to think that none of this physical awareness entered into Emerson's writing. Although he operated frequently within the confines of Platonic and Idealist terminologies, Emerson was an imperfect Platonist at best. Unlike Plotinus, he did not long to escape from his body; for his body, he perceived, was the focus of creative action <u>in</u> the world. Rather than deny the physical or the social, Emerson aspires to transfigure such facts by molding them to the dictates of creative energy, by seeing them as the vehicles of meaning. Although such creative metamorphosis may sound Platonic and visionary when applied to the realms of poetry and philosophy, it refers equally well to material spheres as concrete as the architecture of Emerson's friend, Horatio Greenough. And Emerson's evident admiration for the full-rigged clipper or the well-managed enterprise reveals his appreciation of business affairs as well as affairs of the mind.[26] For every physical fact, he saw, had at least the potential to become an intellectual tool.

But it *is* a striking paradox that Emerson looks both ways -- that his thought could be used as an apologia for manifest destiny as well as the imperial self. Or, in other terms, one is startled to realize that - for Emerson - profound evocations of the unconscious, passages which appear to verge on mysticism, are linked to activity in the world. But then, psychoanalysis and depth psychology, with their differing perceptions of *libido*, study the transformations of that psychic energy into social and cultural manifestations. Depths of subjectivity are linked to the man-made objective world through the dialectic of sublimation. If vital energy is raised from the root to the highest flower (or, to adopt two of the most striking phrases of *Nature*, from the "soiled nest" to the "transparent eyeball"), one sees those extremes as aspects of one organic development, the endpoints of one continuous chain of power, one ascending spire of form.

Many of the above points can be made more concrete by comparing Emerson's *Nature* with a book that influenced it greatly -- Sampson Reed's *Observations of the Growth of the Mind*. Published in 1826, five years after his inspiring "Oration on Genius" (which Emerson had heard as a master's candidate at Harvard), Reed's book formulated an organic style based upon intuitive reception of the "language" of nature. As Perry

Miller explains:

> It announced that the organic principle, if piously observed, cannot fail to achieve coherence by the method of surrender and receptivity, because the correspondence of idea and object, of word and thing, is inherent in the universe.[27]

Emerson's indebtedness to such ideas, especially in the section "Language" is evident. Indeed, early Swedenborgian readers took him as one of their own (Emerson's source, Reed, being one of the foremost American Swedenborgians). But it is important that we read this doctrine of "correspondence" as more than an occult relation which the mind passively receives. For in Sampson Reed's essay, as well as in Emerson's, emphasis is placed upon correspondence revealing itself through action in the world. That is, the mind, expanding its powers, is seen to find the materials of expression ready at hand -- the intellect discovering its contours only through its relatedness to the physical world.

Sampson Reed makes this connection explicit in his explanation of "correspondence." The natural world, he asserts, "was intended to draw forth and mature the latent energies of the soul."[28] Elsewhere, he describes the natural world as "that in which the mind may take root" and "the actual conditions of society" as "the atmosphere which surrounds and protects it; in which it sends forth its branches and bears fruit."[29] For the mind, Reed emphasizes, can only know itself through observing the reflection of its powers:

> The mind will see itself in what it loves and is able to accomplish. Its own works will be its mirror; and when it is present in the natural world,

> feeling the same spirit which gives life to every object by which it is surrounded, in its very union with nature it will catch a glimpse of itself.[30]

It is necessary, Reed asserts throughout his essay, for the mind - if it would know itself - to exist embodied. It is only when the mind is "planted in this world, that the light of heaven may fall upon it with a gentle radiance, and call forth its energies."[31] Illumination is revealed through involvement in the world. For "if we look merely at the truth, it will vanish away, like rays of light falling into vacancy."[32] This optical metaphor should be familiar to readers of Emerson, who also believed - as Sherman Paul expresses it - that the "mind was the lens converging the rays of spirit on the daily affairs of man."[33] For both thinkers, spirit is "invisible" until "it falls on an object" -- the mind's latent power is revealed through natural form.

But if Emerson absorbed Reed's conception of correspondence, he parted company with him over his interpretation of man's lapse from the divine. To Reed's mind, man's vision is so imperfect (was so darkened at the Fall) that only by comparing his condition with "the power of the word of God"[34] can he measure his distance from spiritual perfection:

> The actual condition of man can be seen only from the relation in which he stands to his immutable Creator; and this relation is discovered from the light of revelation.[35]

We must return to the "laws from which we have wandered," Reed proclaims, we must accept the "power of the Lord" by realizing that "go where we will, the paternal roof, the broad canopy of heaven, is extended over us."[36]

We can imagine that the man who could commend his age for building "the sepulchres of the fathers" (CW,I,7) would not be enthralled by the "paternal roof" of divine authority which Reed invokes. For it is this very acceptance of spiritual authority <u>outside</u> the self that Emerson rejects. Although at least one early Swedenborgian reviewer of <u>Nature</u>, taken in by Emerson's exposition of the doctrine of correspondence in "Language," felt that his mind was "imbued with [the] truth" of Swedenborg's writings, the devout were quick to differentiate "the True Light" from the "mock sun of transcendental vanity."[37] Sampson Reed's own preface to the third edition of his <u>Observations on the Growth of the Mind</u> (written two years after the publication of <u>Nature</u>) is especially revealing in this respect. For there, he laments that the "spiritual sense of the Sacred Scripture, which the Lord has now revealed through his servant Emmanuel Swedenborg" has been too readily usurped by "Transcendentalism." "This," he continues,

> is the product of man's own brain; and when the human mind has been compelled to relax its grasp on sensualism, and the philosophy based on the senses, it may be expected first to take refuge here....It may be something gained, when the idolater no longer literally worships the work of his own hands; even though he be in heart an idolater still, and worships the creations of his own imagination. So it may be a step forward from <u>sensualism</u> to <u>transcendentalism</u>....It would seem... that Providence often permits one falsity to be removed by another. <u>Transcendentalism</u> is the parasite of <u>sensualism</u>.[38]

Finally, in a passage which contains a striking insight, Reed alleges: "Imagining themselves spiritual, it is possible that they should be even the lowest of the sensual -- for they may only give to their sensuality wings, by which it may gain an apparent elevation without any real change in its nature."[39]

But it is exactly this giving "sensuality wings" - this attempt to elevate the physical facts of existence to the status of spiritual symbols at the same time the physical is retained ("without any real change in its nature") - that distinguishes Emerson's intention in <u>Nature</u> from Sampson Reed's earlier. What galls Reed is the Transcendentalists' refusal to go all the way -- to step from a recognition of spirit animating man and nature to an open acknowledgement of the priority of God's presence upholding creation. Thus, while both Emerson and Reed long for that apocalyptoc cleansing of vision in which the "world itself again becomes a paradise,"[40] they differ in their interpretation of that transformation. For Reed, it is a sign of God's grace, manifesting His power working through the mind; while for Emerson, it reveals the <u>mind's</u> divine power. This distinction may seem slight, but it measures totally different conceptions of spiritual authority.

One can clarify this by saying that in Emerson's thought the object of faith has shifted from God to the psyche. Writing for unregenerate audiences, both Reed and Emerson must dwell upon the psychological characteristics of faith -- for, as Reed explains, the object of faith only becomes visible after regeneration. Both are confronted with the dilemma of the so-called "hermeneutic circle" -- that one must believe first in order to understand belief. As Reed explains: "Since the fall of man, nothing has been more difficult for him than to know his real condition, since every departure from divine order is attended with the loss of the knowledge of what it is."[41] Consequently, men lack "the chart by which they might determine their moral longitude."[42] If, for Reed, this "chart" is provided by the authority of divine scripture; for Emerson it is found in the successive stages of illumination portrayed by the dialectical structure of Nature. If Reed focus upon the ideal, Emerson (like Hegel) focuses upon both the ideal and the process of attaining it. Thus we have in Emerson's text not just the impersonal voice of prophecy, but also the personal tone of spiritual aspiration. We see here how the interest in psychology necessitated by the erosion of faith can shift into a focus upon psychology itself as an end. Both Reed and Emerson want regenerated vision, but in Emerson's thought it is the process of regeneration (the transfiguration of perception, the play of intuition) which occupies the center of his attention. Psychology emerges here as a separate field of interest from within theology. It is a short step from talking of the revelation of the "God within" to explaining the dynamics of the unconscious.

Let us not forget, however, the extent to which Sampson Reed's discussion of the "power of the mind" and of the unfolding of divinely-inspired intuition displayed for Emerson a psychology of the unconscious. "The mind must grow," Reed asserts, "not from external accretion, but from internal principle."[43] Or again, "the mind will grow and bring forth fruit from its own inherent power of development."[44] Extending this organic metaphor, Reed describes the birth and growth of poetic images in terms which anticipate the observations of Emerson and later Jung:

> we may be conscious of the image in its first conception...we may perceive its beginnings and gradual growth, till at length it becomes distinctly depicted on the retina of the mind.[45]

In Nature, Emerson refines this perception of the emergence of images from the unconscious:

> A man conversing in earnest, if he watch his intellectual processes, will find that always a material image, more or less luminous, arises in his mind, cotemporaneous with every thought, which furnishes the vestment of the thought. Hence, good writing and brilliant discourse are perpetual allegories (CW,I,20).

Thus Emerson, along with Reed, acknowledges "the gleams of a better light" (CW,I,43), that "golden vein of duty, which, if followed aright, will lead to an increasing brightness."[46] For both, this primeval ground of illumination reaches back into the depths of the mind. One need only turn to Hawthorne's "The Old Manse"-to his mention of the "lumps of golden thought, that lay glimmering in the fountain's bed" or to his account of light beaming "through the gates of paradise" which shows us "glimpses far inward"[47]- to see how prevalent was this manner of describing the expression of unconscious forces. In Hawthorne's work especially, this line of figuration revives the alchemical connotation that was an important part of its long inheritance.[48]

Finally, we note that Emerson's psychological emphasis

necessitated a new stance toward the act of writing. Despite his high admiration for Sampson Reed's "genius" (Emerson links him with Dante, Chaucer, and Milton in one passage [JMN,V,54], with Shakespeare in another [JMN,V,232]), Emerson found - when it came to the writing of Nature - that it was difficult to put Reed's precepts into practice. Nature, he discovered, was more intractable than Reed would have us believe; the gleams of the unconscious were more transitory and infrequent. Thus, after jotting down one of the most striking passages eventually to be used in the prophetic utterance of his "poet" in "Prospects" ("A man is a god in ruins...."), Emerson paused to reflect upon the difficulties of composition, recalling in the process one of Reed's more inspiring precepts from his "Oration on Genius":

> How hard to write the truth. "Let a man rejoice in the truth and not that he has found it," said my early oracle. Well, so soon as I have seen the truth I clap my hands & rejoice & go back to see it & forward to tell man. I am so pleased therewith that presently it vanishes. Then am I submiss & it appears "without observation." I write it down, & it is gone (JMN,V,181).

That language is limited and not perfectly suited to the needs of the spirit (despite the bravado of his contrary assertion in parts of Nature) is one of Emerson's more profound observations -- one that he allows to enter his writing in contrast to his yearning for correspondence. This recognition that language will not, as Sampson Reed asserted, always be "one with things" was one of the marks of Emerson's great honesty as a writer. For he realized that "there are many things that refuse to be recorded,-- perhaps the larger half. The unsaid part is the best of every discourse" (JMN,V,51).

Accordingly, Emerson placed the most revolutionary aspects of his vision in Nature into the mouth of his "Orphic" poet:

> "Man is the dwarf of himself. Once he was permeated and dissolved by spirit. He filled nature with his overflowing currents. Out from him sprang the sun and the moon; from man, the sun; from woman, the moon. The laws of his mind, the periods of his actions externized themselves into day and night, into the year and the seasons. But, having made for himself this huge shell, his waters retired; he no longer fills the veins and veinlets; he is shrunk to a drop..." (CW,I,42).

While Sampson Reed had no compunctions about ascending to prophetic levels of utterance, asserting the possibility of rending "the veil by which [the mind] would avoid the direct presence of Jehovah,"[49] Emerson realized that the imperfection of man circumscribed man's vision and hence his rhetoric. He, too, longed for that "apocalypse" of the mind in which the things of the world "shall reappear in their morning lustre" (CW,I,21), but he also acowledged, by placing within quotation marks "A man is a god in ruins," that this regeneration of consciousness stood before him as an aspiration and not an accomplished fact. Such speech was a myth of man's potential (and hence, a realization of his lapse), a myth which helped define man's spiritual longings. But as myth, it existed on a plane discontionuous with daily speech, discontinuous because - as Emerson observed, continuing to reflect on this passage - often "The Reason refuses to play at couples with Understanding" (JMN,V,181). Emerson's sense of this disunity, the rift between the ideal and the aspiration, between the unconscious and consciousness, constituted the motive of his literary quest. It was the existential wounding that his writing attempted to heal.

NOTES: CHAPTER FIVE

[1] Charles Feidelson Jr., *Symbolism and American Literature* (Chicago: Univ. of Chicago Press, 1953), pp.128,129,143.

[2] Feidelson, p.146.

[3] *Ibid*.

[4] To remake F.O. Matthiessen's phrase, "hypnotize himself into rhapsody," in *American Renaissance: Art and Expression in the Age of Emerson and Whitman* (New York: Oxford Univ. Press, 1941), p.48.

[5] Matthiessen, p.61.

[6] Newton Arvin, "The House of Pain," in M.R. Konvitz & S.E. Whicher eds., *Emerson: A Collection of Critical Essays* (Englewood Cliffs, N.J.: Prentice Hall, 1962), p.51.

[7] Roland Barthes, *The Pleasure of the Text*, trans. R. Miller (New York: Hill & Wang, 1975), pp.6-9.

[8] Stanley Cavell, "Thinking of Emerson," *New Literary History* 11 (1979), pp.169,171.

[9] Cavell, pp.172,174,176.

[10] Paul Ricoeur, *Freud and Philosophy: An Essay on Interpretation*, trans. D. Savage (New Haven: Yale Univ. Press, 1970), Book II, Chapter 2: "The Conflict of Interpretations," p.20ff.

[11] Coleridge, *The Statesman's Manual*, in *Complete Works*, ed. W.G.T. Shedd (New York: Harper & Bros.), 1884), I,436.

[12] *Coleridge's Shakespearean Criticism*, ed. T.M. Raysor (Cambridge, Mass.: Harvard Univ. Press, 1930), I,223.

[13] Ibid.

[14] Coleridge, Aids to Reflection, in Complete Works, ed. Shedd, I,129.

[15] This and the preceding quotation are from Heidegger, "Building Dwelling Thinking," in Basic Writings, ed. D. Krell (New York: Harper & Row, 1977), p.332.

[16] Coleridge, Aids to Reflection, in Complete Works, I,154.

[17] This paragraph throughout is indebted to Heidegger's analysis of the poetic process in "The Origin of the Work of Art," Poetry, Language, Thought, trans. A. Hofstadter (New York: Harper & Row, 1971), pp.17-87.

[18] James Hillman, Re-Visioning Psychology (New York: Harper & Row, 1975), Chapter 2: "Pathologizing or Falling Apart," p.56ff.

[19] Paul De Man, Blindness and Insight: Essays in the Rhetoric of Contemporary Criticism (New York: Oxford Univ. Press, 1971), p.148.

[20] Wallace Stevens, Collected Poems (New York: Alfred A. Knopf, 1965), p.380.

[21] Albert Hofstadter, "Introduction" to Heidegger, Poetry, Language, Thought, p.xviii.

[22] Heidegger, Poetry, Language, Thought, p.49.

[23] Paul Ricoeur, Freud and Philosophy, Book III, Chapter 4: "Hermeneutics: The Approaches to Symbol," p.494ff.

[24] Paul D. Sheats, The Making of Wordsworth's Poetry, 1785-1798 (Cambridge, Mass.: Harvard Univ. Press, 1973), pp.92-3.

[25] Bronson Alcott, "Orphic Sayings," in Perry Miller ed., *The Transcendentalists: An Anthology* (Cambridge, Mass.: Harvard Univ. Press, 1950), p.303.

[26] Joel Porte details Emerson's attention to his business affairs in *Representative Man: Ralph Waldo Emerson in His Time* (New York: Oxford Univ. Press, 1979).

[27] Miller, *The Transcendentalists*, p.53.

[28] Sampson Reed, *Observations on the Growth of the Mind* (1826; rptd. New York: Arno Press, 1972), p.45.

[29] Reed, p.61.

[30] Reed, pp.41-2.

[31] Reed, p.30.

[32] Reed, p.29.

[33] Sherman Paul, *Emerson's Angle of Vision* (Cambridge, Mass.: Harvard Univ. Press, 1952), p.86.

[34] Reed, p.67.

[35] Reed, p.11.

[36] Reed, pp.14,35.

[37] John Westall, *The New Jerusalem Magazine* (Boston), XV, No. CLXX (Oct. 1841), p.50. Rptd. in M. Sealts & A. Ferguson, *Emerson's Nature -- Origin, Growth, Meaning* (New York: Dodd, Mead & Co., 1969), p.109.

[38] Reed, pp.vi-vii.

[39] Reed, p.vii.

[40] Reed, p.15.

[41] Reed, p.11.

[42] *Ibid.*

[43] Reed, p.39.

[44] Reed, p.48.

[45] Reed, pp.74-5.

[46] Reed, p.78.

[47] Hawthorne, *Mosses from an Old Manse*, vol. 10 of *The Centenary Edition of the Works of Nathaniel Hawthorne*, ed. W. Charvet, R.H. Pearce, C.M. Simpson (Columbus, Ohio: Ohio State Univ. Press, 1962-   ), pp.24,28.

[48] For a discussion of alchemical themes in Hawthorne, see: Mark Hennelly, "Hawthorne's Opus Alchymicum: 'Ethan Brand,'" *ESQ* 22, No.2 (1976), pp.96-106. Raymona E. Hull, "Hawthorne and the Magic Elixir of Life: The Failure of a Gothic Theme," *ESQ* 18, No.2 (1972), pp.97-102. David M. Van Leer, "Aylmer's Library: Transcendental Alchemy in Hawthorne's 'The Birthmark,'" *ESQ* 22, No.4 (1976), pp.211-221.

[49] Reed, p.28.

CHAPTER SIX

EMERSON'S "PHILOSOPHY OF HISTORY" AND JUNGIAN PSYCHOLOGY

Emerson's writing after Nature amplifies this sense of rift - of the alienation of consciousness from unconscious power - as the occasion of reflection. Like Gnostic thinkers two thousand years before, Emerson takes as his point of departure a sense of divergence between power and being, between inspired consciousness and quotidian care. Man is seen to have fallen away from the "One Mind" whose currents no longer fill consciousness, but only circulate when we sleep: "our mental processes go forward, even when they seem suspended" (EL,II,35). Beneath the surface of life, there is felt to reside a "common law" which connects disparate phenomena (EL,II,27). Like a plant which "struggles up to light," each "thought...arises in the mind" (EL,II,42). In such terms, Emerson analyzes - in his lectures on "The Philosophy of History," delivered the winter following the publication of Nature - his deepening perception of that "large

...portion of ourselves" which "lies within the limits of the unconscious" (EL,II,56).

Significantly, such limits are seen as potential power and not as disinheritance. The unconscious, for Emerson (as later for Jung) constitutes a reservoir of power, of tappable psychic energy, and not an antagonist to the ego's security. There is no indication, as there is for Poe and Melville, that unconscious forces might erupt and usurp consciousness in an uncontrollable paroxysm of demonic energy. Even when he compares the emergence of unconscious energy to volcanic eruption (as Emerson does one half year later in "The American Scholar"), there is no loss of control, no regression to anxiety at the possible extinction of the ego. Overpowering archetypes do not threaten, as they do for Melville. Rather, Apollonian forces rest secure - perhaps too secure - in their contol of the psychic economy. Thus, the danger, for Emerson, resides in excessive control -- in an egotism so strict that it closes down the conduits of the psychic economy.

In terms of Emerson's discovery of the unconscious, his lectures on "The Philosophy of History" serve three functions. First, they define at great length Emerson's sense of the unconscious as a collective, "rational" source which he refers to as "One Mind." Next, they outline the conditions for the unfolding of unconscious energy as constructive power. Finally, they articulate Emerson's sense of a contemporary dissociation from the unconscious. All three duplicate - almost exactly - arguments later made by Carl Jung. If one did not know better, one might accuse Jung of plagiarizing Emerson. However, Jung himself refers to Emerson only four times -- twice in passing, once to commend Emerson's "introspection" and his quotation of St. Augustine on God as an infinite circular figure, and finally to note the similarity of their views upon character as "fate."[1] As we shall see, the thought of these two seminal thinkers bears a closer resemblance. "One of the problems," Martin Bickman writes, "in juxtaposing Emerson and Jung is not that they have so little in common but that they have so much."[2]

We can thank Bickman for enlarging the question of the similarity between Emerson's thought and Jung's. Recognizing their "common Romantic inheritance" (substantiated by Henri Ellenberger's monumental history of psychoanalysis), Bickman suggests fruitful comparisons between their conceptions of symbolism and psychic development.[3] For both, "The very act of creating or apprehending a symbol is...a bridge across the rift, a way of reuniting psyche and world."[4] This bridge heals as well the division <u>within</u> between consciousness and the unconscious. As we have seen, M.H. Abrams' mapping of archetypal Romantic quests provides one model for this dialectic. Bickman confirms this view, focusing in his study upon what he calls "the Romantic unity-division-reintegration pattern" mapped thoroughly by Abrams.[5] Suggesting similarities between Emersonian "self-reliance" and Jungian "individuation"[6] (a point which I shall amplify in the following pages), Bickman focuses upon Emerson's "double consciousness" as a method of reconciling consciousness with the unconscious.[7] Continuing the discussion of Emerson's metamorphic style (his "aesthetics of perpetual transition"), he suggests that this style promotes a balance <u>between</u> consciousness and the unconscious, a multiple perspective that helps assimilate the wisdom of the self to the ego. "Surprise," he comments, "is the Emersonian equivalent of ecstasy, where the painfully constructed ego is abandoned for the ever-new fullness of the self."[8] My conception of "interpretive form" as a variety of Romantic irony extends Bickman's discussion by relating Emerson's literary stance more generally to the Romantic tradition. As we shall see, Emerson's early lectures and addresses continue his search for interpretive structures which might assimilate the powers he intuited within. His early lecture series on "The Philosophy of History" is one of the most important documents of this enterprise.

Like Jung, Emerson finds a "common law at the foundation of terrestrial natures" (<u>EL</u>,II,27). This "deep centre" he calls "the unconscious" (<u>EL</u>,II,29). According to Emerson, we all look nostalgically back upon "the engaging consciousness of childhood" -- our "unconscious period" when we seemed closer to divinity (<u>EL</u>,II,135). Within ourselves, we sense a "power of life" which "grows when we sleep" (<u>EL</u>, II,35). We are aware of a constant "impulse" in the mind -- a "current" which "knows the way to be realized" and which "is the root of all the great arts" (EL,II,36). In similar terms, Jung describes the inner "urge toward self-realization."[9] "Every creative man," Jung argues, "knows that spontaneity is the very essence of creative thought" -- he realizes that "the unconscious is not just a reactive mirror... but an independent, productive activity."[10]

Unfolding from an unseen center, psychic energy - for both Emerson and Jung - emerges into the light of consciousness. "As the mind unfolds," Emerson writes, it begins "... to publish in the colors of the pleasant light the secrets which preexisted in the closet of the mind" (EL,II,176). In every man, there is "some faculty never yet unfolded" (EL,II,9). The only good for the individual is "the fruit of his Nature...which must grow out of him as long as he exists" (EL,II,95). Amplifying a similar conception of the mind's organic growth, Jung comments extensively in his work upon figures of thought which project images of this psychic unfolding. In *Psychology and Alchemy*, for example, Jung equates the Eastern mandala (often imagined as an unfolding lotus blossom) with the alcehmical vessel. In both instances, a center (the calyx of the lotus and the center of the vessel) becomes a field of projection for images of birth corresponding to the emergence of unconscious forces.[11] Through such figures of unfolding, Jung observes, the unseen center moves "once more into the field of consciousness."[12] The mind imagines its own psychic origins.

Emerson's discussion of "relation" extends this conception

of unfolding. Unconscious creative energies, he observes, can only emerge when they have material to work through:

> Put Napoleon into an island prison and let the great faculties of that man find no men to act upon, no Alps to climb, no stake to play for, and he would beat the air and appear stupid. Then transfer him to large countries, dense population, complex interests, and antagonist power and you shall see him unfold his masterful energies (EL,II,17).

Emerson never ceases to marvel over the fact that we are not imprisoned. For the world corresponds to our unlocked potential -- it *fits* as a field for our projections:

> out of the human soul go as it were highways to the heart of every object in nature, and so subject them to the dominion of man. A man is a bundle of relations, a knot of roots, whose flower and fruitage is the world (EL,II,17).

Always the soul "goes forth to the conquest of the world" (EL,II,145). This conquest, Emerson observes, is facilitated by man's "innumerable relations" (EL,II,155). For "each object unlocks that faculty which is exercised upon it and makes it for the first time known to us" (EL,II,18) -- "known" because our projections, once they are perceived as "objective" facts, become accessible to interpretation. Thus, by relating itself to the world through the projection of unconscious patterns upon external reality, the psyche promotes its own self-analysis.

At the heart of Carl Jung's psychology lies a profound understanding of this dialectical relationship between projection and interpretation. "Projections," he writes, "change the world into the replica of one's own unknown face."[13] The point of analysis is to interpret this hitherto-unknown visage.

For only by recognizing our unconscious projections can we free ourselves from them and consciously assimilate the power they embody. Possession gives way to psychic growth. Emerson's comments, in "The Philosophy of History," reveal a similar awareness of interpretation. We observe Emerson here attempting to delineate what he calls the "science of the mind" (EL,II,167) -- a psychology which analyzes the functioning of "deeper causes" within human behavior (EL,II,172). One of the primary laws of being is that all forms of human activity are "signs more or less near of the human will." Our understanding of "history," Emerson continues, involves "inferring the hidden nature of the human soul from these...remote effects" (EL,II,143). Thus, humanity and culture offer themselves as evidence of unconscious powers which we interpret through them.

Just as Jung interprets his patients' symptoms and dreams, Emerson infers "human character" from "the most fugitive deed and word" (EL,II,129). Our "manners," he writes, "evermore publish" the hidden man -- they "proceed directly from the character of which they are the involuntary signs" (Ibid.). Each one of us

>has his proper forms of living, speaking, motion, address, which are independent of his will but wholly dependent on his character and condition, and therefore are the same index of his genius or turn of mind.
>   That circumstance constitutes their value to the historian and philosopher, that they are the unconscious account which [the] party gives of himself (EL,II,130-1).

Along these lines, the value of the hero or the man of genius is that he <u>represents</u> most fully the power within. His life becomes <u>representative</u>, a symbol of the unconscious realizing itself through his active realization to the world. It becomes one of the primary roles of Emerson to interpret for us the psychological and spiritual significance of such representations.

Correlative with representation is the act of interpretation which reads the energy incarnated in such forms. Emerson discusses such interpretation when he exhorts us to recognize the "ideas" which rule our lives:

> We must always be prisoners of Ideas which we are just beginning to apprehend; when by and by we understand them and see how we were guided and led we are already following another clue, or tyrannised over by another Ruling Thought, which we can no more see around (<u>EL</u>,II,170).

Just as Jung taught his patients to recognize the archetypes ruling their lives, Emerson advocates the "act of reflection" which places life "in perspective" (<u>EL</u>,II,144-5). One can overcome unconscious possession only through a process which, as Emerson describes it, "separates for us a truth from our unconscious reason, and makes it an object of consciousness" (<u>EL</u>,II,57). When such "truth" is "separated by the intellect," when "any sentiment or principle" is "disentangled from the web of our unconsciousness" (<u>EL</u>,II,57,58), we learn to "acquire" ourselves by recognizing the hidden face behind the mask. Thus, like Jung, Emerson practices a psychological analysis dedicated to "detaching from the general instinct of life the moral principles which we feel to be the ascendant stars in our inner firmament" (<u>EL</u>,II,58).

Feeling is converted into thought; intuition, into insight.

It is significant that Emerson sees the creation of such interpretive perspectives as the cause of literary impersonality. Since recognition of the unconscious reveals a level of the psyche common to all men, the orator addresses "the common soul" (EL,II,109). Similarly, the artist "must disindivudalize himself, and be a man of no party, and no manner, and no age, but one through whom the soul of all men circulates" (EL,II,48-9). Years before T.S. Eliot argued that artistic activity must involve "a continual self-sacrifice, a continual extinction of personality,"[14] Emerson asserts that the successful artist must "hinder [his] individuality from acting," that he must "shove aside...egotism... prejudice, and will" (EL,II,49). But while Eliot displaces egotism in favor of language, Emerson displaces it in favor of transcendent depths. The artist, Emerson explains, "purges out of his thought every vestige of personal limitation and respires the air of pure truth" (EL,II,12). Emerson's "air of pure truth" and Eliot's "art emotion" (a function of the artist's medium)[15] both defer egotism to a larger ground of meaning.

Jung articulates a similar impersonality when he advocates shifting one's perspective from the ego to the "self" which is "the totality of the psyche," including both conscious and unconscious functions.[16] In so doing, we realize that the

> ego is...subordinate to the self and related to it like a part to the whole....And just as circumstances or outside events "happen" to us and

> limit our freedom, so the self acts upon the ego
> like an <u>objective</u> <u>occurrence</u> which free will can
> do very little to alter.$_{17}$

This awareness limits egotism and depersonalizes the psyche by suggesting a larger perspective which sees the ego itself as the vehicle of unconscious powers which determine its activity. The burden of self-reliant individuation is both to humble the ego's pretensions to self-sufficiency and to create new attitudes which place the ego in contact with previously hidden forces. In this way, the "individual mind" becomes "the vent of the mind of humanity" (<u>EL</u>,II,50) and not a raging volcano possessed by uncontrollable energy. Rather than being the <u>object</u> of the "Lethean stream" which "washes through us and bereaves us of ourselves" (EL,II,85-6), we must learn that we rest upon a vast reservoir of exploitable power.

Paradoxically, while expression of unconscious energies necessitates impersonal perspectives, it leads to greater <u>individuality</u>. According to Jung, the displacement of the ego toward the unconscious allows "the better and more complete fulfillment of the collective qualities of the human being." Instead of the false indivudalism of the egocentric "persona," based upon a stereotyped social role, this realization of unconscious potential promotes the true "idiosyncrasy" of the individual, which is "a unique combination, or general differentiation, of functions and faculties which in themselves are universal."[18] Jung calls this process "self-realization" and, more frequently, "individuation," a concept which we can pair with Emerson's ideal of "self-reliance."[19]

Each man, Emerson argues, occupies a potentially unique relationship to the universal center of power:

> He is differenced both in person and in nature from every other man that ever existed, by having the common faculties under a bias, or determination of character altogether new and original. In him, under him, is the same world as another beholds; but it is the world seen from a new point of view; the more deeply he drinks of the common soul, the more decided does his individuality become (EL,II,100).

Emerson's many later exhortations to self-reliance come out of this perception that the true individual is firmly centered upon the "common soul." By standing squarely "upon the basis of the world" and allowing his will to become the "effluence of...Reason" (EL,II,152), he incarnates and expresses a spiritual authority that gives his being weight and presence. His "point of view" is always his own; he is "wholly his own man" (EL,II,175). Instead of donning a social persona, the true individual realizes a sense of "vocation" and accepts "his own calling, which is determined by his peculiar reception of the Common Reason" (EL,II,147). In other words, he listens to the Muse.

Throughout "The Philosophy of History," Emerson refers to this domesticated unconscious as "one Mind common to all individual men" (EL,II,11). "In all individual men there is but one mind" -- this

> is the mind of the mind. We belong to it, not it to us. It is in all men, even in the worst, and constitutes them men (EL,II,83).

"Of the Universal Mind," Emerson writes elsewhere, "...each individual man is one more incarnation" (EL,II,15). In many respects, Jung's concept of the "collective unconscious" illuminates this vision of "One Mind." Indeed, Jung himself - upon occasion - refers to the collective unconscious as "One Mind": "By means of the transcendent function we...gain access to the 'One Mind.'"[20] Jung attributes this figure to Swedenborg, one of Emerson's most important sources: "we are part of a single, all-embracing psyche, a single 'greatest man,' the homo maximus, to quote Swedenborg.[21] But as Martin Bickman, R.A. Yoder, and others have shown, this is an ancient myth, dating back to antiquity.[22] In the hands of Emerson and Jung, this myth becomes a symbol of transformation which helps to define and assimilate the power of the unconscious.

At this point, let us clarify Jung's conception of the "collective unconscious," an idea which has been the occasion of much misunderstanding and some controversy. First, let us note that even Freud agreed with Jung in recognizing the possibility of what Freud called "a phylogenetic heritage."[23] But for both psychologists, other aspects of the unconscious were more important than the inheritability of certain functions or fantasies. For Freud, as is well known, the repressed personal unconscious became the focus of attention. Jung extends Freud's conception of the unconscious by including an even more primitve level lying below the personal unconscious. It is "collective" because, like cell structure or the chemistry of blood, it represents a capacity shared by all human beings -- in this case, certain <u>universal structural principles of imagination</u>. As Jung explains:

> There are no inborn ideas, but there are inborn possibilities of ideas that set bounds to even the boldest fantasy and keep our fantasy activity within certain categories.[24]

While Jung describes these "categories" as "primordial images" or "archetypes," it is important to recognize that he <u>does not define archetypes as inherited images</u>, as is often assumed, but rather as formal principles shaping the image-making activity. Archetypes, he explicitly states, are not "images filled with content," but rather inborn "<u>forms without content</u>, representing merely the possibility of a certain type of perception and action."[25] They correspond, he adds, to what Henri Hubert and Marcel Mauss call "categories of the imagination."[26] They are the "unthinkable matrices of all our thoughts," "*a priori* conditions of the imagination."[27]

Such definitions bring Jung's thought much closer to contemporary Structuralist theory than is usually assumed. Structuralism, Vernon Gras observes, "opposes the freedom of the fully conscious subject," for the conscious subject is seen to be "the object of the structuring system which has its true initiating agent in the unconscious."[28] While this perspective usually leads to pessimistic commentary upon the "death" of the subject, it is useful to see its kinship to the views of Emerson and Jung examined above.

According to them, it is not the subject which is destroyed, but rather the ego as the center of the individual. Awareness of the unconscious as a "structuring system," it appears, need not lead to nihilism -- for there also exists the possibility of faith as a stance toward the unconscious. Furthermore, we note that Claude Levi-Strauss' description of the unconscious as a "pre-existing structure" which imposes universal "structural laws"[29] is close to Jung's conception of "archetype." Levi-Strauss lamely tries to dispose of Jung by attributing to him belief in universal unconscious "contents,"[30] but such misreading barely covers the similarity between their views. Indeed, Levi-Strauss' method in "The Structural Study of Myth" of collating all the variants of a myth to arrive at an ur-myth is not that far removed from Jung's system of "amplification." In both cases, all accessible variants of a myth are compared in order to illustrate its basic features.

Returning to Emerson and Jung, we observe that both, as inheritors of Romantic psychological tradition, speak of the unconscious as a divine source. The collective unconscious, Jung notes, "contains an indefinite number of motifs or patterns of an archaic character, in principle identical with the root ideas of mythology."[31] More succinctly, he describes archetypes as "unconscious powers, 'gods' in fact, as the ancient world quite rightly conceived them to be."[32] For Emerson also divinity lies within the psyche: "The Unconscious is ever the act of God himself" (EL,II,135). Religion, as Emerson defines it, is "the emotion of reverence which the conscious presence of the Universal Mind inspires" (EL, II,181). It is not surprising, then, to see that both Emerson and Jung admire Christ as one of the most perfect incarnations of this divine, unconscious energy -- as the epitome of the self-reliant individual. Christ was "a minister of the pure Reason," Emerson writes (EL,II,90). Jung concurs with the assertion that Christ, as one of the most perfect models of individuation, "exemplifies the archetype of the self."[33]

Both writers turned to the occult tradition and to Oriental religion for the spiritual wisdom lacking in their cultures. Many of their contemporaries had forgotten divinity altogether as they lost the old terms for godhead. Without the sense of a larger power giving meaning to the individual, there was no ground of being in which to participate. Both Emerson and Jung found in Oriental culture a psychological terminology to replace the failing language of religion. If there are to be gods in the modern world, each realized, they must appear from within. In the East, Jung found an awareness of the mind as "a cosmic factor, the very essence of existence."[34] Eastern thinkers, he observed, saw their gods as projections from the depths of the mind. This perspective relocated the source of divine power: the gods' "potency was really our, and...their significance was our projection."[35] For many, this psychic "origin" cements the conviction that divinity is merely a "fiction,"a "superstition."

But Emerson, like Jung, realized that the power and mystery of religious faith need not be diminished just because its center had shifted. If "Nothing is sacred," as Emerson affirms, "but the integrity of one's own mind" (EL,II,151), this sense of "integrity" does not deny God, but rather relocates His provenance by displacing the sacred from heaven to the psyche. The unconscious, Emerson saw, is ultimately as mysterious as heaven -- we can never see to its "bottom."

Emerson realized acutely the difficulty of preserving a religious spirit in a self-conscious, reflective age. He knew too well the hermeneutic dilemma that one must believe already in order to see. For unless an attitude of faith exists, sacred truths fall upon deaf ears:

> But the Revelation and the Church both labor under one perpetual disadvantage. They need always the presence of the same spirit that created them to make them thoroughly valid. All attempts to confine and transmit the religious feeling of one man or one sect to another age, by means of formulas the most accurate or rites the most punctual, have hitherto proved abortive. You might as easily preserve light or electricity in barrels. The truest state of thought rested in, becomes false. Thought is like manna, that fell out of heaven, which cannot be stored. It will be sour if kept; and tomorrow must be gathered anew (EL,II,92-3).

In order to appreciate the "perfumed breath" of the ancient religious teachers, Emerson continues, we must realize that such flowers grow in our age also (EL,II,93). Yet around him Emerson saw closed nostrils and sleep. Men continued to worship the dead forms of the past, institutions from which the spirit had slowly seeped until only husks remained.

soul has stolen away "leaving a corpse in their hands" (EL, II,97). Given this decay of the objective forms of religion, no alternative existed but to build anew -- to turn within for the religious spirit that had no external habitation.

Emerson's comments in these lectures reveal a profound understanding of the way spirit creates forms for itself in which to dwell. "Only if we are capable of dwelling, only then can we build," Heidegger teaches.[36] Applying such insights to Emerson, Stanley Cavell suggests that the interest of his writing (as well as Thoreau's) resides in such dwelling: "in the fact that what they are building is writing, that their writing is, as it realizes itself daily under their hands, sentence by stunning sentence, the accomplishment of inhabitation."[37] In addition, Emerson's analysis of the founding and decay of churches demonstrates that his comprehension of "inhabitation" extends from practice to theory. For he saw that any public gesture - the institution of a church being the example at hand - objectifies impulses found within, but that also this objectification eventually leads to a divorce between spirit and form, original impulse and solidified gesture. Ideally, form is plastic and continually responsive to the fluctuations of the spirit, to new ideas. But one of the sources of human tragedy is that all form is imperfect and eventually "decays" as it progressively fails to express the spirit which once wore it like a close-fitting garment.

As Charles Feidelson was one of the first to notice, the

process of objectification at the heart of Emerson's vision of being entails a concept of symbolic form. Thus, when Emerson blames spiritual decay upon the "obstinate tendency to personify and bring under the eye-sight what should be the contemplation of Reason alone" (EL,II,96), we find a critique of the symbol-making process at the base of human culture. Symbols "personify and bring under the eye-sight" what had been hidden -- they incarnate and embody impulses once unconscious. But this process, Emerson notices, leads eventually to a sense of alienation. For symbols, once created, are fixed and immobile; while the spirit constantly changes. Thus, cognitive dissonance unavoidably arises from a sense of discrepancy between fixed rites and spiritual need. "But having made for himself this huge shell, his waters retired; he no longer fills the veins and veinlets; he is shrunk to a drop."[38]

This is what happened during the spiritual crisis of Emerson's age. Although existing churches had once succeeded in fully expressing the inner man, spiritual needs had changed until such forms seemed to the introspective individual "another and not himself" (EL,II,96):

> Something like this has been the recent condition of Christendom. Its established churches have become old and ossified under the accumulation of creeds and usages. They who held to the establishment so fast did not see that they could not imprison the Soul and it was stealing away from them, forming itself a new body and leaving a corpse in their hands (EL,II,97).

Although "flat idolatry appears" (EL,II,96) among those holding onto the husks of the old religion, Emerson is heartened by the observation that the spirit cannot long remain unexpressed -- "new communities of faith form" (EL,II, 97). As long as men exist who can assume "a deeper tone," the hidden spirit of man "finds a vent" (EL,II,97).

Any gesture, any creation or act - Emerson realized - will decay if held too long. The therapies of Freud and especially Jung were later designed to heal the rift caused by such repression, to create new symbolic forms (for example, the discourse of therapist and patient) which might release stifled spirit. Emerson's lectures and essays, as attempts toward new dwelling, fulfilled a similar function. For they try to startle "the soul awake" (EL,II,84) by creating new forms which might express its hidden contours. Significantly, this expression takes the form of a discourse upon the unconscious and the ego's relation to that center of power. Psychology, Emerson realized, must accept the mantle theology had let drop. Accordingly, Emerson identifies the inner spiritual impulse with a psychological function, "Reason."

Thus "The Philosophy of History" analyzes the psychology of spiritual alienation. "Inertia, habit, the love of repose, the lucrative skill we have acquired" are all seen to impede the spiritual process (EL,II,159). Egotism, man's "individual as contradistinguished from his universal nature" (EL,II,137), leads to the "little and contemptible." More seriously, reflection itself seems to impede instinctive spontaneity, the free flow of unconscious impulse:

> It is alleged that the habit of the cultivated
> intellect of the present day is reflection, not
> instinct. Ours is distinguished from the Greek
> and Roman and Gothic ages and all the periods of
> childhood and youth by being the age of the sec-
> ond thought. The golden age is gone and the sil-
> ver is gone -- the blessed areas of unconscious
> life, of intuition, of genius (EL,II,168).

Indeed, the introspection which Emerson himself utilizes seems part of the problem:

> we, as soon as we have thought, turn short upon
> ourselves to inquire how the thought arose....
> The ancients were self-united. We have found out
> the difference of outer and inner (EL,II,168).

"We are become philosophic," Emerson later complains: "The age is infected with the malady of Hamlet, 'Sicklied o'er with a pale cast of thought'" (EL,II,180).

Part of Emerson's and Jung's solutions for such divisive self-consciousness, Martin Bickman argues, was to use this awareness as the starting point of a Romantic quest for unifying symbolic form:

> The search for a viable relation, a "disposition
> to reconcile" the Soul and the Understanding, is
> also a search for a medium, a redeeming language
> through which there can be commerce between the
> two.[39]

"Double consciousness" or "self-consciousness" is opposed to what Geoffrey Hartman terms "antiself-consciousness."[40] An alienating sense of self-division defines the possibility of a unified sensibility aimed at through symbolism.

According to Paul Ricoeur, proper attention to literary symbols can restore the fullness of meaning. "The symbol gives rise to thought," he asserts at the conclusion of The Symbolism of Evil.[41] Fullness appears again because we must imitate an act of faith in order to plumb the symbol's depths. We criticize in order to believe; but we cannot interpret without a prior belief in the value of what we are interpreting: "We must believe in order to understand: never, in fact, does the interpreter get near to what his text says unless he lives in the <u>aura</u> of the meaning he is inquiring after."[42] (Thus we attempt here to dwell in the aura of Emerson's meaning.) We are still able to "communicate with the sacred," Ricoeur continues, "by making explicit the prior understanding that gives life to the interpretation."[43] Through such a "hermeneutic" perspective (which Ricoeur finds in Schelling, Eliade, and Jung, among others[44]), the meaning of the sacred is restored as a living truth framed by interpretation. Without this "frame," the sacred as a viable picture of the world cannot exist. Ultimately, consciousness discovers its roots by seeing that "the very act by which it abstracts itself from the whole does not cease to share in the being that challenges it in every symbol."[45] Or, as Edward Whitmont declares, "The conversation between unconscious and consciousness, between Self and ego, between God - infinite life - and finite man, never ceases."[46] In the above, I have attempted to show that this "conversation," as a dialectic between "projective" and "interpretive" form, lies at the heart of both Emerson's and Jung's self-realizations.

Finally, Emerson affirms, reflection is "welcome" as the latest stage of "unfolded human nature" (<u>EL</u>,II,180). It is welcome as a "transition state, whilst...man sees the hollowness of traditions and does not yet know the resources of the soul" (EL,II,170). But so long as reflection helps us to see the meaning of statements such as the following - "The slumber as of centuries weighs down the iron lids of Reason" (EL,II,158) - or this - "Into our little bay ebb and flow the tides of the great ocean" (EL,II,188) - it sets the conditions for a belief which can coexist with interpretation. Ultimately, Emerson argues in "The Philosophy of History," this belief entails a stance of faith toward the unconscious from which such symbols emerge. For openness to the possibilities of language and openness to the mysterious turns of self-expression are the same thing.

In "The Philosophy of History," Nature, identified with the unconscious, is seen as a limit which the curve of man's thought never reaches. His ideas of things only approximate the extent of the phenomenal world. His ideas of mind only approximate the depth of the soul. In these lectures, Emer- communicates a sense of a whole transcending the human -- of the context, physical and spiritual, in which man orients himself and strives toward self-definition. This awareness of the limits of human expression and endeavor is equivalent to Romantic irony -- the sense that all aspiration falls short, that all communication is imperfect. But such limitation is not taken as an occasion for despair, but rather for hope. Man's glory is his struggle for order -- his capacity to imagine a transcendent whole that defines his particular being, giving it meaning as the ground of symbolic participation. At this stage of his career, Emerson imagines that whole as a divine, unconscious, rational order.

Emerson's intuition of "One Mind," of a universal ground of being uniting all individuals, orients him toward reunion with rather than isolation from humanity. Sensing this transcendent whole deep within the mind, he is motivated to surpass isolating intellection in a quest for what Yeats was to call "unity of being" -- a reunion of isolating egotism with spontaneous, intuitive roots which ground the self in a larger meaning. The danger, Emerson saw, is <u>disembodied</u> thought, abstract intellection which isolates consciousness in a self-indulgent solipsism. Opposed to such solipsism is thought which sees both the mind's responsibility to its own sources of energy and to other individuals as carriers of the same spark of intuition, the same light of "Reason." In this way, all humanity is potentially united in a common enterprise -- the reconstruction of the fragmented "Mind" of which their own individual egos represent bits and pieces. This process of reunification, of reconnection, returns to man his sense of relation, his awareness of belonging to a historical community. Man immerses himself again in an aura of participation, a communion in which each individual being becomes a symbol of Being.

NOTES: CHAPTER SIX

[1] Jung, CW 11, par.92; CW 5, par.102 note.
[2] Martin Bickman, The Unsounded Centre: Jungian Studies in American Romanticism (Chapel Hill, N.C.: Univ. of North Carolina Press, 1980), p.81.
[3] Bickman, pp.80,45-7.
[4] Bickman, p.45.
[5] Bickman, p.43.
[6] Bickman, p.39.
[7] Bickman, pp.82-3.
[8] Bickman, p.92.
[9] Jung, PJ, 134 (CW 7, par.291).
[10] Jung, PJ, 135 (CW 7, par.292).
[11] Jung, PJ, 423 (CW 12, par.246 & note).
[12] Jung, PJ, 420 (CW 12, par. 237).
[13] Jung, PJ, 146 (CW 9,ii, par. 17).
[14] T.S. Eliot, Selected Essays, New Edition (New York: Harcourt, Brace & World, 1932), p.7.
[15] Eliot, p.10.
[16] Jung, PJ, 324 (CW 12, par. 144).
[17] Jung, PJ, 142 (CW 9,ii, par. 9).
[18] Jung, PJ, 122 (CW 7, par. 267).
[19] Jung, PJ, 122 (CW 7, par. 266).
[20] Jung, PJ, 499 (CW 11, par. 784).
[21] Jung, PJ, 470 (CW 10, par. 175).
[22] Bickman, p.43.

23 Freud, SE 17:97.

24 Jung, PJ, 319 (CW 15, par. 126).

25 Jung, PJ, 66 (CW 9,i, par. 99).

26 Jung, PJ, 60 (CW 9,i, par. 89).

27 Jung, PJ, 21 (CW 8, par. 794).

28 Vernon Gras, "Introduction" to European Literary Theory and Practice: From Existential Phenomenology to Structuralism (New York: Dell, Delta Book, 1973), pp.15-16.

29 Claude Lévi-Strauss, Structural Anthropology, trans. C. Jacobson & B.G. Schoepf (Garden City, N.J.: Doubleday, Anchor Book, 1967), pp.198,199.

30 Lévi-Strauss, pp.65,204.

31 Jung, PJ, 498 (CW 11, par. 781).

32 Jung, PJ, 160 (CW 9,ii, par. 41).

33 Jung, PJ, 428 (CW 12, par. 253); and CW 9,ii, par. 70.

34 Jung, PJ, 485 (CW 11, par.768).

35 Jung, PJ, 482 (CW 11, par. 761).

36 Heidegger, Basic Writings, ed. D.F. Krell (New York: Harper & Row, 1977), p.338.

37 Stanley Cavell, "Thinking of Emerson," New Literary History 11 (1979), p.174.

38 For a fuller discussion of this passage, see chapter three.

39 Bickman, p.84.

40 Geoffrey Hartman, "Romanticism and Antiself-Consciousness," in R.F. Gleckner & G.E. Enscoe eds., Romanticism: Points of View (Englewood Cliffs, N.J.: Prentice Hall, 1970).

[41] Paul Ricoeur, The Symbolism of Evil, trans. E. Buchanon (Boston: Beacon Press, 1969), p.348.

[42] Ricoeur, p.351.

[43] Ricoeur, p.352.

[44] Ricoeur, p.350.

[45] Ricoeur, p.356.

[46] Quoted by Bickman, p.87.

CHAPTER SEVEN

INTERPRETING THE SELF

In this chapter, I would like to pursue further the outlines of the Emersonian hermeneutic. In essence, I argued in the last chapter that the circle of faith posited by Emerson in his lectures and essays is analogous to the openness structured into the Jungian therapeutic situation. In both instances, images of power (or to use Jung's term, "symbols of transformation") are embedded within interpretive contexts designed to assimilate their power. At the heart of such methods lies a profound insight into the mechanics of faith. Both Emerson and Jung saw that acceptance of these symbols brought with it an implicit faith in their hidden message, in the transcendent ground which gives them meaning. Through representation, symbols of transformation incarnate the unseen, the <u>unfolded</u>. Their "translucence," pointing toward that source, challenges consciousness to relate itself to a larger ground of being, which both Emerson and Jung found within.

As Paul Tillich shows us in The Courage To Be, one can leap from ontological insecurity, from angst, into the security of participation:

> Doubt is based on man's separation from the whole of reality, on his lack of universal participation, on the isolation of his individual self. So he tries to break out of this situation, to identify himself with something transindividual, to surrender his separation and self-relatedness.[1]

Rather than accepting non-being as an integral aspect of being, one can escape from the burden of freedom through "collective self-affirmation."[2] It is not surprising, Tillich observes, that with the decay of the Church, substitute religions have risen to replace it. Rather than accept the burden and terror of individualism, modern man has turned toward self-defintion in terms of "movements of a neo-collectivist character" -- in the twentieth century, "fascism, nazism, and communism."[3]

In the nineteenth century, Romantic organicism (with its theory of symbolism) epitomized a similar longing for group identity -- for a unifying whole imagined in Nature.[4] As participation became problematic, there arose self-conscious examination of central themes of individualism. Thus, both Emerson and Jung strive to connect individual being with transcendent wholes that orient and animate indivudal consciousness. But both were also aware of the dangers of this quest for participation. It can break down into collectivist identification. If one comes too close to the center of power (whether Unconscious, Church, or State), one's individuality will be swallowed. To prevent this loss of being, both aspire toward patterns of relation which maintain contact with the unconscious at the same time they insure the integrity of individual consciousness. Emerson's pleas for "enthusiasm" are clearly subordinated to the Apollonian expansion of the self. Jung's analyses attempt to help his patients steer clear of the maelstrom of "inflation."[5]

We have seen how the "unconscious" serves both Emerson and Jung as a participatory vehicle. Consciousness, they argue, "represents" the unconscious by expressing its hidden potential. The individual ego represents the hidden "sea" on which it floats. Similar metaphors of "depth" and "surface," of "seed" and "unfolded" being, of "center" and "circumference," proliferate in their works. "The life of man," Emerson observes,

> is a self-evolving circle, which, from a ring imperceptibly small, rushes on all sides outwards to new and larger circles, and that without end. The extent to which this generation of circles, wheel without wheel, will go, depends upon the force or truth of the individual soul (W,II,304).

At the center, stands "the heart," which "refuses to be imprisoned," "a residuum unknown, unanalyzable," an unconscious source which Emerson identifies with divine power (W,II,304, 306). Opening ourselves to "the energizing spirit," to "waves of God," we float outward on a sacred pulse of becoming (W,II,320,317). At the highpoint of Emerson's enthusiasm,

"Circles," along with many of its companion pieces in Essays, First Series, expresses the dream of a perfect, frictionless sublimation. With virtually no resistance, psychological cause will be translated into effect, potential being into power.

But even at this cresting wave of enthusiasm, let us note the interpretive, hermeneutic aspect of Emerson's rhetoric. In "Circles," for example, this "optative mood" - expressed through a racing series of short and potent sentences - predicates enthusiasm upon belief in Emerson's symbols of transformation. We suspend disbelief in order to understand, and then find - breathless at the conclusion - that disbelief has left us open to inspiration. You cannot read "Circles" without being uplifted -- for each metaphoric leap, each verbal audacity, compels you to carry it upon a responding wave of imagination. As James M. Cox succinctly observes:

> The sentences, sufficiently independent to be epigrammatic, create a momentary but decisive gap between each other, which the eye and ear of the reader and listener bridge with a responsive intellectual leap.[6]

Accepting the terms of Emerson's "argument," we find these terms directed toward the end of locating power within us. The "eternal generation of the soul" (W,II,314), Emerson would show us, is within him, is within us, is within everyone.

But as Emerson himself comments, this generation only appears within the context of an imaginative perspective which posits the unconscious as spiritual origin:

> Yet this incessant movement and progression which all things partake could never become sensible to us but by contrast to some principle of fixture or stability in the soul (W,II,318).

This same perception recurs throughout Essays, First Series. Contrasting unconscious vitality with self-conscious reflection, Emerson links the two as the poles defining our relationship to unconscious power. Opposed to the "power of fortune," the unseen fate written in our character, is the interpretive perspective of reflection which consciously assimilates what had once been unconscious. Thus Emerson observes in "Intellect,"

> a truth, separated by the intellect, is no longer a subject of destiny. We behold it as a god upraised above care and fear. And so any fact in our life, or any record of our fancies or reflections, disentangled from the web of our unconscious, becomes an object impersonal and immortal (W,II,327).

From the era of "instinctive action" we move to the "era of reflection" in which our unconscious life becomes "detached" and drops like ripe fruit into our waiting hands (W,II,331). In the case of artistic creation, these two processes are closely integrated as unconscious projection is framed and controlled:

> The thought of genius is spontaneous; but the power of picture or expression, in the most enriched and flowing nature, implies a mixture of will, a certain control over the spontaneous states, without which no production is possible. It is the conversion of all nature into the rhetoric of thought, under the eye of judgment, with a strenuous exercise of choice (W,II,336).

Looking back to "The American Scholar," we find the same

awareness of interpretation as an arena in which emblems of spontaneity are presented to the self. Let us now turn to that address and examine its interpretive rhetorical form.

Implicit in Emerson's argument and essential to his method of presentation in "The American Scholar" is the recognition that the lessons of the unconscious can be assimilated through establishing interpretive relations to myth. Rather than treating myth as something dead and buried, it is assumed that the mind must intuit the potential energy of myth and - through a stance of openness and faith - reconnect itself to the living "germ" of mystery. Hence, Emerson does not view myth allegorically, translating its lessons term by term into ideas; but instead, he relates to it as a symbol of transformation, as a field of energy in which the interpreter can participate. In this way, he overcomes the "Cartesian" detachment which eschews action in the world in favor of sterile contemplation. The detached observer is replaced by the related participant. From this perspective, Emerson's argument contributes to our definition of the "spiritual problem" of modern man. The discovery of the unconscious offers one way out of this impasse.

For Carl Jung, modern man's alienation, his lost sense of participation, coincides with the decay of conventional religious symbols. But at the same time, this sense of disparity between religious form and spiritual need, between the husk of consciousness and the kernel of buried energies, occasions "the 'discovery' of psychology":[7]

> While man still lives as a herd animal he has no
> psyche of his own, nor does he need any, except
> the usual belief in the immortality of the soul.
> But as soon as he has outgrown whatever local
> form of religion he was born to - as soon as this
> religion can no longer embrace his life in all
> its fullness - then the psyche becomes a factor
> in its own right which cannot be dealt with by
> the customary measures. It is for this reason
> that we today have a psychology founded on expe-
> rience, and not upon articles of faith or the
> postulates of any philosophical system.[8]

Jung's comments can be taken as a cogent analysis of Emerson's intellectual position, of the spiritual task perceived by Transcendentalism.

In the mid-nineteenth century, awareness of the "inside," of psychic depths, mirrors the failure of the unconscious to find adequate reflection in "some external form, be it an ideal or a ritual, by which all the yearnings and hopes of the soul are adequately expressed."[9] According to Jung, the advance of consciousness eroded religion until the self-conscious individual felt torn "loose from the maternal womb of unconsciousness in which the mass of men dwells."[10] The solution to such alienation, Jung argues, is to "voluntarily declar[e] oneself bankrupt," to slip from the "burden of guilt" fostered by self-division through a reawakening to the unconscious ground of consciousness.[11] By chastening the ego, a sense of the self is able to appear. Limiting the ego's aspirations, its will-to-power, the individual shifts the center of his being from self-certainty to a stance of faith. In "The American Scholar" (and later, in "The Divinity School Address"), we observe Emerson displacing egotism in favor of the unconscious. Emerson's awareness of the failure of conventional religious and intellectual forms provides the opening, the spiritual vacuum, which faith in the unconscious must fill. Thus his goal in "The American Scholar" is to awaken his audience and point them in the "right" direction -- that is to say, inward.

This discovery of the unconscious proceeds through "the gradual <u>domestication</u> of the idea of Culture" (<u>CW</u>,I,65). Culture is "domesticated" as man learns to "<u>plant</u> himself indomitably on his instincts" and sees that as "a globule of sap ascends," so unconscious energy emerges through sublimation into "Reason" (<u>CW</u>,I,69). In so doing, man learns that in himself is "the law of all nature" (<u>Ibid</u>.). Such remarks reveal Emerson's intention to reconnect self-consciousness with spontaneous unconscious activity. The stance of "the Reflective or Philosophical age" is regrounded in prereflective activity (<u>CW</u>,I,66). By showing his audience that "the sublime presence of the highest spiritual cause lurks" in the familiar (<u>CW</u>,I,67), Emerson hopes to awaken them to a recognition of the unconscious processes underlying everyday life. He hopes to show them that the molten core of being "flowing now out of the lips of Etna...now out of the throat of Vesuvius" (<u>CW</u>,I,66) has the potential to flame out of their throats and lips as well. Only in this way can he rouse them from that idolatrous stupor which sees creation as completed, the cosmos as fixed, which forgets that "in proportion as a man has anything in him divine, the firmament flows before him, and takes his signet and form" (CW,I,64).

In "The American Scholar," Emerson comments upon the interpretive perspective which is central to the assimilation of this instinct. For example, his discussion of the influences of action upon the intellectual development of the scholar provides one of his major treatments of unconscious projection and its relation to interpretive consciousness. "The preamble of thought," Emerson explains, "the transition through which it passes from the unconscious to the conscious, is action" (CW,I,59). Through action, the unconscious is able to emerge and establish contact with the world by means of unobserved processes of projection. In action, "The stream retreats to its source" (CW,I,61); the individual relates to the world whose "attractions are the keys which unlock [his] thoughts" (CW,I,59). He is "taught by an instinct" (CW,I,59). He "unfolds the sacred germ of his instinct" (CW,I,61).

Afterwards, in the calmness of reflection, the individual can step back and analyze the flower which has sprouted, the silk which has been woven:

> A strange process too, this, by which experience is converted into thought, as a mulberry leaf is converted into satin. The manufacture goes forward at all hours (CW,I,59).

But the deed ceases to remain "immersed in our unconscious life." We emerge from unconsciousness as, in "some contemplative hour, it detaches itself from the life like ripe fruit, to become a thought of the mind" (CW,I,60). At that moment, projection is circumscribed and examined by interpretation. The "affections" cease to "circulate" through our actions as we step back to discover in those actions laws of circulation -- for example, the "great principle of Undulation" which connects night and day, unconscious and consciousness (CW,I,61). Consequently, the "actions and events of our childhood" become "matters of clamest observation," lying like "fair pictures in the air" (CW,I,60). From the perspective of reflection, unmediated activity is "framed" by consciousness into pictures and emblems revealing unconscious energy.

"The American Scholar" resonates with such emblems of unconscious wholeness and activity. For Emerson's rhetorical strategy is to give his audience a sense of the energy waiting to be transformed into meaningful action. Man's lack of meaning, Emerson's argues, results from his inability "to possess himself" (CW,I,53). His partiality is that of consciousness alienated from the unconscious. Materializing labor, he closes his mind to activity as self-expression -- as the unfolding of unconscious potential. In this way, Emerson complains, our acts confront as things, amputated limbs of the "One Man," fragments isolated from our untapped psychic potential. Our goal, Emerson suggests through this symbol, must be to reunite the broken god, to reconnect the severed limbs of Dionysius. Functioning both as a myth of the regenerated psyche and as a democratic ideal, the myth of "One Man" combines individual and polis. For the salvation of self is seen also as the salvation of society.

By joining together isolated particles of energy, the scattered drops of the original "fountain of power" (CW,I,53), one fuses together the disorder of once random actions, the previously jumbled activities of disconnected individuals. In this way, myth serves the cause of spiritual recalibration. For action is defined in relation to the archetype of "One Man." At the same time, praxis is given a new charge, a stronger motivation, through this relation. Emerson's myth sets up a gap - which must be bridged - between the individual and transcendent being. The distance between my state and the ideal extends as an area to be traversed, a potential which must be bridged by the spark of action. One aspires toward the ideal as a dream of one's better self, as a necessary fiction. Emerson clarifies this dynamic in the introductory lecture to his series on "Human Culture" when he observes, "The basis of Culture is that part of human nature which in philosophy is called the Ideal" (EL,II,217). Constantly aware of the gap between the Actual and the Ideal, Emersonian man aspires toward an ever-receding self-perfection. But no matter how fast he travels, "the ideal still craves a speed like a cannon ball, a speed like a wish" (EL, II,218). Emerson's function as orator and essayist is to awaken us to this quest by projecting before us myths which define the angle of our desire toward the limit of transcendence.

In a leap of faith which characterizes Romantic idealism,

Emerson's myth of "One Man" takes form as a transcendent field analogous to Jung's "collective unconscious." The "circular journey" of consciousness, M.H. Abrams notes, aspires to end where it began -- as figures of man's spiritual destination are projected as images of an alienated origin, a "lost home."[12] The "highest" consciousness is linked to the unconscious as two ends of a psychic totality which forever eludes man. Thus, the Romantic quest can be seen as the dream of a perfect sublimation -- of the maintenance of a steady bridge between psychic potential and psychic reality, between the "pool" of the unconscious and flourishing psychic life. Emerson's many images of growth, relation, connection, budding, and unfolding all lead to this end. For Emerson's dream is that which has lured all explicators of psychic dynamics -- the ideal of pure expression, frictionless unfolding, sublimation as ceaseless growth. If one could communicate the exact correspondence which matches unconscious potential to realized idea, nature to thought, then being could be turned "inside out." We might leap from imperfection into the transfigured, ecstatic state in which even our fingertips would burst into flame and our psyche unfurl "beautiful wings" (CW,I,60).

A second major symbol of unconscious wholeness in "The American Scholar" is the figure of an infinite circle. "There is never a beginning, there is never and end to the inexplicable continuity" of Nature, Emerson comments,

>but always circular power returning into itself.

> Therein it resembles his own spirit, whose beginning, whose ending he never can find -- so entire, so boundless (CW,I,54).

This image, of "circular power returning into itself," recurs throughout the world as a symbol of cosmic and psychic origin. So asserts Erich Neumann, who in The Origins and History of Consciousness, details the "birth, suffering, and emancipation" of consciousness from the unconscious.[13]

At the beginning of every creation myth, Neumann observes, before the ego recognizes its dignity through myths of the hero, one encounters cosmic symbols of wholeness.[14] Before the psyche is differentiated into consciousness and the unconscious, before Emerson's "One Man" fragments into partial human beings isolated from unity, there is the endless circle of identity. Before the distinction of "I" and "thou," "me" and "not-me," "self" and "other," one finds "Plato's Original Man," "the Chinese t'ai, chi, a round containing black and white, day and night, heaven and earth, male and female," and "the circular snake, the primal dragon of the beginning that bites its own tail, the self-begetting Uroboros."[15] Clearly, Emerson's "circular power returning into itself" belongs to this class of figures -- a matrix of symbols which Neumann finds in Babylonia, Phoenicia, Egypt, Africa, Mexico, India, indeed in virtually every great mythological tradition.[16] Neumann concludes,

> so long as man shall exist, perfection will continue to appear as the circle, the sphere, and the round; and the Primal Deity who is sufficient unto himself, and the self who has gone beyond the opposites, will reappear in the image of the round, the mandala.[17]

Differentiated consciousness returns to its roots, to chthonic powers projected from the unconscious, by reflecting upon such symbols. The ego, tapping the depths of the psyche by "discovering roots running under ground" (CW,I,54), learns the avenues of power which connect root, leaf, and flower. By securing contact with an endless fund of myth, man "shall look forward to an ever expanding knowledge as to a becoming creator" (CW,I,55). Such is the dream of regenration which Emerson holds before his audience.

As in Nature, we return to the mystery of correspondence -- to the fact that nature and the mind illuminate each other. Emerson never ceases to wonder over this:

> The very existence of thought and speech supposes and is a new nature totally distinct from the material world; yet we find it impossible to speak of it and its laws in any other language than that borrowed from our experience in the material world (EL,I,24).

For Emerson, this was the great discovery of Swedenborg, who "saw and showed the connexion between nature and the affections of the soul" (CW,I,68). That this connection might be one of analogy is the great dream inherited from the Swedish sage. For then, "the whole of Nature is a metaphor or image of the human mind" (EL,I,24). The "visible, audible, tangible world" becomes an emblem or sybol of the spirit, a map to the unconscious (CW,I,68). Meditating upon the order of nature, man discovers in that order, in the process of ordering, "laws of his own mind":

> Nature then becomes to him the measure of his attainments. So much of nature as he is ignorant of, so much of his own mind does he not yet possess (CW,I,55).

Accordingly, Emerson exhorts his audience to expand the limits of their being by relating to the world through activity, to immerse themselves in experience. "So much only of life as I know by experience," Emerson writes, "so much of the wilderness have I vanquished and planted, or so far have I extended my being, my dominion" (CW,I,59). If the tree of wisdom is to flourish, man must nourish psychological development by firmly rooting the mind in the rich soil of experience. Without a web of relations connecting the unconscious to the things of the world, the psyche is not allowed to become "an angel of wisdom" which "unfurls beautiful wings" (CW, I,60).

But we must not forget Emerson's keen awareness of the failure of sublimation, of the perpetual degradation of living symbols into objects of idolatry. This awareness represents his great advance over Swedenborg -- for Emerson's realism forces him to recognize that no process of "distillation" is "quite perfect":

> As no air-pump can by any means make a perfect vacuum, so neither can any artist entirely exclude the conventional, the local, the perishable from his book, or write a book of pure thought that shall be as efficient, in all respects, to a remote posterity, as to our contemporaries, or rather to the second age (CW,I,55-6).

This insight into the inefficiency of the mechanics of correspondence, the ratio of inertia impeding expression, marks the measure of Emerson's self-consciousness. For if the poet in him could project and believe in living symbols of unconscious power, the critic and scientist in Emerson saw the necessity of interpreting messages which always lost something in the process of transmission.

Even worse, to Emerson's mind, than the gradual erosion of inspiration is the reification of symbols into objects of idolatry. If process is allowed to become product, then the saint, the poet, the genius become things to be used and then discarded by the crowd of frustrated consumers. If piety and worship (that is, openness to the power of symbols) are allowed to decay, then the "light" of the great man transforms into artificial illumination -- the sun, to risk an anachronism, is worshipped in the form of neon lights. It was Emerson's painful role to stand squarely in the middle of an accelerating process of secularization that threatened to bury once and for all the methods whereby man might remain "open to the incursions of Reason" (CW,I,56). Modern man was in danger of forgetting how to send taproots into the unconscious, thereby condemning himself to live unconsciously myths already written out for him.

Fifteen years later, Melville's Pierre stands that much closer to psychological and spiritual chaos. Lacking the capacity to determine in advance his relations to the unconscious, he wakes from enthusiasm to the dire reflection that he has been driven by obsession. Emerson, in 1837, anticipates the dislocation that makes Melville's hero possible. His avowed purpose, in opposition to this moral decay, is to awaken his audience from the slumber of unconsciousness to an awareness of the psychic processes underlying their lives. As contemporary rites failed, those processes went underground or became displaced into various symptoms (such as Hawthorne's sexual imagery).[18] In too many cases, divinity resided within unheard. But Melville's great question was to be: if we hearken to that call, how do we know that the hidden gods of the psyche do not lie?

As is well known, Emerson's rhetoric - as he matured - shifted from the enthusiasm of addresses like "The American Scholar" to a more pragmatic viewpoint. Robert Spiller sees this shift as a move from persuasion to "dialectic," from the strong faith of Essays, First Series to the "dialectical counterpoint" of essays like "Experience" (CW,I,161,218). At one point, Spiller describes this later perspective as an "acceptance of a suspended dualism of attitude in the world of reality while holding to the singleness of an absolute faith" -- a vision of "the scholar as mediator between the world of actuality and that of the moral absolute" (CW,I,165). Whether we focus upon Emerson's "dialectic," his "double consciousness," or his sense of "progressive" and "regressive metamorphosis,"[19] it is necessary to come to terms with the self-limiting aspect of his thought. Vision does not remain unchallenged in Emerson, but instead forms part of a "process, perpetually, of defining and redefining itself."[20]

By the time of Essays, Second Series, Emerson's presentation of the self is much more explicitly an interpretive process. Each man, he declares at the opening of "Nominalist and Realist," is "a relative and representative nature" — "a hint of the truth, but far enough from being that truth which yet he quite newly and inevitably suggests to us" (W, III,225). Such statements reveal a felt distance from the expansive proejction of "Circles," a sense of distance between the unconscious projection of power and the conscious realization of the limits of aspiration. Here, projection is framed by an interpretation which easily sees around the inspiration it nourishes. Yet Emerson's "double consciousness" is not the occasion of despair or nihilism, but rather the condition of faith. Emerson is still oriented toward an infinite ground, toward "nature" without and the "unconscious" within, but now he realizes that he will never exhaust its meaning.

An important aspect of this sense of self-limitation and self-reference involves Romantic irony. Acutely aware of the silence bounding speech, Emerson's style and literary presentation are predicated upon the necessary limitation of each articulation. "Since the paradox of language is that 'words are finite organs of the infinite mind,'" Albert Gelpi observes, "even the successful poem will be an incomplete articulation."[21] This sense of incompleteness, Gelpi argues, arises from Emerson's awareness that the "infinite mind" behind his writing resides in his unconscious. Emerson intuits a field of potential meaning which transcends any single action, address, or essay. Or, in Emerson's terms, quoting from "Nominalist and Realist," each "man is a channel through which heaven floweth," but a channel which is "partial" (W,III,242). "Nature" transcends every system, every perspective upon its meaning. By necessity, we have only a partial view of the world's "plenum," its infinite perfection (W,III,243). By now, we should be able to read "heaven," "Nature," and "plenum" as frequently used symbols of the unconscious. Each posits an infinite field constituting the individual's incarnation of its power. Attempting to "unfold" this potential, each individual succumbs to disproportion. Literary awareness of the unconscious, of the unknown and the uncontained, necessitates Romantic irony as the interface between finite speech and infinite potential for meaning.

One of the persistent challenges to our understanding of Emerson has been to articulate the dual perspective which tempered and focused his thought. At least since Friedrich Schlegel, literature has looked at itself; self-reference has been central to the literary quest. As a part of modern "subjectivism," leading to the "birth" of psychology and the "discovery" of the unconscious, this literary position, as a stance "between two worlds" with one's feet in both,[22] has constituted nineteenth and twentieth-century writing as a literature of "crisis." Indeed, a sense of juncture, of the self as interface, comprises one of the central themes available to nineteenth-century writers. Caught outside of faith, outside of nature, outside of the unconscious, they struggled to regain the old certainties -- the security of a period when "God" and "man," "essence" and "existence," "unconscious" and "consciousness" were not disparate terms. To this end, we have observed Emerson positing within his writing interpretive structures which attempt to keep open the question of faith by framing unconscious myth within critical consciousness. In this way, consciousness can root itself again without sacrificing the integrity of self-knowledge. For <u>un</u>consciousness, the lost innocence of culture's childhood, is no longer a real possibility. But through self-conscious openness faith might remain viable. Aware of the "horizon" of thought and aspiration (<u>CW</u>,I,106), one might intuit the forces waiting beyond it. One might attempt to "re-collect the spirits" fallen out of focus into disunity (<u>CW</u>,I,110).

As early as 1838, in Emerson's address on "Literary Ethics" (from which I have just been quoting), this "reorientation" entails a turning <u>inward</u>.[23] In contrast to the perspective of "Circles" which focused upon creative energy expanding outward from a potent center within the self, Emerson speaks here <u>outside</u> of power. We notice that "the state of being and power" (<u>CW</u>,I,105) to which he refers is a memory of a former plenitude, a fullness that we might recover if we point ourselves in the right direction. While this is a difference in degree and not in kind from "The American Scholar," the proportion here between projection and interpretation shifts toward interpretation:

> To feel the full value of these facts, of these lives, as occasions of hope and provocation, one

> must rightly ponder the mystery of our common
> soul. You must come to know, that each admirable
> genius is but a successful diver in that sea whose
> floor of pearls is all your own (CW,I,103).

Here, Emerson speaks out of a sense of "surface" hiding us from "the grandeur and secret of our being." Only by "diving" toward the unconscious, can we "bring up out of the secular darkness, the sublimities of the moral constitution" (CW,I,110). The alterantive is to be a "ghostly" creature, sapped of psychic and spiritual energy. In order to achieve fullness of life, one must allow the inner powers "an unobstructed channel" through which "the soul...easily and gladly flows" (CW,I,113). Only through such expression, a "mutual reaction of thought and life," can one "make thought solid, and life wise" (Ibid.). This "channel" of expression appears only if the "man of genius" learns to balance essence and existence, learns to relate unconscious depth to consciously-perceived social form. We have been examining one aspect of this relation -- the structured contact between myth and language.

By 1841, Emerson's faith in such expression had become more problematic. In "Man the Reformer," for example, external limits threaten to inhibit and perhaps extinguish the fire of genius. If the reformer acts as "mediator between the spiritual and actual world" (CW,I,159), we see this mediation dislocated by the loss of faith which Emerson sees around him:

> The Americans have no faith. They rely on the
> power of a dollar; they are deaf to sentiment.

> They think you may talk the north wind down as
> easily as raise society; and no class is more
> faithless than the scholars or intellectual men
> (CW,I,156-7).

Such faithlessness, Emerson realized, leads to the loss of power. For it erodes the channels of creative energy, closing off contact with the unconscious:

> The power, which is at once spring and regulator
> in all efforts of reform, is faith in Man, the
> conviction that <u>there is</u> an <u>infinite worthiness
> in him</u> which will appear at the call of worth
> (CW,I,156,emphasis mine).

Without this perception of "an infinite worthiness" <u>within</u> man, the individual forgoes self-definition in favor of definition by society. Power resides elsewhere, as the property of a selfish society dedicated to maintaining its prerogatives. Man is reduced to a functionary, an instrument, from being the vehicle of creative power. Again, Emerson structures his argument as a pattern of relationship to infinite potential -- in this case, man's infinite potential which will be unfolded in the future:

> There is a sublime prudence, which is the very
> highest that we know of man, which, believing in
> a vast future,- sure of more to come than is yet
> seen,- postpones always the present hour to the
> whole life; postpones always talent to genius,
> and special results to character (CW,I,160).

"Genius" and "character," we know (for example, from Emerson's essay on "Character"), depend upon access to unconscious forces. Here, significantly, the unconscious is potential; its expression is deferred to the future.

"The Method of Nature" continues this deferral. In that address, Emerson argues that we need "reception," an awareness of psychological depth, because "we have lost our miraculous power" (CW,I,123). If "nature" (nature without and nature within) is an infinite ground that promises "ecstasy" as the pattern of relation to it, that ecstasy has become even more problematic. For we need now, Emerson asserts, to reconstruct "the channel through which heaven flows to earth," to recreate nature within us through "enthusiasm," "the fulness of its reception" (CW,I,130). Inspiration, here, appears to be totally out of man's control: "There is the incoming or the receding of God: that is all we can affirm; and we can show neither how nor why" (CW,I,127). Desiring to be a "bridge," a "mediator" between God and man, unconscious and consciousness, genius now must struggle to focus infinite potential upon the "point" of action (CW,I, 129). Only in this way can his actions become "vents for the currents of inward life" (CW,I,129), for the "cause and life" which "proceeds from within outward" (134). We have lost the old piety of the Puritans, Emerson laments. What we have left to worship is "the mighty and transcendent Soul" (CW,I,135). Our project, he continues, must be "to annul that adulterous divorce which the superstition of many ages has effected between the intellect and holiness" (CW,I,135).

It is not surprising, therefore, to see this address concerned with the relation between conscious thought and unconscious depths (the site of whatever "holiness" remains). "Confine" the sea "by granite rocks," Emerson comments, "let it wash a shore where wise men dwell, and it is filled with expression; and the point of greatest interest is where the land and water meet" (CW,I,127). It is that point of contact, the area of "crisis," that was Emerson's focus in speaking and writing. This region, he explains, is the locale of "language": "Each individual soul" has the "power to translate the world into some particular language of its own" (CW,I,128). It was Emerson's project to focus upon the "shoreline" -- that area where power is translated into speech, the "neutral territory" (as Hawthorne called it) where myth and thought intermingle and dwell as an incarnation of released psychic energy. Sensing the unconscious as an unseen speaker addressing us from behind (CW,I,129), Emerson asserts our need for that voice as a "divine" influence. Our imagination, he realizes, needs infinite ends in order to enlarge its potential. If an external God has been taken from us, we must return to the source of our images of God. We must find the "light" within, must aim inward toward an infinite and ultimately unattainable ground -- the unconscious.

NOTES: CHAPTER SEVEN

1 Paul Tillich, <u>The Courage To Be</u> (New Haven: Yale Univ. Press, 1952), p.49.

2 Tillich, p.91.

3 Tillich, p.96.

4 Tillich discusses the twentieth-century "longing for the collectivist pole," p.117.

5 For a more detailed discussion of "inflation," see chapter nine.

6 James M. Cox, "R.W. Emerson: The Circles of the Eye" in D. Levin ed., <u>Emerson: Prophecy, Metamorphosis, Influence</u> (New York: Columbia Univ. Press, 1975), p.68.

7 Jung, <u>PJ</u>, 462 (<u>CW</u> 10, par. 159).

8 Jung, <u>PJ</u>, 462 (<u>CW</u> 10, par. 160).

9 Jung, <u>PJ</u>, 461 (<u>CW</u> 10, par. 159).

10 Jung, <u>PJ</u>, 457 (<u>CW</u> 10, par. 150).

11 Jung, <u>PJ</u>, 458 (<u>CW</u> 10, par. 152).

12 M.H. Abrams, <u>Natural Supernaturalism: Tradition and Revolution in Romantic Literature</u> (New York: Norton, 1973), p.255.

13 Erich Neumann, <u>The Origins and History of Consciousness</u>, trans. R.F.C. Hull (Princeton Univ. Press: Bollingen Series XLII, 1970), p.5.

14 <u>Ibid</u>.

15 Neumann, pp.8-10.

16 Neumann, pp.10-11.

17 Neumann, p.11.

[18] Frederick C. Crews, The Sins of the Fathers: Hawthorne's Psychological Themes (New York: Oxford Univ. Press, 1966), p.17.

[19] Daniel B. Shea, "Emerson and the American Metamorphosis," in D. Levin ed., Emerson: Prophecy, Metamorphosis, and Influence (New York: Columbia Univ. Press, 1975), p.44.

[20] Joel Porte, Representative Man: Ralph Waldo Emerson in His Time (New York: Oxford Univ. Press, 1979), p.xii.

[21] Albert Gelpi, "Emerson: The Paradox of Organic Form," in D. Levin ed., Emerson: Prophecy, Metamorphosis, and Influence, p.157.

[22] Martin Bickman, The Unsounded Centre: Jungian Studies in American Romanticism (Chapel Hill, N.C.: Univ. of North Carolina Press, 1980), pp.82-6.

[23] Joel Porte discusses Emerson's "orientation" as a turning eastward in Representative Man, p.50.

CHAPTER EIGHT

ASPECTS OF POWER: TOWARD A PHENOMENOLOGY OF THE SELF

"The only way into nature," Emerson asserts at the conclusion of "The Method of Nature,"

> is to enact our best insight. Instantly we are higher poets and can speak a deeper law. Do what you know, and perception is converted into character, as islands and continents were built by invisible infusories, or as these forest leaves absorb light, electricity, and volatile gases, and the gnarled oak to live a thousand years is the arrest and fixation of the most volatile and etherial currents (<u>CW</u>,I,136).

Let us stop for a moment and contemplate these metaphors. "Light," "electricity," "gases," "etherial currents" -- we see Emerson here groping for terms to express his sense of what we have learned to call psychic energy or <u>libido</u>. Brooding from the beginning of his career upon the problem of individual creative growth, Emerson came to see that growth as the expression of an energy, a quasi-physical power. From the vicissitudes of light to the fluid mechanics of what has been called a "spermatic economy,"[1] Emerson concerned himself with the <u>economics</u> of the psyche, with laws of psychic energy. In our own century, Freud continues this enterprise. But the counter-example of Jung keeps us alert to the fact that <u>libido</u> is open to both materialistic and spiritual interpretations. Indeed, we cannot decide between Freud and Jung; for each view, as a different perspective upon the mind and its dynamics, has its own validity.

Returning to Emerson, we note that he combines the physical roots of power and its spiritual aspirations in different proportions at different stages of his career. From the beginning, one suspects, Emerson sensed the natural origin of libido in the body's physical energy. But in his early works, this physical aspect is lost in the glare of spiritual illumination. As he aged and illumination became less frequent, the physical took on more and more importance in Emerson's thought -- until, like the aged Yeats, he seemed obsessed in the end with performance and potency. This is not a surprising development, and can be paralleled in the careers of many Romantic and post-Romantic writers who, like Wordsworth, came to observe that

> the hiding places of man's power
> Open; I would approach them, but they close.
> I see by glimpses now; when age comes on,
> May scarcely see at all....$_2$

This compares with Emerson's later complaints about his "flash-of-lightning faith" which he would gladly exchange "for continuous daylight" (<u>CW</u>,I,213). In both cases, inspiration - as it grew less frequent - came to be seen as an occasional and treasured visitant. Not surprisingly, this intellectual decay and physical decline came to be associated.

This association is typical of the growing materialization of Romantic culture in general. For if Emerson came to replace "spirit" with "power" as his central term for psychic energy, this development seems to parallel a massive cultural shift. By the 1850's, when Hawthorne and Melville were writing their major romances and Emerson was composing The Conduct of Life, the sexual aspects of libido had become much more apparent. Indeed, Joel Porte has documented instances of the "spermatic economy" throughout the 1830's and 1840's.[3] Such observations prove that the sexual themes of The Scarlet Letter and Pierre (to name only two instances) were no accident, but reflections of a growing articulation of sexual energy and its vicissitudes. The materials were available in 1852 for Melville to use the disguised sexual motivation of Pierre to deconstruct his spiritual (and "Transcendentalist") illusions. This deconstruction, we can see, adumbrates in many respects the later debate between Freud and Jung over the aspect of libido.

It is important to see that the mid-nineteenth century also wavered over the aspect of power, with spiritual and materialistic interpretations competing in works as late as Emerson's "Fate," where he contrasts the "vital force" motivating genius (W,VI,12) with "insight" and "light" (25). Man, Emerson decides, is a dual nature:

> On one side elemental order, sandstone and granite, rock-ledges, peat-bog, forest, sea and shore; on the other part thought, the spirit which composes and decomposes nature (W,VI,22).

At the same time, Emerson's comments elsewhere in The Conduct of Life suggest that he sees sexuality and spirituality, physical vitality and thought, as two aspects of the same "power" which is sublimated up the spire of form: "As we refine, our checks become finer. If we rise to spiritual culture, the antagonism takes on a spiritual form....The limitations refine as the soul purifies" (W,VI,338).

This awareness of psychological dynamics - expressive of Emerson's conviction that "thought...must act according to eternal laws" (W,VI,21) - reveals an insight not that far removed from Freud's. For example, Emerson speaks in surprisingly modern terms of "the laws of repression" -- "the terms by which our life is walled up" (W,VI,19). Similarly, in "Power" he reveals a fundamental insight into displacement and sublimation:

> The luxury of fire is to have a little on our hearth; and of electricity, not volleys of the charged cloud, but the manageable stream on the battery-wires. So of spirit, or energy; the rests or remains of it in the civil or moral man are worth all the cannibals in the Pacific (W,VI,70).

Like Freud, Emerson is aware of psychic compensation: "any excess of power in one part is usually paid for at once by some defect in a contiguous part" (W,VI,131). Indeed, we see the two sharing a similar conception of the psychic economy as a system of fluid dynamics:

> But this force or spirit...is as much a subject
> of exact law and arithmetic as fluids and gases
> are; it may be husbanded or wasted; every man
> is efficient only as he is a container or ves-
> sel of this force, and never was any signal act
> or achievement in history but by this expendi-
> ture (W,VI,80).

It is tempting - after such comments - to align Emerson with Freud as a proponent of the physical nature of libido.

However, let us note that Emerson equivocates -- he speaks of "force or spirit." And while he talks frequently of "spending" (a timeless sexual metaphor, Porte observes[4]), not all of Emerson's spending is sexual. "We live in a transition period, when the old faiths which comforted nations, and not only so but made nations, seem to have spent their force" (W,VI,207). Is Emerson asserting here that religion has a sexual basis? Perhaps. But this economy, it is clear from the context, transcends its physical roots -- it sublimates physical energy into something else. The danger is to equate sublimated spirit with physical cause; for at a certain point, they are different in kind. Jung saw this when he complained of Freud's "causal" perspective, which is only one of several possible viewpoints on the psyche.[5]

In his article "On Psychic Energy," Jung is careful to maintain the very distinction that Emerson blurs. We must not equate the psyche with its biological roots, Jung argues, for at a certain point the "mechanistic" hypothesis fails to account for the psyche "as a phenomenon in its own right."[6] To clarify this point, Jung distinguishes the concept of psychic "energy" from mechanistic "force":

> The idea of energy is not that of a substance moved in space; it is a concept abstracted from relations of movement. The concept, therefore, is founded not on the substances themselves but on their relations, whereas the moving substance itself is the basis of the mechanistic view.[7]

However, such distinctions, Jung later observes, are difficult to make:

> In delimiting a concept of psychic energy we are...faced with certain difficulties, because we have absolutely no means of dividing what is psychic from the biological process as such.[8]

Although he is willing to "enlarge the narrower concept of psychic energy to a broader one of life-energy, which includes 'psychic energy' as a specific part," Jung maintains that psychology and biology must "form their own concepts."[9]

It is this differentiation between psychic and biological facts that many of Emerson's contemporaries failed to maintain. By equating psychic with sexual energy, thought with its biological roots, they saw all psychological phenomena as sexual in nature. By hypostatizing psychic energy into a substance and then confusing psychic form with this "content," they seem to deny the possibility of sublimation. Although psychic energy frequently expresses itself through sexual forms, that energy - once released - carries those forms into new contexts. Indeed, Jung argues, psychic energy as it metamorphoses *always* carries with it "parts or characteristics of the previous structure with which it was connected."[10] Even the field of Christianity, he observes, is "rich in striking examples...the sexual character of which only the blind could fail to see."[11] This "sexual character" is much different from "sexual nature":

> libido does not leave a structure as pure intensity and pass without a trace into another, but ...it takes the character of the old function over into the new. This peculiarity is so striking that it gives rise to false conclusions.... For instance, say a sum of libido having a certain sexual form passes over into another structure, taking with it some of the peculiarities of its previous application. It is then very tempting to think that the dynamism of the new structure will be sexual too.[12]

Although Emerson and many of his contemporaries did not entirely resist the temptation to see psychic as sexual energy - a confusion engendered by the organic models of Romanticism - they did not always equate the two. To the extent that they adopted <u>causal</u> perspectives, hunting for the origins of consciousness in the dank cellar of the psyche, they performed a necessary deconstruction of moribund nineteenth-century ideals which had lost their vital energy. But at the same time, we must see that Emerson and many others subordinated psychic causation to the quest for new values sublimating the very sexual energy they had discovered.

For Jung, the process of symbolism facilitates this psychic transformation. Symbols of power - even crudely sexual symbols - release psychic energy which becomes available for metamorphosis. In the case of sexual symbolism, the sexual aspect of libido is the form that allows its release. Libido is transformed <u>through</u> the symbol, a "psychic mechanism" which "imitates the instinct and is thereby enabled to apply

its energy for special purposes."[13] A paradigm of this
transformation is the "earth-impregnation ceremony" of the
Wachandi tribe in Australia. Although this ceremony imitates the sexual act (with the thrusting of phallic spears
into a pit decorated to look "like a woman's genitals"), it
is not equivalent to sexual performance. Rather,

> It is a magical act for the purpose of transferring libido to the earth, whereby the earth acquires a special psychic value and becomes an object of expectation. The mind then busies itself with the earth....The instinctual energy becomes closely associated with the field, so that the cultivation of it acquires the value of a sexual act.[14]

At the other extreme, we might place the sexual symbolism
of Ezra Pound, for example his portrayal of Anchises' union
with Aphrodite in Canto 76:

> or Anchises that laid hold of her flanks of air
> drawing her to him
>   Cythera potens, Κύθηρα δεινά
>
> no cloud, but the crystal body
>   the tangent formed in the hand's cup
> as live wind in the beech grove
>   as strong air amid cypress[15]

Focusing the mind's energy through the archetype of the goddess, Pound releases the "live wind," the "fluid" of the
"moving crystal."

According to Jung, such release is the function of all
symbols of psychic energy, which he terms "symbols of transformation." They make psychic energy available for use by
focusing it through manipulable units. In this sense, the
symbol is a "transformer of energy...a machine."[16] It fuels
the will, which Jung defines as "disposable energy."[17] Thus,

the "will-to-power" - the quest toward greater and greater circumference to the self (v. Emerson's "Circles") - is promoted through the creation of an effective language which can symbolize psychic energy. One must use a language which establishes "connecting bridges" between unconscious and consciousness.[18] Indeed, one cannot discuss the psyche and its economy without such a language -- for example, some concept of psychic energy, whether Emerson's "power," Schopenhauer's "Will," or the "elan vital" of Bergson.[19] Each concept functions as a "terministic screen" which "directs the attention into some channels rather than others."[20] But only through such direction is the mind able to operate upon its own energy, by treating it "as though it were hypostatized."[21] Thus, in order to speak of the psyche, Jung (like Emerson) must contrast "surface" to "depths" and write about the "flow" of libido like electricity through "channels."[22] Without such images of power, the power itself would be inaccessible.

Let us turn back to Emerson's Essays, Second Series to clarify these processes. For if this volume resonates with images of power, it also illustrates Emerson's growing awareness of the vicissitudes of psychic energy. In the essay "Character," for instance, Emerson suggests that character is the product of a physical force that obeys the "same laws which control the tides and the sun, numbers and quantities" (W,III,91). During the course of his argument, Emerson characterizes this power as a "motive force," an "energy," "a natural power, like light and heat," and as "magnetic currents" (W,III,93,95,97). Strong character, he continues, gives us "a sense of mass" -- of action resting upon a man's "substance" (W,III,99,101). Clearly, such terms involve a concept of psychic energy as physical force.

But at the same time, this psychic energy takes on spiritual connotations. By the conclusion of Emerson's essay, we see that our reaching down "into the profound," into the "deep root" of the psyche (106,111), leads to "glad rays" shining "out of that far celestial land" and to the "holy sentiment" which opens "into a flower" (115). While this progression emphasizes the mechanics of sublimation, Emerson's comments reveal that this sublimation of physical into spiritual power is problematic. That "clestial land" is "far" and, by most, can only be observed from a distance: "If we cannot attain at a bound to these grandeurs, at least let us do them homage" (114). Striving to link the organic source of libido with its spiritual manifestation, Emerson here clearly does not know how to connect the "root" to the "flower." Inspiration seems to lack the symbols which might give it full expression.

In "Nature," to continue this theme, Emerson asserts that we need "the right energy" in order to sparkle "with real fire" (W,III,178-9). But what sets energy "right"? The answer, we know from Emerson's doctrine of correspondence, is a symbolism derived from nature. But here, nature is no longer a "symbol of spirit" (CW,I,17), but rather "a differential thermometer, detecting the presence or absence of the divine sentiment in man" (W,III,178). Nature no longer serves as a symbol of power, but rather as a reminder of the failure of inspiration. Needing to feel the power of the soul streaming through us, we find that we cannot connect, no longer know the proper symbols. "Nature is still elsewhere" (W,III,192); and we live "always a referred existence, never a presence and satisfaction" (193). Lacking what Emerson elsewhere calls a sense of "magnetism" (W,III, 228), the alignment of our energies through the symbol, we sense that "the old aims have been lost sight of, and to remove friction has come to be the end" (W,III,191). Although Emerson opens this essay with an evocation of those rare perfect days which give us a sense of nature's "sanctity," we are unable to "escape the sophistication and second thought, and suffer nature to intrance us" (W,III,170). Instead, we remain in a state of "dejection" like that painted years earlier by Coleridge in his great ode.

In "The Poet," Emerson asserts the doctrine of symbolism which might rescue him from dejection:

>It is proof of the shallowness of the doctrine of beauty as it lies in the minds of our amateurs, that men seem to have lost the perception of the instant dependence of form upon soul. There is no doctrine of forms in our philosophy. We were put into our bodies, as fire is put into a pan to be carried about; but there is no accurate adjustment between the spirit and the organ, much less is the latter the germination of the former (W, III,3).

Lacking a sense of the psyche's energy, contemporary writers have lost sight of its expressive potential, have forgotten

that we are "children of the fire, made of it" (W,III,4).
For much of the remainder of this essay, Emerson defines
this psychic potential through his myth of "the poet" --
that "man without impediments" who "is representative of
man, in virtue of being the largest power to receive and to
impart" (W,III,6). In other words, Emerson's "poet" is a
figure symbolic of perfect sublimation. He is an idealized
individual, perfectly self-reliant, through whom psychic
energy flows as through a frictionless channel. Psychic
energy is not "natural power" in his hands, but "divine energy" (W,III,8). His thought unfolds "like the spirit of
a plant or animal" without the impediment of self-consciousness or irony (W,III,9-10). As a perfect vehicle for unfurling libido, the poet stands as an "interpreter" of the
"profound" -- he is a figure of the original psychic explorer.
Perfect correspondence is not a dream in his hands. The hidden psyche and the universe match like figure and shadow:
"The Universe is the externization of the soul" (W,III,14).
All of nature stands before him as a field of projection,
available as a symbol of the psyche.

But such perfect transparency, as Emerson well knew, is
an impossible dream. For any articulation is "partial" --
it is limited by what Emerson called "friction." Thus, the
audacity of Emerson's "diastole," his attempt to see all of
nature as a "neutral territory" open to mythic projection,
was balanced by his awareness of "systole," the ego's limited identity. The distance between diastole and systole,

between Dionysian power and Apollonian individuation, measures the space of Romantic irony. Inspiration is countered by dejection; "progressive," by "regressive metamorphosis."[23] Carl Jung, in order to describe this dynamic, goes back (like Emerson) to Goethe. "Progression and regression," Jung observes,

> correspond to what Goethe has aptly described as systole and diastole. Diastole is an extraversion of libido spreading through the entire universe; systole is its contraction into the individual, the monad.[24]

Reception and action, Jung comments (in a point reminiscent of one of Emerson's most basic themes), must balance each other: "to remain in either of these attitudes means death."[25] Psychological insight, we realize from this, arises from disinheritance. For as the currents of power retreat again to their hidden center, consciousness learns to measure the gap between spiritual aspiration and disinherited "reality." At this point, patterns of interpretation can be structured which aim to conserve, if not rekindle, the failing spark of energy.

In "The Poet" Emerson's method of presentation serves such a function. For we sense that Emerson's vision of power speaks to a corresponding poverty. In part, this poverty is an erosion of participation in nature and its processes. This loss manifests itself as a "dislocation and detachment from the life of God," as a detachment from "nature and the Whole" (W,III,18). "On the brink of the waters of life and truth," Emerson laments, "we are miserably dying" (W,III,33).

Each thought, every symbol, threatens to become "a prison" which ceases "to flow" (W,III,33-4). In response, Emerson offers a vision of metamorphosis so continuous that the poet can resign himself to the unimpeded release of psychic energy, "to the divine aura which breathes through forms" (W, III,26). By trusting wholly in "instinct," by releasing himself to its motives, he floats on the "etherial tides" of "a great public power" (W,III,27.26). "The poet," Emerson explains, "resigns himself to his mood" (24) and, through this resignation, realizes "enthusiasm," spiritual exhileration, the rush of joy. Surrendering himself to the "dream-power" within himself, he realizes in his person the vision of man as a "conductor of the whole river of electricity" (W,III,40).

While surrender to the power of the unconscious leads to creative metamorphosis in "The Poet," in "Experience" Emerson deconstructs this idealistic vision of psychic potential. For here, surrender to one's moods leads not to illumination, but to illusion:

> Dream delivers us to dream, and there is no end to illusion. Life is a train of moods like a string of beads, and as we pass through them they prove to be many-colored lenses which paint the world their own hue, and each shows only what lies in its focus (W,III,50).

Nowhere can Emerson find a stable center from which to view the psyche:

> The secret of the illusoriness is in the necessity of a succession of moods or objects. Gladly we would anchor, but the anchorage is quicksand. This onward trick of nature is too strong for us: Pero si muove. ("Still it moves")   (W,III,55)

Trapped within his "temperament," a "prison of glass which we cannot see," he reaches for a spiritual and psychological security which forever eludes his grasp. The unconscious and its energy seem disturbingly distant. It has receded farther within: "Power keeps quite another road than the turnpikes of choice and will; namely the subterranean and invisible tunnels and channels of life (W,III,67). More desperately, libido itself has receded. We "have no superfluity of spirit for new creation," "not an ounce to impart or to invest"; we "have exhausted the water" (W,III,45-6).

Rather than repeating the much fine commentary on this essay, I wish to focus on one point -- that Emerson's acute self-consciousness in "Experience" sharpens his psychological insight. While at one extreme, "the rapacity of self-consciousness causes it to incorporate all things into its own null center,"[26] at the other end this acute sense of negation allows Emerson to define positive power. If the death of Waldo has "wounded Emerson in his genius, his generative power,"[27] this brooding sense of impotence forces Emerson to re-call the energy that he now lacks. Although this "unbounded substance," as Emerson calls it, "refuses to be named," yet

> every fine genius has essayed to represent [it] by some emphatic symbol, as, Thales by water, Anaximenes by air, Anaxagoras by (Noûs) thought, Zoroaster by fire, Jesus and the moderns by love; and the metaphor of each has become a national religion (W,III,72-3).

Mencius, Emerson continues, called this power "vast-flowing vigor"; while, "In our more correct writing we give to this generalization the name of Being, and thereby confess that we have arrived as far as we can go" (W,III,73).

Like Emerson's earlier works, "Experience" portrays his stance toward unfolding (or folding) power. Where fulfillment and presence once reigned, there is now deferment and absence: "Men seem to have learned of the horizon the art of perpetual retreating and reference" (W,III,46). As power recedes, perspective (one's attitude toward power) moves to the center of interest. Throughout this essay, Emerson focuses upon the way phenomena present themselves to the mind. His verbs reveal this emphasis: "I am grown...I am thankful ...I find that I begin...I accept...I find...I awake" (W,III, 61-2). Here, the ego is careful to define the precise nature of its relationship to experience. This relationship, Emerson adds, is colored by temperament and point of view. Thus, he is aware of experiences as "subjective phenomena," as objects determined in part by the act of vision: "As I am, so I see" (W,III,79).

What we find here is the emergence of a "phenomenological" perspective. Indeed, to the extent that Emerson focuses upon the patterning of his thought and feeling, he inclines toward perspectives similar to modern phenomenologies of the self. This direction is especially evident in "Experience." The present "illusoriness" of experience "brackets" it by making it appear as a succession of phenomena, the reality of which Emerson refuses to judge. Changes in mood have revealed the world under a new aspect. Previously, things had profundity, depth; now they appear slippery and superficial. Losing hold of once firm "reality," Emerson focuses sharply upon how he sees, how objects present themselves today within the field of awareness. As vision becomes problematic, he attends more closely to its processes and patterning. Edmund Husserl responded to a similar crisis, developing his phenomenology in reaction to the threat of solipsism, as a bridge attempting to reunite subject and world. Let us turn now to a brief look at Husserl's concept of "phenomenological reduction" in order to compare it with Emerson's perspective in "Experience."

Basically, this process - which Husserl describes as a "bracketing" of experience - suspends all one's ordinary expectations as to the reality or meaning of the objective world. (In this regard, it does not seem unlike Coleridge's "willing suspension of disbelief," except that the field of perception is not limited to literature.) In this way, Husserl explains, one retains the "natural standpoint" at the same time one alters the "fact-world" by viewing it as a phenomenon which appears to consciousness. Whether this world exists or not is irrelevant; what is important is that one self-consciously observes one's _relation to the world_, thus allowing this relation to emerge as a subject of inquiry. Husserl describes this as an "abstention" from judgment[28] which allows the world to remain in existence for us at the same time we examine it as a phenomenon:

> this entire natural world therefore which is continually "there for us," "present to our hand,"

>and will ever remain there, is a "fact-world" of which we continue to be conscious, even though it pleases us to put it in brackets.$_{29}$

We observe Emerson doing something of this kind in <u>Nature</u>, when he examines the "hypothesis" of Idealism and then suspends it, thus allowing the natural world to stand for him both as phenomenon and as physical fact. As we have seen, the sense in "Experience" of the world as both real and "illusion" heightens Emerson's attention to his structuring of reality as he knows it. More important for our purposes, this "phenomenological bracketing" opens up consciousness as a subject which can be examined in its processes and dimensions. Emerson pursues such examination throughout his career. Later, William James' description of the "stream of consciousness" entails a similar phenomenological perspective, as does Carl Jung's description of the images unfolding in his patients' dreams.

A second aspect of Emerson's "phenomenology" involves his awareness of the subjective coloration of phenomena. What we know, he realizes, are our ideas of things and not the things in themselves. There is "the world I converse with," as well as "the world I think," "your world," and, occasionally, "a new and excellent region of life" (<u>W</u>,III, 84-5,71). This sense of the lived-world, the <u>lebenswelt</u>, entails an awareness of perception as an "intentional" act. Robert Magliola explains the significance of this concept of "intentionality" for phenomenology:

>Consciousness is an act wherein the subject intends

> (or directs himself towards the object), and the object is intended (or functions as a target for the intending act, though the object transcends this act). The subject intending and the object intended are reciprocally implicated (and, it should be added, the subject is real and the object is real, that is, truly emanating from the outside).[30]

Extended by Heidegger and Merleau-Ponty to include one's entire life-situation and pattern, the concept of intentionality focuses upon one's <u>being-in-the-world</u> as an indivisible phenomenon. While we can <u>speak</u> of "subject" and "object," we must realize that the two are abstractions. For we cannot cleanse objects of their "subjective" coloring, or perceive the subject except through the world. This, years before, was Emerson's argument.

For Emerson, we recall, started making similar points as early as <u>Nature</u>, where he stresses that mind and nature could only be known <u>through</u> each other. Subject and object, Emerson's remarks imply, are united in the act of perception. The subject discovers his contours, the world takes shape, simultaneously, as two facets of the same process. Of course, Emerson slips frequently into dualistic terminology. But the emphasis, from early on in his career, was upon the <u>relation</u> of subject and object, <u>the</u> <u>way</u> <u>the</u> <u>mind</u> <u>unfolds</u> <u>through</u> <u>action</u>. Indeed, there can be no thought, Emerson has constantly told us, without this relation to action. Thought, it is clear, was not seen by Emerson as a solipsistic function, but as an activity. We think <u>through</u> images, because there is no other way. We may dream of pure spirit, but even our dreams present themselves in terms of natural images. The point that Emerson constantly stresses is that we exist "incarnated." And this sense of incarnation, of existing through and by means of natural forms, leads toward a phenomenological perspective.

But if Emerson's self-conscious awareness of reflection allows him to attend to the process of his understanding, this interpretive stance - as we have seen - dates back to the earliest Romantic writers. Paul Sheats, for example, finds it in Wordsworth's poetry. Examining the awakening of Wordsworth's "genius to the exercise of its own powers," Sheats argues that Wordsworth's oscillation between the subjective "abyss of idealism" and an objective realism was one of the motives for his development of an "epistemologically critical" poetry.[31] Wordsworth, Sheats argues, "sought ...to recover a relationship in which both poles, inner and outer, guarantee and support each other."[32] His attempt to maintain this balance led Wordsworth to "presentational imagery" which attempts "to reproduce the presentation of phenomena to the mind in experience" (a phenomenological undertaking).[33] By presenting images of both the mind and the objects it perceives, Wordsworth was able to examine critically the epistemological stance of his personae.[34]

Again, we observe that a sense of crisis motivates attention to the process of thinking. Processes of projection are examined by an interpretive stance aimed toward the recovery of receding energy. As thinking loses exterior spiritual validation, thought examines its own creation of values as part of its quest for new spiritual authority. Disoriented by the erosion of exterior norms, the mind attends to the process of orientation -- how, for example, we aim toward the ideal, which "journeys" constantly "before us" (Emerson,W,III,75). Such a reorientation, we have seen, leads to the "discovery" of the unconscious. Since the psyche is no longer defined as being outside of us, Jung explains, we must search for its definition within.[35] In the process, we develop concepts of psychic dynamics and energy. But let us not delude ourselves into thinking we know the unconscious, Jung reminds us; what we know are only its manifestations:

> I trust I have given no cause for the misunderstanding that I know anything about the nature of the "centre" -- for it is simply unknowable and can only be expressed symbolically through its phenomenology.[36]

Thus, we must scrutinize the aspects of power in consciousness in order to revitalize ourselves from its hidden source.

"The phenomenology of the involuntary," Paul Ricoeur explains, "becomes the phenomenology of the power which the body offers to voluntary action."[37] In pursuit of its goals, the mind shapes its motivation through images raised from hunger and desire to the level of symbols. Conscious of the process of symbolism, as a formal relation to power, the cogito (if I may slip into that term) sees itself as a blend of the voluntary and the involuntary, of will and psychic energy. Concurrently, the cogito becomes aware that its passion for order is limited by "fate," by the unconscious, by defects in vision. Paul Ricoeur's exposition of this point stands as a virtual paraphrase of Emerson:

> the experience of a voluntary force which has begun to deploy itself in the body, has as its constant counterpart a background of invincible nature, necessity. Let us go straight to the most subtle forms of necessity...those which are involved in the very exercise of will: this means primarily the partiality of my motives, the partiality of my action. This <u>partiality</u>, which constitutes each indivi<u>dual</u>'s character, far from merely occurring in a scale of values, <u>is</u> rather <u>the unique perspective from which all value appears</u>.$_{38}$ (emphasis mine)

The aspect of nature, Emerson wrote, "depends on the mood of the man...depends on structure or temperament" (<u>W</u>,III,50). This structure, he emphasized throughout <u>Essays, Second Series</u>, is "partial."

Given this structural limitation of human action, a product of physical being (of "thrownness," Heidegger would say), the best we can do is to adjust as finely as possible the proportions of the voluntary and the involuntary, the conscious and the unconscious. "The mid-world is best," Emerson reflects, advocating in "Experience" a mediation between what he calls "power" and "form":

> Human life is made up of the two elements, power and form, and the proportion must be invariably kept if we would have it sweet and sound. Each of these elements in excess makes a mischief as hurtful as its defect (<u>W</u>,III,66).

One meaning of "power," we have seen, is psychic energy derived from the body; "form" then becoming the shaping principle, "intellect" or "spirit," which contains and focuses expression. But the forms of our expression, Emerson finally realized, are far from perfect. Repression of vital energy is too easily countered by an opposite excess. In the unfolding of the mind, the "hair's breadth" of sanity and happiness is difficult to maintain (W,III,66).

NOTES: CHAPTER EIGHT

[1] Joel Porte, *Representative Man: Ralph Waldo Emerson in His Time* (New York: Oxford Univ. Press, 1979), p.277.

[2] Wordsworth, 1850 *Prelude*, XII, 11.279-282.

[3] See the chapter "Economizing" in Porte, *Representative Man*.

[4] Porte, pp.257-8.

[5] Jung, *CW* 8, par.462.

[6] Jung, *CW* 8, par.10.

[7] Jung, *CW* 8, par.3.

[8] Jung, *CW* 8, par.30.

[9] Jung, *CW* 8, pars.31 & 32.

[10] Jung, *CW* 8, par.38.

[11] Jung, *CW* 8, par.36.

[12] Jung, *CW* 8, par.38.

[13] Jung, *CW* 8, par.13.

[14] Jung, *CW* 8, par.85.

[15] Ezra Pound, *The Cantos* (New York: New Directions, 1973), pp.456-7.

[16] Jung, *CW* 8, par.81.

[17] Jung, *CW* 8, par.87.

[18] Jung, *CW* 8, par.19 note.

[19] The last two examples are Jung's: *CW* 8, par.55.

[20] Kenneth Burke, *Language as Symbolic Action: Essays on Life, Literature, and Method* (Berkeley: Univ. of Calif. Press, 1966), p.45.

[21] Jung, <u>CW</u> 8, par.56.

[22] Jung, <u>CW</u> 8, par.72.

[23] Daniel Shea, "Emerson and the American Metamorphosis," in D. Levin ed., <u>Emerson: Prophecy, Metamorphosis, and Influence</u> (New York: Columbia Univ. Press, 1975), p.44.

[24] Jung, <u>CW</u> 8, par.70 & note.

[25] <u>Ibid</u>.

[26] Porte, p.185.

[27] Joel Porte, private conversation, 1980.

[28] Edmund Husserl, <u>Ideas: General Introduction to Pure Phenomenology</u>, trans. W.R.B. Gibson (New York: Collier, 1962), p.98.

[29] Husserl, pp.99-100.

[30] Robert Magliola, <u>Phenomenology and Literature: An Introduction</u> (West Lafayette, Indiana: Purdue Univ. Press, 1977), p.4.

[31] Paul Sheats, <u>The Making of Wordsworth's Poetry, 1785-1798</u> (Cambridge, Mass.: Harvard Univ. Press, 1973), pp.1,19.

[32] Sheats, p.19.

[33] Sheats, p.88.

[34] Sheats, pp.92-3.

[35] Jung, <u>PJ</u>, 461-2 (<u>CW</u> 10, par.151).

[36] Jung, <u>PJ</u>, 451 (<u>CW</u> 12, par. 327).

[37] <u>The Philosophy of Paul Ricoeur: An Anthology of His Work</u>, ed. C.E. Reagan & D. Stewart (Boston: Beacon Press, 1978), p.13.

[38] Ricoeur, p.8.

CHAPTER NINE

MASKS OF DIONYSIUS:

ENTHUSIASM AND INFLATION IN THE NINETEENTH CENTURY

In anticipation of Melville after him, Emerson came to "deconstruct" the aspirations of the Transcendentalist self. For his realization of the "regressive" phase of metamorphosis - the "systole" or contraction of power - emphasized critical detachment at the expense of faith in the unconscious. Openness toward psychic depths could still be maintained, but inspiration became less a product of will and more the gift of an "other" outside the self. In "Fate," for example, external grace seems to replace internal illumination. Furthermore, from the perspective of contraction, Emerson was forced to recognize, earlier enthusiasm could look like illusion -- the product of quixotic "moods" and not of divine illumination.

In the mid-nineteenth century, an even more decisive deconstruction of Transcendentalist enthusiasm took place at the hands of writers like Poe, Hawthorne, and Melville. Turning the psychological metaphors of Gothic romance upon similar problems of motivation and inspiration, romancers in America constructed a model of the psyche which emphasized sinister aspects of the unconscious. Much of this difference in vision, of course, can be attributed to the dominant figurative patterns of Gothic romance. But significantly, such figures spoke to the psychological needs of writers like Poe who used them as means of mapping the psyche. Although Emerson and his Gothic contemporaries share a Romantic vision of the mind which focuses upon the unconscious as the source of creative energy, they disagree profoundly as to the proper relationship to that source.

The operant mode of contact with the unconscious, as we have seen, was the imaginative projection of hitherto-buried psychological powers into forms of consciousness which then grew to the organic shape of that inspiration. As Robert Langbaum reminds us, Romantic writers "came to know the world, not from outside by applying ideas to it, or by passively responding to it, but by playing roles in it -- by projecting themselves into nature, the past and other people."[1] But if Romantic writers "evolved a sense of identity" through such projection, in many cases that identity was precarious. With the ebb of psychic power - as in Coleridge's "Dejection" or Emerson's "Experience" - identity seemed more like a hollow shell than a potent, creatively-driven self.

More frightening was the discovery that the adaptation

of Gothic archetypes to the personal exigencies of creation could uncover powers which were often malign and threatened to engulf the self. From this perspective, opening the door to the unconscious through reliance on intuition (as Emerson had advocated) unleashed the potential for monomania or madness, and not creative expansion. Thus, while Emerson preaches <u>faith</u> in the unconscious as the power driving the expanding circumference of Apollonian egotism, Poe, Hawthorne, and Melville all reveal in their works a <u>distrust</u> and a <u>fear</u> of Dionysian depths. In the universe of American Gothic archetypes, the unconscious is a dungeon containing a murderous goddess (Poe), a closet or cave filled with disturbing images of sexuality (Hawthorne), the boudless depths of the sea from which emerges murderous force (Melville).

While Transcendentalist writers articulate an ultimate faith in intuition as the creative force behind psychological and spiritual growth, Poe, Hawthorne, and Melville all express profound ambivalence over the safety of placing consciousness in contact with the unconscious. For they perceived that the ego could become fascinated - if not possessed - by the very creative energy it tried to harness, that psychic energy could assume malevolent as well as beneficent forms. Understanding that the imagination projects unconscious energy into symbols which are invested with its power, they saw that these symbols could carry negative as well as positive valences. If natural facts could become symbols of the mind's unconscious power (as Emerson had argued in <u>Nature</u>), that power did not always choose benign symbols to reveal its previously hidden face. Through ironic presentations and even parodies of conventional Gothic archetypes (dark lady, dungeon, quest), American romancers subjected those symbols and the process of symbolization itself to the scrutiny of a critical self-consciousness which increasingly called into question a literature based upon Emersonian intuition.[2] For the unconscious was seen not as a locus of moral order, but rather as the source of amoral if not dangerous forces. Eros, and not Christ, was found at the heart of faith.

Harriet Beecher Stowe, commenting in 1852 on the psychology of her Gothic villain in <u>Uncle Tom's Cabin</u>, gives a perceptive reading of the processes involved:

> No one is so thoroughly superstitious as the godless man. The Christian is composed by the belief of a wise, all-ruling Father, whose presence fills the void unknown with light and order; but to the man who has dethroned God, the spirit land is, indeed, in the words of the Hebrew poet, "a land of darkness and the shadow of death," without any order, where the light is as darkness. Life and death to him are haunted grounds, filled with goblin forms of vague and shadowy dread.[3]

Composed by a traditional Christian archetype - "the all-ruling Father" - the psyche reflects a focused energy. The "void unknown," the unconscious "spirit land" of dreams organizes itself like iron filings around the central magnetism of sanctioned myth. But what about those like Melville's Ahab and Pierre for whom the Father has been replaced by darker and less controllable gods who have not entered yet into any binding covenants? The spirit does not disappear, rather it manifests itself as nightmare, as "goblin forms of vague and shadowy dread." Harriet Beecher Stowe's observations help us recall that antebellum piety was founded, not upon sterile intellectualism, but instead upon the management of psychic forces intuited within.

The decay, in mid-nineteenth century America, of conventional forms of Spirit opened the door for spirits -- pagan divinities buried since their exile and repression during the Renaissance. One recalls Milton's exile of the pagan gods in "On the Morning of Christ's Nativity" -- for example, the binding of the "Dragon" (prototype of Moby-Dick):

> Th'old Dragon under ground
> In straiter limits bound,
>   Not half so far casts his usurped sway,
> And wrath to see his Kingdom fail,
> Swinges the scaly Horror of his folded tail.[4]

One has to believe that these lines involve more than mere poetic ornamentation, a pleasing conceit -- that the energy of the Dragon was as dangerous and as feared as all those gods persecuted and exiled by seventeenth-century American Puritans. Edward Johnson, for example, took the threat of pagan religion very seriously. He opens his <u>Wonder-Working Providence</u> with the assertion that the Puritans removed from England to avoid contamination by "prophane persons" who celebrated "a Sabbath like the Heathen to Venus, Baccus and Ceres."[5] All gods had to be repressed who threatened the authority of the Father and his visible image, the Church. But by the 1850's, such repressions were eroding. Paternal-istic religious forms were giving way to new centers of imaginative energy. The "dark ladies" of Gothic romance revealed the extent to which essentially religious energies could be carried by female forms. For some, the energy of the Great Mother was replacing that of Christ -- the figure of Dionysius becoming the carrier of her ecstatic and destructive power.[6]

The stakes were high. For opposed to Emerson's <u>universe of sacrament</u>, Poe inhabited a <u>universe of sacrifice</u> and death. Rather than aspiring toward the unity of "Oversoul" or "One Mind," his characters encounter the fragmentation of divinity into isolated parts which - like Berenice's teeth - maintain value only as tokens of lost plenitude, as fetishes. (In a similar fashion, a white whale serves as Ahab's fetish.) The Dionysian forces of the psyche lead here not to transfiguration, but dismemberment -- to the dark side of the Dionysian myth, the tearing apart by uncontrollable energies of those who dare to assume the mask of the god. Images once filled with life, partaking through symbolic relation of the power of the unconscious, become emblems of death. For they embody projected energies which consciousness can pursue but not wholly assimilate without disintegration, cannot approach without seeing its outlines blur before the obsessive power of dangerous archetypes.

Over and over again, Poe's characters break off at the edge of the abyss, rejecting that final plunge into the psychic depth which absorbs the ego in oblivion and unconsciousness. Unlike the triumphant hero of myth, they cannot return with the maiden and the gold.[7] Vanished is the hope of regenerated identity in which the self, opening itself fully to the unconscious, puts on a transfiguring mantle of power and prophecy, illuminated by the grace of "divinity." Instead, Poe and his Gothic kin imagine a universe of disintegration, a crumbling mansion animated by others who emerge from the cellar as dangerous and self-destructive power.

As a result of the malevolent aspect of the unconscious in American Gothic romance, interpretive structures - designed to relate to and assimilate deeply-buried energies - are transformed into <u>patterns of defense</u>. Unconscious sources of inspiration remain an object of literary quest, but a profound ambivalence develops over undertaking what well may be self-destructive enterprises. In Poe's "The Fall of the House of Usher," for example, a myopic, rationalizing narrator is used to distance us from the dark depths of Roderick Usher's dungeon. In this way, Poe approaches, yet shields himself from, the full power of the "realm of the submerged - the underside of human consciousness - which is the peculiar province of romance."[8] Similarly, Hawthorne uses multiple plots (for example, the mythic tales within <u>The House of the Seven Gables</u> and <u>The Blithedale Romance</u>) to examine psychological dynamics. In addition, Hawthorne's famous "ambiguity" and his use of multiple explanations of fictive events allow him to explore the possibilities of myth without committing himself to them. Finally, Melville exploits narrative distance and ironic voice as defenses against the power embodied in Moby Dick and Isabel Banford (_Pierre_) respectively.

In the universes of Poe, Hawthorne, and Melville, interpretive form - by necessity - constitutes a pattern of defense against the awesome power of the other. None of these writers wants to get too close to the demonic strength of whatever gods lie within. For in the Gothic universe, one usually can escape alienation only through annihilation and death -- Roderick Usher and Ahab are pulled down into the maelstrom. Similarly, one notes the disturbing frequency with which the carriers of unconscious energy (especially Hawthorne's "dark ladies") are placed within destructive interpretive forms. Beatrice Rappaccini ("Rappaccini's Daughter"), Georgiana ("The Birthmark"), and Zenobia (_The Blithedale Romance_) are all repressed and destroyed as carriers of threatening unconscious energies (often recognizable as Freudian _libido_). If on the one hand, the feminine became a powerful field of projection for male writers in the mid-nineteenth century, one wonders about an age when goddess-figures are destroyed by men who are terrified by their energy. Zenobia, a flower-goddess, is cast as a sacrificial victim upon the waters of Hawthorne's _Blithedale Romance_; Madeline Usher is buried alive; while Melville's Isabel Banford takes Pierre down with her. Frequently, it is not just the protagonist who goes down. Often, the integrity of the ego (I mean here the "phenomenological ego" embodied in the text) can be maintained only at the expense of the entire fictive universe. The House of Usher and the Pequod both sink, with their narrators just escaping from the doomed world of Gothic romance.

For Hawthorne, the depths of the self were so threatening that he often closed the doors to the unconscious. By killing off his dark ladies in favor of feminine images leached of their sexuality (Phoebe, Priscilla, Hilda), Hawthorne represses disturbing images released from the unconscious in favor of a rigid psychic economy. In this light, we can see Hawthorne's killing of Zenobia in <u>The Blithedale Romance</u> as a ritualistic exorcism of the sexually-overpowering feminine. This is the sinister side of the sentimental love-religion expressed in his letters to Sophia Peabody (his future wife). It is no surprise that Hawthorne's portrayal of Hester Prynne is alleged to have given her a headache. For Hester embodies a sexuality forbidden to respectable nineteenth-century women. The tension between this repressive norm and Hawthorne's fascination with the figure of the forbidden "dark lady" provides much of the creative energy of his work, which ultimately enforces a painfully-achieved sublimation through the "cleansing" of libido.

In the case of Melville (I am thinking here of <u>Pierre</u>), such cleansing seems an impossibility. Pierre attempts to repress the unconscious, but its disturbing themes keep coming back.[9] In both <u>Moby-Dick</u> and <u>Pierre</u>, the unconscious cannot be walled up or buried or drowned -- it keeps knocking at the gate of consciousness, threatening to come in. (Earlier, Poe created especially terrifying examples of this pattern.) Thus, in <u>Pierre</u> Melville is forced to confront head-on the disturbing question of the physical, even sexual, origin of imaginative energy. Like Byron's Manfred, who opens himself to destructive sexually-colored powers buried in his psyche, Pierre succumbs to the seductive lure of his half-sister Isabel. This "fascination of the terrible" casts him adrift upon "appalling" depths of soul.[10] It leads not to revelation, but to unbearable moral ambiguity. Similar instances, reinforcing the ambiguous provenance of psychological power, could be cited from practically anywhere in the complex corpus of Gothic fiction. In contrast to the mythic participation (the "correspondence") longed for by Emerson, such ambiguity measures a dissonance between the aspirations of the ego toward transcendence and the threatening tonality of descendent unconscious energies. A self-destructive lure toward the unconscious overcomes the Apollonian aspirations of the ego. By the end of <u>Pierre</u>, especially after the bald phallic imagery of Pierre's vision of Enceladus, the tension between fascination and sublimation becomes unbearable. Suicide seems the only alternative -- for Pierre finally begins to see that he cannot reconcile his ideals with his urges, and that he will never escape the demonic forces tormenting him.

In Pierre's case, psychic energy takes on a more and more manifest sexual form. While it is difficult to avoid quibbles with Freudian critics who <u>equate</u> Pierre's sexuality with his libido, it is important to see that Freudian terminology obscures part of the meaning of Melville's fiction. In contrast to an Oedipal reading of <u>Pierre</u> (which does map much of its dynamics), Henry Murray suggests that the relationship between Pierre and Isabel Banford has a spiritual component. Murray argues, for example, that the passage describing Pierre's fascinated reverie upon the face of his unknown half-sister "is the best description in literature ...of the autonomous inward operation of the aroused soul-image, or anima, as Jung has named it."[11] From this perspective, Pierre's relationship to Isabel is that of a spiritual devotee to a "femme inspiratrice" who shapes his devotions.[12] Clearly, Pierre's involvement with Isabel is <u>both</u> <u>spiritual</u> <u>and</u> sexual. Indeed, the tension between two conflicting attitudes toward her generates much of his turmoil. Murray's eclectic approach to Melville, blending together both Freudian and Jungian themes, suggests the multiple interpretive perspectives needed to comprehend the theme of the unconscious.

To continue our Jungian analysis of Melville, we see portrayed in the figures of Ahab and Pierre the dangers of excessive power, a psychological stance which Jung labels "inflation." Robert Richardson's commentary on Ahab's "possesion" can serve to introduce this theme -- for Richardson's viewpoint is essentially congenial with Jung's. Melville's "elaborate psychological portrayal of Ahab," Richardson argues,

> is intended to anchor...mythmaking in undeniable realities of the mind. We have been accustomed, after all, since Freud, to finding myth reduced to psychology or explained in terms of psychology. It is one of Melville's great achievements to have done just the opposite. If we follow the portrayal of Ahab with sufficient care, we will find that Melville has enlarged psychology into myth. Melville validates psychology by myth, rather than the other way round.[13]

As we have seen, Jung also "validates psychology by myth," grounding consciousness upon a more primitive reality intuited beneath. It was one of the key perceptions of Melville that this mythic psyche could manifest itself in demonic terms. Ahab, Richardson observes, "is an <u>inverted</u> enthusiast" -- for he embodies "enthusiasm as the <u>evil god in us</u>."[14] This "demon-intoxication" (a phenomenon thoroughly documented by Jung) stands Emersonian faith on its head. Here, faith in the unconscious casts one adrift upon terrifying processes of possession. The unconscious reveals itself as too strong to be tamed by the ego and channeled into its expansive projects. Instead, the ego is warped to the curve of an overpowering energy which transforms and magnifies consciousness to mythic proportions. This "mythic investiture" (as Richardson calls it) verges constantly - in Melville - toward "inflation."

For both Ahab and Pierre are disposed by forces which have possessed their egos. Opening the gates to the unconscious, they release pent-up energies which overwhelm them and transform their conscious beings to the shape of trans-human power. As Melville well knew, this release brings with it feelings of "super-human capacity" as the ego is inspired by the god-like power rushing through it.[15] Ahab and Pierre are exhilarated by quests which seem, to them, divinely-inspired missions. Each figure is caught up in the rush of forces that lifts him beyond the pale of ordinary humanity into a region of divine motivation. Each is possessed by energies which he just barely keeps under control, energies which ultimately destroy him. For the obverse of such Dionysian inspiration is dismemberment or crucifixion. As Melville drily observes of Pierre near the fatal climax of his career: "But man does never give himself up thus, a doorless and shutterless house for the four loosened winds of heaven to howl through, without still additional dilapidations."[16] The "additional dilapidations" for Ahab and Pierre are those of self-destruction.

An equally-telling example of inflation (one that Jung returns to constantly as a cautionary example) is the final madness of Nietzsche. For Jung, Nietzsche was the great example of inflation, one of those whose consciousness was possessed by an archetype

> so powerfully that it identifies with it and thinks it desires and needs nothing further. In this way a craze develops, a monomania or possession, an acute one-sidedness which seriously imperils the psychic equilibrium.[17]

Nietzsche's ruling myth, as is well known, was Dionysius. From The Birth of Tragedy to the final notes collected in The Will to Power, Nietzsche reminds us constantly of the vital Dionysian forces trapped within. He was, Jung asserts, one of those "trying to restore the lost Dionysos who is somehow lacking in modern man."[18] Melville was another. Both men apprehended within mythic forces which counterbalanced failing religious forms without. Consequently, both Moby-Dick and Zarathustra embody processes of mythmaking. But the danger apprehended by Melville and experienced by Nietzsche is that Dionysius is a more primitive and dangerous god than Christ. He is closer to the id, to the primordial level of untamed animal instinct. Wild beasts, Walter Otto reminds us, have always been the god's avatars.[19] Ezra Pound, who associates Dionysius with the lynx and the leopard in The Cantos, knew this well.[20]

At the end, Jung obsrves, as Nietzsche slipped into madness,

> There can be no doubt that he knew...that the dismal fate of Zagreus was reserved for him. Dionysius is the abyss of impassioned dissolution, where all human distinctions are merged in the animal divinity of the primordial psyche.[21]

If Nietzsche was able to transcend nihilism and to attain a vision of "a Dionysian relationship to existence" (see, for example, his account in Ecce Homo of the inspired creation of Zarathustra), that ecstasy was maintained only briefly before he realized the darker side of the Dionsyian myth. The form of Nietzsche's final, catastrophic madness was to live the myth of the crucified Christ, the dismembered Dionysius:

> it is just the "inspired soul"...that becomes god and demon, and as such suffers the divine

> punishment of being torn asunder like Zagreus.
> This was what Nietzsche experienced at the onset
> of his malady.[22]

Thus, we see Nietzsche signing those last, excruciating letters, written just before his hospitalization, "The Crucified" and "Dionysius."[23]

But if Nietzsche's life, at the end, was <u>structured by</u> the very forces with which he was contending, we must not forget the affirmation preceding his collapse -- his intense vision of the possibility of rising above self-division through a self-overcoming of negation and loss. Another way of stating this is to say that Nietzsche's vision of the unconscious subsumed both Freud's and Jung's. On the one hand, he saw - in an archeology of consciousness pointing toward the Freudian unconscious - the self-delusion of states of mind structured by forces out of man's reach.[24] But on the other hand, this "deconstructive" perspective is tempered by a vision of forces leading to spiritual growth, a position articulated more fully in Jung's psychology. "From the pressure of plenitude," Nietzsche wrote,

> from the tension of forces that continually increase in us and do not yet know how to discharge themselves, there arises a condition like that preceding a storm.[25]

That Nietzsche was able to release that "storm" and achieve heights of creative rapture, we know from <u>Ecce Homo</u> where he describes how - during the composition of <u>Thus Spoke Zarathustra</u> - he reached that state of mind in which

> Everything happens involuntarily in the highest
> degree but as in a gale of a feeling of freedom,

of absoluteness, of power, of divinity.[26]

Thus, we can read Nietzsche as a paradigm of the nineteenth-century vision of the unconscious, comprehending extremes of inspiration and self-destructive inflation. The triumphant sublimation of unconscious power is balanced - in his life and work - by the impending threat of chaos, the disintegration of spiraling aspiration into a Dionysian maelstrom which submerges the ego.

Turning to the American Renaissance, we see Nietzsche's struggle for form enacted within our greatest writers. On the one hand, the threat of fragmentation is never far off. For if Emerson and Whitman embody affirmations of psychic wholeness, of the resurrection of the "One Man" fallen into self-division, Poe and Melville (and to a lesser extent, Hawthorne) realize in their work visions of the opposite extreme -- the dismemberment of Dionysius. Roderick Usher - like Melville's Pierre and Ahab - is torn apart by forces he cannot control; he is rent by the cataclysm of a psychic storm. But even more important, we see both sides of this conflict - the struggle between unconscious power and the spirit's quest for form - enacted <u>within</u> the greatest writers of this period. Emerson as well as Melville, Poe as well as Hawthorne, all attempt to reconcile the power of the unconscious (potentially both creative and destructive) with the need of consciousness for Apollonian self-definition. The untamed wild calls for cultivation, the drawing of boundaries, the laying of streets -- secure avenues leading out from the comfortable light of the hearth into the somber forest. Depending upon the success of such enterprises, upon the temperament of each writer, the Dionysian core of being embodies itself as ecstatic joy or self-destruction, in the "perpetual youth" found by Emerson in the woods or the dark covenant attended by Hawthorne's Young Goodman Brown. The sacramental universe envisioned by Emerson is countered by the sacrificial universe dreaded by Poe, avoided by Hawthorne, flirted with by Melville. But even Emerson, as we have seen, had to come to terms with sacrifice. For Dionysius, depending upon the stance of his suppliant, can be the god either of violence or of ecstasy. That, long ago, was the lesson of Euripides' The Bacchae -- a lesson that writers in the nineteenth century had to relearn.

Paul Tillich's analysis of power and being in Love, Power, and Justice provides a theoretical framework which confirms these views. For Tillich describes the various "power-relations" which can be adopted, stances which correspond to the differeing attitudes possible toward the Dionsyian power of the unconscious:

> 1) "The mental power of a human being...can express itself in three forms. It can suppress elements which belong to it, as special desires or hopes or ideas. In this case the suppressed elements remain and turn the mind against itself, driving it toward disintegration." (For example, Poe's repression leads to what D.H. Lawrence describes as "a great continuous convulsion of disintegration.")
>
> 2) "Or the mental power of a human being can receive resisting elements which belong to it, elevating them into unity with the whole." (Compare this with Emerson's spiritual aspiration as a successful process of aufhebung or sublimation.)

3) "Or the mental power can throw them out radically as foreign bodies whose claim to belong to the whole is successfuly rejected." (Consider Hawthorne's rejection of the dark elements at the end of The House of Seven Gables.)[27]

In summary, repression, assimilation, and exorcism are three ritual attitudes toward the unconscious -- three possible boundaries defining the frontier separating the "wild" from "civilization." Each boundary, we note, establishes a different psychological polity.

Dionysius, Walter Otto explains in Dionysius: Myth and Cult, was "the genuine mask god."[28] He was often worshipped in the form of huge masks planted on draped columns firmly rooted in the ground.[29] It is important, Otto asserts, that we realize that these masks were not empty signs, but symbols of the god's presence: "It was Dionysius, himself... who appeared in the mask."[30] Confronting us with its "penetrating eyes," each mask projects a "stare" which "cannot be avoided":

> its face, with its inexorable immobility, is quite different from other images which seem ready to move, to turn around, to step aside. Here there is nothing but encounter, from which there is no withdrawal -- an immovable, spell-binding antipode. This must be our point of departure for understanding that the mask, which was always a sacred object, could also be put on over a human face to depict the god or spirit who appears.[31]

To the extent that they opened themselves to unconscious currents, our writers slipped into personae, into masks, that threatened them with the consuming, ritualized stare of confrontation -- in the most extreme form, with the sacrifice of individual differences to the spellbinding gaze of the other. Without such openness, they were faced with the bleaker prospect of hollow, stereotyped masks - outworn social roles - from which the god's power had departed. For their lives - as Emerson stringently reminded them in "The American Scholar" - threatened to become "things," rather than living participants in community, the resurrected body of the "One Man."

Somewhere <u>between</u> stereotype and myth, both of which threatened the individual with extinction, lay that "neutral territory" where one could exchange gifts with the gods, safely imbibing their power without being consumed like Semele by their radiance. Self-consciousness, reflecting upon its own structure, sought to embed within itself that "sacred fount" which might nourish - but not inundate - creativity. Such a labor necessitated the ability to bracket consciousness, examining the differential which provided an opening for meaning to emerge, a space cleared of outmoded convention. But it also entailed the ability to clear, to clarify, that "bare common" to the transparency needed to allow room for the transfiguring energies of the unconscious. Aware again of our own powers, we remember what it means to be "embosomed in nature, whose floods of life stream around and through us."[32] Dismissing the "masquerade" of outworn ideas, we place consciousness back in the body, in contact with sources of myth in the unconscious. Instead of abstract intellection, divorced from the ground, we have an embodied thought in which spirit and physical energy, "Reason" and libido, can celebrate their marriage.

NOTES: CHAPTER NINE

[1] Robert Langbaum, *The Mysteries of Identity* (New York: Oxford Univ. Press, 1977), p.165.

[2] This, essentially, is the argument of Joel Porte's *The Romance in America* (Middletown, Conn.: Wesleyan Univ. Press, 1969).

[3] Harriet Beecher Stowe, *Uncle Tom's Cabin* (New York: New American Library, Signet Classic, 1966), p.427.

[4] John Milton, "On the Morning of Christ's Nativity," ll. 168-172, in *Complete Poems and Major Prose*, ed. M.Y. Hughes (Indianapolis: Bobbs-Merrill, Odyssey Press, 1957), pp.47-8.

[5] Edward Johnson, *Johnson's Wonder-Working Providence 1628-1651*, ed. J.F. Jameson (New York: Barnes & Noble, 1967), p.23.

[6] Erich Neumann documents the relationship of Dionysius to the archetype of the Great Mother in *The Origins and History of Consciousness*, trans. R.F.C. Hull (Princeton Univ. Press: Bollingen Series XLII, 1970), p.79ff.

[7] For a discussion of the hero archetype, see Neumann above and Joseph Campbell, *The Hero With a Thousand Faces* (Cleveland & New York: World Pub. Co., Meridian Book, 1956).

[8] Porte, p.67.

[9] Porte, p.179.

[10] Herman Melville, *Pierre; or the Ambiguities*, vol. 7 of *The Writings of Herman Melville*, ed. H. Hayford, H. Parker, G.T. Tanselle (Evanston & Chicago: Northwestern Univ. Press & The Newberry Library, 1971), p.327.

[11] Henry Murray, "Introduction" to Melville, *Pierre* (Hendricks House, 1949), p.xliv.

[12] Murray, pp.lii-liii.

[13] Robert D. Richardson Jr., *Myth and Literature in the American Renaissance* (Bloomington: Indiana Univ. Press, 1978), p.222.

[14] Richardson, pp.222,223.

[15] Carl Jung, *Two Essays on Analytical Psychology*, trans. R.F.C. Hull (New York: Meridian, 1956), p.162: "for identity with the collective psyche always brings with it a feeling of universal validity - 'godlikeness' - which completely ignores all differences in the personal psyche of his fellows."

[16] Melville, pp.339,340.

[17] Jung, *Two Essays*, p.82.

[18] Jung, *PJ*, 391 (*CW* 12, par.181).

[19] Walter F. Otto, *Dionysius: Myth and Cult*, trans. R.B. Palmer (Bloomington: Indiana Univ. Press, 1973), pp.110-113.

[20] Ezra Pound, *The Cantos* (New York: New Directions, 1973), p.8.

[21] Jung, *PJ*, 357 (*CW* 12, par.118).

[22] Jung, *Two Essays*, p.83.

[23] *Selected Letters of Friedrich Nietzsche*, ed. & trans. C. Middleton (Chicago: Univ. of Chicago Press, 1969), pp.345-6.

[24] For a discussion of "archeology," see Paul Ricoeur, *Freud and Philosophy: An Essay on Interpretation*, trans. D. Savage (New Haven: Yale Univ. Press, 1970), Book III, Chapter 2: "Reflection: An Archeology of the Subject," p.419ff. For an example of Nietzsche's examination of states of mind structured

by forces out of man's reach, see "On Truth and Lie in an Extra-Moral Sense," in The Portable Nietzsche, ed. & trans. Walter Kaufmann (New York: Viking Press, 1954), pp.42-7.

[25] Nietzsche, The Will to Power, ed. Walter Kaufmann, trans. Kaufmann & R.J. Hollingdale (New York: Random House, Vintage Book, 1968), #1022 (p.529).

[26] Nietzsche, On the Genealogy of Morals & Ecce Homo, ed. W. Kaufmann, trans. Kaufmann & R.J. Hollingdale (New York: Random House, Vintage Book, 1967), pp.300-1.

[27] Paul Tillich, Love, Power, and Justice: Ontological Analyses and Ethical Applications (New York: Oxford Univ. Press, 1954), p.68.

[28] Walter Otto, Dionysius: Myth and Cult, p.88.

[29] Otto, p.87.

[30] Otto, p.87.

[31] Otto, p.90.

[32] Emerson, CW,I,7.

CHAPTER TEN

DECONSTRUCTION AND RECONSTRUCTION

To conclude, let me discuss some of the methodological assumptions of a study of the unconscious. One of the aims of this study has been to complement literary insights derived from Freudian theory with Jungian analyses. One cannot hold to Jung's and to Freud's views of the unconscious at the same time; for they exclude each other by definition. Not only does this contrast teach us something about the theoretical limitations of any study of the unconscious, it suggests that Jung's and Freud's differing views of their subjects result from complementary perspectives. Now that the essential relativity of critical viewpoints - the limitation of any one view as opposed to another - has become an axiom of interpretation, it is possible to survey the strengths and weaknesses of these competing visions as they illuminate the self-limitations imposed by different interpretive stances. At the same time, we can discern some of the differences between "exclusive" and "eclectic" interpretive strategies.

As opposed to Freudian exclusivity, Jung takes the latter view, suggesting that his psychological perspective does not usurp Freud's but rather complements it. Contrasting his interpretive stance with Freud's, Jung differentiates them according to their perspective toward psychological process. Freud, Jung suggests, looks <u>back</u> to the causes of psychic phenomena, to their antecedents; while he looks <u>forward</u> to their purpose within the individual's unfolding of his unique meaning:[1]

> We know that every psychic structure, regarded from the causal standpoint, is the result of antecedent psychic contents. We know, furthermore, that every psychic structure, regarded from the final standpoint, has its own peculiar meaning and purpose in the actual psychic process.[2]

Both views, Jung insists, are necessary for a full view of the psyche: "only a combination of points of view...can give us a more complete conception of the nature of dreams."[3] Unlike Freud, who dogmatically excludes the competing theories of his rebellious "sons," Jung emphasizes that his position does not replace Freud's, but merely reverses its critical perspective by adding the perspective of "finality" to that of "causality":

> Considering a dream from the standpoint of finality, which I contrast with the causal standpoint of Freud, does not - as I would expressly like to emphasize - involve a denial of the dream's cause, but rather a different interpretation of the associative material gathered round the dream.[4]

Following Jung's assertion of the need for multiple

interpretive perspectives, we ask how Freudian and Jungian insights can be used together to illuminate a literature devoted to exploring the unconscious. Furthermore, we wonder if there is any link between "causal" perspectives and critical exclusivity. From the causal point of view does each interpretation threaten every other?

Conveniently, the French philosopher Paul Ricoeur addresses himself to the problematic interrelationship of multiple interpretive perspectives. At the climax of Freud and Philosophy, for example, Ricoeur argues that the "archeological" perspective of Freud finds its inverted double in Hegelian "teleology." Like much recent Structuralist criticism allied with Freudian premises, Freudian theory - according to Ricoeur - raises the "question of the subject" by teaching us "that the subject is never the subject one thinks it is."[5] Suspending all consideration of "the existential and thinking subject," Freud turns instead to an "archeology" of the underlying causes of thought.[6] As a "discipline of reflection," this stance dispossesses the subject's self-certitude by "a decentering of the home of significations, a displacement of the birthplace of meaning."[7] The locus of meaning, for the Freudian, is shifted "from consciousness toward the unconscious."[8]

Such dispossession should seem familiar to students of the French psychoanalyst Jacques Lacan, who asserts in his psychology the deferral of consciousness to unconscious forces which are never fully recoverable by the conscious mind. Focusing upon the "inmixing of otherness" in conscious states, Lacan shows us how the priority of the conscious mind is displaced by messages which come "from the Other," from alien forces deep within the psyche:[9]

> It speaks in the Other, I say, designating by the Other the very locus evoked by the recourse to speech in any relation in which the Other intervenes. If it speaks in the Other, whether or not the subject hears it with his ear, it is because it is there that the subject, by means of a logic anterior to any awakening of the signified, finds its signifying place.[10]

From Lacan's perspective, a radical "splitting" cleaves the subject into conscious illusion and unconscious force.[11] The subject is no longer seen as a unified and stable observer, "present" to itself, but as "intermittent."[12] Thus, Lacan sees assertions of the unity of the mind as necessary fictions. Against "the idea of unity as the most important and characteristic trait" of the mind, he asserts that "the mind is not a totality in itself."[13] Recognition of this radical split in the psyche, Lacan observes, refutes the unitary psychological assumptions of the "Gestalt school" and of the "phenomenological movement."[14] Vision of a radical alterity at the heart of the psyche represses the interpretive perspective of phenomenology, which focuses instead upon the appearance of phenomenon within the field of consciousness.

Returning to Ricoeur's analysis of the Freudian perspective, we see that he too recognizes the essential antagonism between Freudianism and phenomenology. Ricoeur's strategy is to analyze Freudian psychology as the preliminary stage in a dialectic of reflection. As such, it is "an antiphenomenology...dispossessing me of that illusory Cogito which at the outset occupies the place of the founding act, <u>I</u> think, <u>I</u> am."[15] But this "antiphenomenology," Ricoeur continues, "must now be seen by us as a phase of reflection, the moment of the divestiture of reflection."[16] In order to complete the dialectical movement, one must return from the unmasking of desire <u>behind</u> consciousness to a comprehension of desire as it unfolds <u>within</u> the flow of conscious thought:

> since desire is accessible only in the disguises in which it displaces itself, it is only by interpreting the signs of desire that one can recapture in reflection the emergence of desire and thus enlarge reflection to the point where it regains what it had lost.[17]

From the first step of perceiving "the inadequacy of consciousness," we "must now take a further step and speak... in positive terms of the emergence or positing of desire through which I am posited, and find myself already posited."[18]

In order to interpret this emergence, Ricoeur contrasts the Freudian "archeology of the subject" with "the complementary concept of teleology." Indeed, Ricoeur insists that we cannot comprehend either perspective without the other: "In order to have an <u>archê</u> a subject must have a <u>telos</u>."[19] There is no beginning without an implied end. This dialectical maneuvre (calling to mind Jung's contrast between Freud's "causality" and his own "finality") expands our comprehension of the interrelationship of competing interpretive perspectives. If "the only way to understand the notion of archeology is in its dialectical relationship to a teleology,"[20] then contemporary views of the unconscious as "Other" (Lacan) and of the subject's displacement (Structuralism) must be complemented by competing teleological perspectives:

> if the subject is to attain its true being, it is not enough for it to discover the inadequacy of its self-awareness, or even to discover the power of desire that posits it in existence. The subject must also discover that the process of "becoming conscious," through which it <u>appropriates</u> the meaning of its existence as desire and effort, does not belong to it, but belongs to the meaning that is formed in it. The subject must mediate self-consciousness through spirit or mind, that is, through the figures that give a telos to this "becoming conscious."[21]

In order to clarify this mediation of "self-consciousness through spirit or mind," Ricoeur goes on to contrast Freudian "archeology" with the "teleological" orientation he finds in Hegel. But we can stop here; for we have already encountered a similar contrast in the conflicting interpretations of Freud and Jung.

Ricoeur's analysis suggests the existence of two basic stances toward figurative language. On the one hand, we can see figures as "swerves" from prior "causes"; or we can analyze them as definitions of spiritual aspiration aiming toward the future. As an example of the first view, Harold Bloom's "poetics of revisionism" is illuminating, especially since Bloom's archeology defines itself against a corresponding teleology. However, for Bloom (as for Freud) the prior, the causative, the "precursor," is posited as the point of departure against which poetry takes its stand as defense. The "proper use of Freud, for the literary critic," Bloom argues, "is not to apply Freud (or even revise Freud) as to arrive at an Oedipal interpretation of poetic history."[22] By analyzing the assumptions of this "Oedipal" stance we can clarify one of the interpretive poles in the dialectic of critical reflection.

In Bloom's analysis of poetic creation, the stance of the poet is defined as a "defense" against the potentially withering influence of a "strong precursor." Against the threatening pressures of "engulfment" and "oblivion," Bloom's poet asserts his identity (this identity, by definition, is masculine).[23] In order to exist as an authentic voice, "he must repress the causes, including the precursor-poems," which overshadow and inhibit creativity.[24] By means of this repression, a creative "misreading" of the past, the poet is able to "clear a space for himself" and hence receive "a new name all his own."[25] The poet, from this perspective, becomes the "Over-poet," an incarnation of "the Over-man, as prophesied by Nietzsche's Zarathustra."[26] His strength becomes a function of the Other's weakness; his "divination," a usurpation of prior authority which he now possesses in "a declaration of property that is made figuratively."[27] "Poetic image" and "trope," for Bloom, are thus imagined as forms of defense similar to the Freudian notion of defense.

"The trope-as-defense," Bloom continues, "...might be called at once a warding-off by turning and yet also a way of striking or a manner of hurting."[28] Against the threat of annihilation, of powerlessness, of impotence, the poet strikes a stance of aggression. In this way, he confirms his power and identity.

But if Harold Bloom's poetics constitutes one "phenomenology of power-relations," there are others. "The typical forms in which powers of being encounter each other," Paul Tillich writes,

> are a fascinating subject of phenomenological descriptions....One draws another power into oneself and is either strengthened or weakened by it. One throws the foreign power of being out or assimilates it completely. One transforms the resisting powers or one adapts oneself to them. One is absorbed by them and loses one's power of being, one grows together with them and increases their and one's own power of being.[29]

Later, Tillich identifies three fundamental stances toward power: repression, assimilation, and exorcism.[30] Such insights suggest that a criticism founded upon repression (the exclusion of threatening elements) must be complemented by visions of the creative process which emphasize assimilation and identification. One can associate these latter stances with the perspective of phenomenological criticism, such as that found in the non-directed reveries of Gaston Bachelard.

But to be fair, we must observe that Harold Bloom's poetics contains within it a vision of assimilation, which he terms "restitution." For example, Bloom offers us as model Luria's revision of "the *Zohar*'s dialectics of creation into an ingoing or regressive process, a creation by contraction, destruction, and subsequent restitution."[31] In this dialectical view, negation - "a regression, a holding-in of the Divine breath" - clears a space for new creation.[32] In Bloom's Freudian terms, initial repression is compensated by the "restitution" of "symbolic representation." In Gnostic terms, "the breaking-of-the-vessels" is repaired by "an antithetical completion, the device of recognition that fits together the broken parts of a vessel, to make a whole again."[33] While Bloom complicates this scheme considerably (outlining three dialectical phases of destruction and reconstruction), let us not lose sight of his central insight (similar to Ricoeur's) -- that dispossession and possession, repression and compensatory expression, constitute the poles of the creative process.

As Bloom himself acknowledges, focus upon <u>either</u> of these two extremes leads to one of two equally valid, but mutually contradictory, forms of criticism:

> Language, in relation to poetry, can be conceived in two valid ways, as I have learned, slowly and reluctantly. Either one can believe in a magical theory of all language, as the Kabbalists, many poets, and Walter Benjamin did, or else one must yield to a thoroughgoing linguisitc nihilism, which in its most refined form is the mode now called Deconstruction. But these two ways turn into one another at their outward limits.[34]

J. Hillis Miller, a fellow "deconstructive critic (at least for the sake of the anthology <u>Deconstruction</u> & <u>Criticism</u>) concurs. The "obvious or univocal reading," he argues,

> always contains the "deconstructive reading" as
> a parasite encrypted within itself as part of it-
> self. On the other hand, the "deconstructive"
> reading can by no means free itself from the
> metaphysical reading it means to contest.[35]

Without going, at this point, into the subtleties of the "deconstructive" critical stance, we can recognize that deconstruction and construction engage in a circular hermeneutic dance which can never be resolved. If the emphasis of Freudian psychology (especially in its contemporary revisions) falls upon defenses against threatening psychic contents which "defer" or engulf the ego, other stances (notably, the Jungian and phenomenological) stress the opposite pole -- the assimilation and unfolding of unconscious energy.

At this point, we can stand back and examine some of the existential assumptions underlying recent critical revisions of Freud. (I am thinking here, primarily, of the theories of Bloom, Lacan, and Derrida.) For psychoanalytic criticism (whatever its guise) carries as part of its "prefiguration" certain attitudes toward being, acting, and energy. Power is imagined as something "other," originating elsewhere. It is alien and frequently threatening. It manifests itself as the uncanny, the <u>unheimlich</u> (the unhomely, alienated). As a messenger from elsewhere, from the "scene of the other" (Lacan), it "deconstructs" the pretensions of the ego. For it reveals rational thought being undermined by irrational urge, reason as the unwitting vehicle of unseen forces. "Where it was, there I shall be": the preferred attitude toward <u>it</u>, toward the wild, is one of domination. Psychic imperialism - for the Freudian - is the plot most commonly imitated. Harold Bloom, as we have seen, imagines literary creation as a power-struggle for domination. Ritualized "murder" of the "precursor" and theft of his power, his "authority," is the Oedipal model of this stance. The poet (and critic) as hero ventures against a dangerous foe whom he must subdue or be extinguished. The Father threatens to monopolize psychic energy which must be wrested from him. Father or son, "precursor" or "ephebe" -- only one can maintain priority. The other must be "belated" and fall to second rank in the literary pecking order.

But this "otherness" - deconstructing the pretensions of the ego - becomes, at the hands of Bloom's "strong poet," the occasion for speech. In a dialectical reversal, imaginative poverty - what I have called a sense of "rift" - defines an opening for creation. "A poem begins because there is an absence," Bloom observes.[36] Elsewhere, he reminds us that Emerson's concept of "Fate" or "Necessity" defines the limits of being that Emerson overcomes through willed freedom. Bloom writes,

> the Transcendentalist vision...turns transumptive, projecting all the past as a lame, blind, deaf march, and introjecting a sublime future, mounted over fate, the finite, the cosmos. What Emerson represses is Ananke, the Fate he has learned already to call "compensation."[37]

This recognition of a "dualizing split," a "catastrophe," as the "invariable inaugural act for consciousness" relates to those readings which stress Emerson's recognition of "Fate" within and without -- that is, his sense of the Fall.[38] To the extent that criticism reminds us of this fate and of its necessary interrelationship with freedom, it centers upon the dialectical struggle of being against non-being at the heart of the greatest art. "The power of being is greater," Tillich reminds us, "the more non-being is taken into its self-affirmation."[39]

In this light, "deconstructive" criticism serves to remind us of the non-being, of the "nihilism" (as Hillis Miller calls it) which is the "uncanny guest" within creative affirmation. Metaphysics, Hillis Miller argues, "attempts to cover over the unhealable by annihilating the nothingness hidden within itself."[40] Similarly, the "unconscious" - "the term...given by consciousness to that part of itself which it cannot face directly"[41]- defines the condition of absence, of otherness, against which consciousness responds. Or does it? The danger of this view of the unconscious as non-being, as the "alien," is that it sees the unconscious as the negation (the annihilation) of consciousness and not as an active principle in its own right. Harold Bloom rejects the unconscious as a useful literary term.[42] Perhaps he is right. But the consequence of such a stance is that consciousness appears as a function of will and not as a dialogue with emerging unconscious forces. Reading Bloom, one has the impression that poetic creation is a power-struggle between fully-conscious gods, Nietzschean ubermenschen. But the strong poet (and the strong critic) - inflating consciousness at the expense of the unconscious - soars like Icarus toward unattainable illumination. For when does one reach the asymptote of the receding curve of ego-gratification, the secure stance of perfectly-willed dominance? The "never-resting mind" (as Wallace Stevens called it) will never be satisfied -- for there will always be more "precursors" to conquer and new threats to the ego. Without denying, then, the will-to-power manifest in creation and criticism, let us also see that the perspective of the will distorts the unconscious.

For if the poet clears a space for himself against his precursor's vision, we must remember that this "space" is the area not only of will, but also of "will-less" inner forces that would write our destiny for us -- of the "alien god" of Gnosticism which must somehow be acclimated to conscious being. Thus, the dialectic between "freedom" and "fate" becomes the site of a struggle between conscious and unconscious motivation, between self-reliance and possible inscription by the Other. Opening ourselves to the unpredictable power within, we do not know whether Apollonian impulse can demarcate the boundary of the Dionysian. Such boundaries, according to Hillis Miller, must be "permeable," "connecting inside and outside," "allowing the inside in, making the inside out, dividing them and joining them."[43] Harold Bloom's theory of tropes meets this test of "permeability," since it focuses upon defenses which <u>express</u>, in distorted form, original power. Bloom's perspective reminds

us that all we know of the unconscious are its "symptoms,"
its tropes. But this epistemological limitation should not
blind us to the power of the unconscious which resists and
disciplines the will.

If libido "swerves" (as Bloom says) from unnamed and inarticulate energy into vital speech, critical focus upon
that swerve as <u>defense</u> colors our vision of the unconscious.
Since the unconscious does not always manifest itself as a
threatening force, there are more stances of being than those
which emphasize defense or vicissitude. However, if one
looks from the stance of defense and vicissitude, one can
see nothing else. Lost is any sense of unconscious power as
a freely-given "grace." Obscured is the sense of the unconscious as a mysterious power transcending consciousness.
From the perspective of defensiveness, personality is stressed
over impersonality, the ego over the ego's <u>relation to</u> the unconscious. Without phenomenological openness, one may see
creative being as "writing"; but not as "vision." Admittedly, our strongest poets - as Bloom asserts - have wrestled
with the "anxiety of influence." But that struggle was for
the sake, not merely of ego-gratification, but of spiritual
vision. In order to see that vision, we have to move from
Freudian defense to a criticism founded upon the openness of
"hermeneutic" understanding.

It seems ironic to have to insist upon maintaining an
openness to the spiritual meanings of literature. But contemporary demythologizing perspectives have often led to the

dismissal of spiritual wisdom as error, illusion, "centrist metaphysics" (as if centrism were a bad thing). Rather than giving in to the pressure of such skepticism, let us preserve a wisdom which daily seems to be annulled. The concept of the "unconscious" reminds us that ego psychology and emphasis upon psychic defense represent narrow bands in the total psychological spectrum. Wordsworth, Emerson, Pound (among many others) explore ranges of light which transcend the ego's light of "common day." Indeed, for all these writers, egotism threatened to darken creativity. The stances of many recent critics obscure such vision by rejecting the existence of any power transcending the confines of the ego. For example, the recent shift of critical attention to the signifier (writing with its tropes and defenses) over the signified threatens to eclipse the signified altogether. A concept of writing as willed expression seems to replace writing as reference. "Deconstruction," Geoffrey Hartman explains,

> refuses to identify the force of literature with any concept of embodied meaning and shows how deeply such logocentric or incarnationist perspectives have influenced the way we think about art.[44]

As the ("photographic") negative of earlier interpretive stances, this highlights what had been obscure, what J. Hillis Miller describes as the "inalienable alien presence within Occidental metaphysics."[45]

But at the same time, by cutting figuration loose from the ground ("any concept of embodied meaning"), deconstruction darkens what had once been clear. We can see this obscurity as a function of our current "cultural crisis," manifested here as a preference for the "medium" over the "message," for the "written" over the "seen" or "spoken." There are fewer voices to attend to, either within or without. We contribute to this "silence" by denigrating the "signified" (especially the "transcendental signified") and by magnifying instead the role of the "signifier." Focus then shifts to the act of writing from its reference -- whether "God," "Being," "Nature," or the "Unconscious." Without privileging any one conception of the transcendent, we still must see that without such a concept faith evaporates as a viable structure of consciousness. For the object of faith is then suspended. With such a suspension, writing ceases to be shaped in response to any spiritual authority defining its contours. Nothing lies outside of the written. Homo scriptum (written man) exists in a spiritual vacuum.

The appearance or disappearance of God reflects our openness or closure to the possibility of godhead. Without the terminology of divinity, no god will be visible. That terminology has been rapidly receding since the age of Emerson. Opposed to skeptical materialism, hermeneutic philosophy (Ricoeur) and psychology (Jung) propose to keep the "wager" of faith open. Unless interpretation keeps open the possibility that signification does point to something larger and more profound (which transcends the self-referentiality of language), the aura of symbol and myth stands in danger of disappearing. The significance of Emerson for us today is that he offers the possibility of such faith - a faith in the "god within" - in the face of radical skepticism.

A criticism oriented toward the unconscious responds to this spiritual need. For if the unconscious is accepted as a "transcendental signified," then signification can be seen as a process which intends more than willful patterning. It opens out instead into the "unsounded center" of psychic depth. But acknowledging the unseen and ultimately mysterious currents within does not, as Freudian revisionists assert, mean handing over the psychic economy to the Other. Such definition of the unconscious as alien, uncanny, other, alters our very stance toward creative expression. It shuts certain doors to the house of spirit. We can begin the process of reopening those doors by noting the similarity between stances oriented toward the unconscious-as-other and what has been labelled "patriarchal consciousness" by feminist critics.[46]

For Wordsworth, the unconscious was not always other or paternal. Frequently, it was felt as a familiar breeze or as maternal nurture. For Emerson, it was an essential life-process, as inalienable as breathing. Without this sense of the unconscious as familiar, many of the most profound psychological observations of the last two hundred years are meaningless. Without an openness to currents of life within, stances of fear, aggression, and violence toward the "Other" seem justified. Susan Griffin identifies such attitudes with patterns of "patriarchal consciousness" which defend against the physical, the incarnate, the sexual -- all of which are associated with the feminine. Griffin's theory allows us to see clearly that alternatives exist to the patriarchal modes of consciousness promulgated by Freud and critics influenced by him. What it suggests is that there exist "matriarchal" patterns of consciousness as well. Without pushing the analogy too far, let us note that striking similarities can be discerned between Carl Jung's emphasis upon nurturance and empathy as patterns of relationship to the unconscious and feminist theories which question the necessity of embracing aggressive, imperialistic motives as models of creativity.

Jungian psychology aims to replace patriarchal will-to-power over the unconscious with what might be termed "matriarchal acceptance." For Jung, one's relation to psychic energy, to "nature" within, ideally follows the curve of beneficent nurturance. Demeter and Sophia are projected as figures of the matriarchal psyche, nursing consciousness. (Contrast this with the violence associated with Oedipus.) The ego and the unconscious are no longer seen as antagonists, but as two related aspects of being. Contrasting Freud and Jung, we see that either the "Father" or the "Mother" can be the focus of relation, the strong signifier of an entire semiotics. In the family romance, either the unconscious-as-father or the unconscious-as-mother can define the terminology of power-relations, which can be mapped either as "vicissitude" and "misprision" or as "self-reliance" and "individuation." Thus, the Jungian economy challenges Freud's point by point, offering maternal figures of the unconscious instead of paternal ones -- visions of what Jung calls the anima.

Gaston Bachelard's contrast of conceptual with imaginative modes of thought confirms this distinction. According to Bachelard, "The virility of knowledge grows with each victory of constructive abstraction."[47] But opposed to the "masculine" power of abstraction (the stance of Freudian rationalism), Bachelard places the undirected dreaming of "images as they gather in the state of reverie," immersed within the fertile ambiance of a "feminine" imaginative response:

> If one loves concepts and images, the masculine and feminine poles of the psyche, one must love mental powers with two different loves.[48]

Let us look beyond what seems sexual stereotype (the "rational" male, the "imaginative" female) to see the insight conveyed by Bachelard's sexual metaphor -- that there is an essential difference between objective and subjective cognitive styles. These two stances - which we could relabel "imperialistic" and "nurturing" - lead to two very different conceptions of the unconscious. (We should add that Bachelard, like Jung, reflects upon the basic "androgyny" of the unconscious, which he sees as both male and female.)

As a phenomenological "stance," consciousness can adopt a variety of attitudes toward its myth of the self, attitudes ranging from fear and aggression to acceptance and identification. The myth of psychic origin - the "unconscious" - changes its character according to the stance of the observer, the attitude of consciousness. As Jung observed, manifestations of the unconscious (for example, dream images) change their appearance according to the stance of consciousness toward primordial power intuited within. The appearance of myth - the "face" the unconscious assumes - reciprocates the existential attitude of the ego, what Ludwig Binswanger calls its "key."[49] Thus, a sense of vulnerability and fragility meets its reflection in the image of a dangerous world with threatening powers. Dwelling within vulnerability, the "I" fears dismemberment and castration.

It was Carl Jung's contribution to depth psychology to insist upon this <u>reciprocal relation</u> between the ego and unconscious, which are seen as two facets of the same organism.[50] On the one hand, it has been argued (by Freud and his followers) that the ego is weak because of the overpowering authority of the unconscious which manifests itself as threatening energy. But it is also true - Jung adds - that the unconscious appears overpowering and threatening because the ego is weak. Strengthen the ego and change its stance toward the unconscious, and the unconscious will change its appearance accordingly. This insight is allied with the critical perspective of hermeneutic interpretation: one sees what one believes, one must believe in order to see. It is upon this latter point - belief - that Jung applies full pressure, insisting upon a stance of openness and faith toward the unconscious, rather than one of defense and closure. Like Coleridge, Jung advocates a "willing suspension of disbelief."

One needs to accept the <u>presence</u> of the unconscious, Jung realized, not construe the grammar of its absence. For if the unconscious is "an empty space, a blank, an 'absence,'"[51] it is also a presence shaping the very attitude of those conscious stances defining the distance of the unconscious. It does no good, Jung argues, to define the unconscious as <u>other</u>, to place <u>it</u> underground, to attempt to overcome <u>its</u> influence ("Where it was, there I shall be."). For <u>it</u> is here all the time, along with me. Our attempts to distance ourselves from myth, to classify and contain it, are countervailed by the living power within which will not be killed, dissected, or restrained. Poe's demons, we remember, always return from the grave. It is foolhardy to attempt to imprison Dionysius, King Pentheus learned. Rather than repressing the unconscious, Jung asserts, you must strive to realize the myth you are living so that you can know the shape of your destiny. The alternative is to be "inscribed" by the unconscious -- to be condemned to live unconsciously a myth which is always other, a script which you never see.

Similarly to "deconstructive" critics, Jung recognized that Freud "like an Old Testament prophet...overthrew false idols and pitilessly exposed to the light of day the rottenness of the contemporary psyche."[52] But for Jung, this deconstruction of the psyche's ideals, of its "idols," is just the opening gambit in what should be a constructive dialogue with the unconscious. According to Jung, analysis must pass through early perceptions of the unconscious as alien and other, as the "shadow-side" of the self, to a more familiar and cooperative relationship with the psyche.[53] At the beginning of analysis, while the analysand is still dominated by unconscious projections, he is in the position of Lacan's subject, "a product rather than an originator."[54] But Jung sees the course of analysis as the progressively-conscious realization of forces once unconscious, as a movement toward unique moments of psychic growth in which the subject establishes firm pathways to the unconscious and assimilates once-unconscious power. Thus, while Jungian psychology includes a vision of the possibility of being "written" by impersonal psychic forces, it advocates an overcoming of such unconscious motivation through a stance of openness to the unconscious and its hidden message. By accepting the unconscious as a necessary fiction, Jung's analysand realigns the perspective of consciousness away from the self-certitude of the ego. Like Lacan, Jung sees consciousness as determined by forces within. But instead of "deferring" the ego, these forces suggest the importance of "bracketing" it. Then the ego is seen as part of something larger. From this stance of faith, the unconscious becomes the necessary complement of consciousness (indeed, its ground) and not an alienated "Other." *It* becomes the context of consciousness, the ground from which consciousness emerged, and not a victimizing antagonist.

Like Jung, phenomenological critics question the need for viewing the unconscious as other, deferring consciousness. Gaston Bachelard, for example, focuses upon the manifestation of unconscious energies <u>within consciousness</u> -- upon what Bachelard describes as "the <u>onset of the image</u> in an individual consciousness."[55] Instead of focusing upon the unconscious as an antagonistic force <u>below</u> consciousness, Bachelard examines unconscious motivation as an inextricable part <u>of</u> consciousness. As Colette Gaudin explains:

> Bachelard wants to maintain his analyses at a level which he describes as a botanical <u>graft</u>. He refuses to explore the organic sources of imagination and, in particular, sexual complexes. Rather, he seeks man above the graft, where "<u>a culture has left its traces on nature</u>." Finally, the psychoanalyst, by seeking reality beneath the fable, destroys the primacy of the image. He gives to the symbol a conceptual rigidity -- he "<u>explains the flower by the fertilizer</u>." A graft is a true human mark; thus, it is by their "<u>cultural signs</u>" that Bachelard identifies complexes.[56]

Accordingly, the "poetic image," for Bachelard, "is a sudden salience on the surface of the psyche"[57] -- a text which parallels Jung's phenomenological description of dream-images appearing to consciousness. (By contrast, Freudian and Structuralist critics look below consciousness.) In addition, Bachelard comments upon the "reverberation" of the poetic image, its "sonority of being";[58] while Jung analyzes the "numinous" quality of appearing archetypes.[59] By rejecting the analysis of "psychological antecedents" in favor of an examination of the unique qualities of the image before him, Bachelard develops a concept of the image very close to Jung's "archetype."[60] Gaudin notes this similarity and cites Bachelard's regret at encountering Jung's work "too late."[61] Significantly, both Jung and Bachelard turned to the imagery of alchemy to aid them in their anatomizing of imagination.[62]

Contrasting Jung's assimilation of the unconscious with Lacan's view of the unconscious as other, we ask why must it be "other"? Is it really "other"? Or is the uncanny (the unheimlich) really at home within us all the time? Aren't our moods (irrationally arising within us and as mysteriously disappearing) confirmation of the unseen companion within? (Coleridge's "stranger" in "Frost at Midnight" is really there all the time performing its "secret minisrty.") We can attempt to stand back, like Freud, and define feeling in terms of a "reason" cleansed as much as possible of the irrational, the spontaneous -- which now appears as "absent" and "other." But isn't this "rationality" itself a myth shaped by prefigurations outside the scope of its vision? Appearing as "trope," as "swerve," as "differance," consciousness measures its own distance from power which always appears elsewhere until stolen. From the perspective of reason (obsessed with its difference from the center, from the source), the unconscious is other. But why must consciousness accept the pattern of alienated rationality? Why must it mold itself on ironic stances distant from power?

Why not, instead, accept the possibility of familiarity and nearness, of participation in <u>nourishing</u> unconscious processes. To do so as critics changes one's stance toward the literary work.

Jung, Binswanger, and Bachelard address such questions, defining consciousness as a pattern of relationship to the psychic ground -- a pattern which is part of the ground itself, its "surface." But it is misleading to speak of consciousness as the "surface" of the psyche, lying above hidden depths, if the psychic surface is seen as divorced from the profound. Instead, consciousness must be seen as a responsive film reflecting the depressions and bulges of what lies "beneath." In this way, the psyche is given a "density," a "substance."[63] In contrast to the stance of analytical consciousness (the Cartesian <u>cogito</u>) emphasizing psychic surface at the expense of the deep, consciousness here is seen to shape itself as an expression of the total psyche, conscious and unconscious, known and unknown. From the perspective of scientific analysis, the "mind is not a totality," according to Lacan.[64] But is the perspective of scientific analysis the best stance toward the unconscious (its adversary, by definition)? What we need, instead, are perspectives in which surface and depth need not be seen as antagonists, but rather as two facets of the same process.

One finds such a stance in the "hermeneutic" philosophy of Paul Ricoeur. The "question of faith," Ricoeur writes,

> becomes a hermeneutic question, for what annihilates itself in our flesh is the Wholly Other as

> logos. Thereby it becomes an event of human speech and can be recognized only in the movement of interpretation of this human speech. The "hermeneutic circle" is born: to believe is to listen to the call, but to hear the call we must interpret the message. Thus we must believe in order to understand and understand in order to believe.
>   By thus making itself "immanent" to human speech, the Wholly Other becomes discernible in and through the dialectic of teleology and archeology. Although it is completely different from any origin assignable by reflection, the radical origin now becomes discernible as the question of my archeology; although it is completely different from any anticipation of myself I am capable of making, the final end becomes recognizable through the question of my teleology. Creation and eschatology present themselves as the <u>horizon</u> of my archeology and the <u>horizon</u> of my <u>teleology</u>.[65]

What lies beyond the horizon (let us call it the "unconscious") is outside of human vision. What we know are manifestations of the Other as they appear within the field of consciousness. We can "deconstruct" such appearances by focusing upon their hidden causes, stressing the irreducible gap between sign and its unconscious system. Or we can take these appearances as embodiments of a power which is made present through their manifestation. What that power is we shall never know. But labelling it as the "divine," as "being," as the Jungian "unconscious" allows us to inhabit postures that remain open to the possibility of transcendence. Rather than defining the causes of psychic phenomena, we remain open to their essential unfolding. By realizing the ultimate mystery of the life-process, and thus bracketing the need for causal explanations of being, we are able to focus upon the evolving shape of life, of thought, of literary creation. We can identify this perspective as that of phenomenology -- as an openness to processes unfolding within the field of our vision.

Carl Jung, Ludwig Binswanger, and Gaston Bachelard all give us different visions of that phenomenology. But embedded within their interpretations we find Hillis Miller's "uncanny guest." For the mind must circumscribe itself as part of its dialectic of growth, limiting itself through the acceptance of non-being as boundary. From this perspective, we see the projections of faith chastened by a stoic recognition of the limits of aspiration. We see how self-consciousness defines the edge of unconscious processes of symbolic projection, placing them within self-critical contexts which define their meaning. We realize that Jungian faith <u>needs</u> Freudian skepticism to clarify its contours. For an unlimited process of faith would lack any awareness of its own direction. But conversely, interpretation must imaginatively nourish its subject or it disappears from the field of vision, distorted or darkened beyond recognition. Thus Freudian defense <u>needs</u> Jungian faith to allow the implications of cultural products to unfold. It is the alternation - or rather the co-existence - of faith and skepticism, of projection and interpretation, of self-assurance and irony, that allows meaning to emerge. In contemporary critical terms, the subject as a self-conscious entity cannot exist without a "deconstruction" of its aspirations; but that deconstruction remains a dead abstraction outside of the context of the "presence" which it defines. Light stands out only as the antithesis of darkness. Figures of life and thought can only take existence in relation to the psychic ground.

NOTES: CHAPTER TEN

1 Jung, <u>CW</u> 8, pars.451 & 456.

2 Jung, <u>CW</u> 8, par.451.

3 Jung, <u>CW</u> 8, par.473.

4 Jung, <u>CW</u> 8, par.462.

5 Paul Ricoeur, <u>Freud and Philosophy: An Essay on Interpretation</u>, trans. D. Savage (New Haven: Yale Univ. Press, 1970), p.420.

6 <u>Ibid</u>.

7 Ricoeur, p.422.

8 Ricoeur, p.423.

9 Jacques Lacan, "Of Structure as an Inmixing of an Otherness Prerequisite to Any Subject Whatever," in R. Macksey & E. Donato eds., <u>The Languages of Criticism and the Sciences of Man: The Structuralist Controversy</u> (Baltimore: Johns Hopkins Univ. Press, 1970), p.186.

10 Lacan, <u>Écrits: A Selection</u>, trans. A. Sheridan (New York: Norton, 1977), p.285.

11 <u>Ibid</u>.

12 Lacan, "Inmixing of Otherness," p.189.

13 Lacan, "Inmixing of Otherness," p.190.

14 <u>Ibid</u>.

15 Ricoeur, pp.422-3.

16 Ricoeur, p.424.

17 <u>Ibid</u>.

18 Ricoeur, p.439.

[19] Ricoeur, p.459.

[20] Ricoeur, p.460.

[21] Ricoeur, p.459.

[22] Harold Bloom, Poetry and Repression: Revisionism From Blake to Stevens (New Haven: Yale Univ. Press, 1976), p.25.

[23] Bloom, pp.3,27.

[24] Bloom, p.5.

[25] Ibid.

[26] Bloom, p.6.

[27] Ibid.

[28] Bloom, pp.9,10.

[29] Paul Tillich, Love, Power, and Justice: Ontological Analyses and Ethical Applications (New York: Oxford Univ. Press, 1954), pp.41-2.

[30] Tillich, p.68.

[31] Bloom, p.15.

[32] Bloom, p.16.

[33] Bloom, p.17.

[34] Harold Bloom, "The Breaking of Form," in Bloom, De Man, Derrida, Hartman, Miller, Deconstruction and Criticism (New York: Continuum, 1979), p.4.

[35] J. Hillis Miller, "The Critic as Host," in Deconstruction and Criticism, pp.224-5.

[36] Harold Bloom, Wallace Stevens: The Poems of Our Climate (Ithaca: Cornell Univ. Press, 1976), p.375.

[37] Bloom, Poetry and Repression, p.237.

[38] For a discussion of Emerson's vision of the Fall, see Joel Porte, Representative Man: Ralph Waldo Emerson in His Time

(New York: Oxford Univ. Press, 1979), "Descending," pp.165-178.

39 Tillich, p.48.

40 J. Hillis Miller, Deconstruction and Criticism, p.228.

41 Ibid.

42 Bloom, Poetry and Repression, p.24.

43 Hillis Miller, p.219.

44 Geoffrey Hartman, Deconstruction and Criticism, p.vii.

45 Hillis Miller, p.226.

46 For a thorough examination of the destructive, imperialistic aspect of "patriarchal consciousness," see Susan Griffin, Woman and Nature: The Roaring Inside Her (New York: Harper & Row, 1980).

47 Gaston Bachelard, On Poetic Imagination and Reverie: Selections from the Works of Gaston Bachelard, ed. & trans. Colette Gaudin (New York: Bobbs-Merrill, 1971), p.6.

48 Bachelard, p.7.

49 Ludwig Binswanger, "The Existential Analysis School of Thought," in R. May, E. Angel, H.F. Ellenberger eds., Existence: A New Dimension in Psychiatry and Psychology (New York: Simon & Schuster, 1958), p.194.

50 Jung, PJ, 273 (CW 8, par.132): "the unconscious behaves in a compensatory or complementary manner towards the conscious."

51 André Green, "The Unbinding Process," New Literary History 12 (Autumn 1980), p.26.

52 Jung, CW 15, par.51.

53 Jung, PJ, 146 (CW 9,ii, par.16).

[54] Vernon Gras, "Introduction" to *European Literary Theory and Practice: From Existential Phenomenology to Structuralism* (New York: Dell, Delta Book, 1973), pp.15-16.

[55] Gaston Bachelard, *The Poetics of Space*, trans. M. Jolas (Boston: Beacon Press, 1969), p.xv.

[56] Colette Gaudin, "Introduction" to *On Poetic Imagination and Reverie: Selections from the Works of Gaston Bachelard*, p.xvii.

[57] Bachelard, *The Poetics of Space*, p.xi.

[58] Bachelard, *The Poetics of Space*, p.xii.

[59] Jung, *CW* 18, par.547.

[60] Bachelard, *The Poetics of Space*, p.xxviii.

[61] Colette Gaudin, p.xvi.

[62] See Jung, *Psychology and Alchemy*, vol. 12 of the *Collected Works*. Colette Gaudin discusses Bachelard's use of alchemy in *On Poetic Imagination and Reverie*, p.xv.

[63] Gaudin observes of Bachelard's "material imagination": "Materiality...is not a superfluous property added to images, not a characteristic quickly attributed to objects; it is the imaginary act itself, by means of which images acquire density, their wordly weight," *On Poetic Imagination and Reverie*, p.xxiv.

[64] Lacan, "Inmixing of Otherness," p.190.

[65] Ricoeur, *Freud and Philosophy*, pp.525-6.

BIBLIOGRAPHY

Abrams, Meyer H. *The Mirror and the Lamp: Romantic Theory and the Critical Tradition*. New York: W.W. Norton & Co., 1958.

----------, *Natural Supernaturalism: Tradition and Revolution in Romantic Literature*. New York: W.W. Norton & Co., 1973.

Alcott, Bronson, "Orphic Sayings." In *The Transcendentalists: An Anthology*. Ed. Perry Miller. Cambridge, Mass.: Harvard Univ. Press, 1950.

Anderson, Quentin. *The Imperial Self*. New York: Alfred A. Knopf, 1971.

Arvin, Newton. "The House of Pain." In *Emerson: A Collection of Critical Essays*. Ed. Milton R. Konvitz and Stephen E. Whicher. Englewood Cliffs, New Jersey: Prentice Hall, 1962.

Bachelard, Gaston. *On Poetic Imagination and Reverie: Selections from the Works of Gaston Bachelard*. Ed. and trans. Colette Gaudin. New York: Bobbs-Merrill Co., 1971.

----------, *The Poetics of Space*. Trans. Maria Jolas. Boston: Beacon Press, 1969.

Barthes, Roland. *The Pleasure of the Text*. Trans. Richard Miller. New York: Hill and Wang, 1975.

Bate, Walter Jackson, ed. *Criticism: The Major Texts*. New York: Harcourt Brace Jovanovich, 1970.

Bickman, Martin. *The Unsounded Centre: Jungian Studies in American Romanticism*. Chapel Hill, N.C.: Univ. of North Carolina Press, 1980.

Binswanger, Ludwig. "The Existential Analysis School of Thought." In *Existence: A New Dimension in Psychiatry and Psychology*. Ed. Rollo May, Ernest Angel, Henri Ellenberger. New York: Simon and Schuster, 1958.

Bishop, Jonathan. *Emerson on the Soul*. Cambridge, Mass.: Harvard Univ. Press, 1964.

Bloom, Harold. "The Breaking of Form." In *Deconstruction and Criticism*. Ed. Harold Bloom, Paul De Man, Jacques Derrida, Geoffrey Hartman, J. Hillis Miller. New York: Continuum Pub. Co., 1979.

----------, "Emerson: The Glory and Sorrows of American Romanticism." In *Romanticism: Vistas, Instances, Continuities*. Ed. David Thorburn and Geoffrey Hartman. Ithaca and London: Cornell Univ. Press, 1973.

----------, *Poetry and Repression: Revisionism from Blake to Stevens*. New Haven and London: Yale Univ. Press, 1976.

----------, *Wallace Stevens: The Poems of Our Climate*. Ithaca and London: Cornell Univ. Press, 1976.

Bowen, Francis. Review of Emerson. *The Christian Examiner*, XXI (Jan. 1837), 377-8. Rptd. in *Emerson's Nature -- Origin, Growth, Meaning*. Ed. Merton Sealts and Alfred Ferguson. New York: Dodd, Mead, and Co., 1969.

Burke, Kenneth. "I, Eye, Aye -- Emerson's Early Essay on 'Nature': Thoughts on the Machinery of Transcendence."

In *Transcendentalism and Its Legacy*. Ed. Myron Simon and Thornton H. Parson. Ann Arbor: Univ. of Mich. Press, 1966.

----------, *Language as Symbolic Action: Essays on Life, Literature, and Method*. Berkeley and Los Angeles: Univ. of California Press, 1966.

Campbell, Joseph. *The Hero With a Thousand Faces*. Cleveland and New York: World Pub. Co., Meridian Book, 1956.

Carlyle, Thomas. "Characteristics." In *Critical and Miscellaneous Essays*. New York: Charles Scribner's Sons, 1899.

----------, *Sartor Resartus: The Life and Opinions of Herr Teufelsdröckh*. Ed. Charles Frederick Harrold. New York: Odyssey Press, 1937.

Carpenter, Frederic. *Emerson Handbook*. New York: Hendricks House, 1953.

Cassirer, Ernst. *The Philosophy of Symbolic Forms*. Trans. Ralph Manheim. 3 vols. New Haven and London: Yale Univ. Press, 1955-7.

Cavell, Stanley. "Thinking of Emerson." *New Literary History* 11 (1979), 167-176.

Chase, Richard. *The American Novel and Its Tradition*. Garden City, New York: Doubleday, Anchor Book, 1957.

Cohn, Jan and Miles, Thomas H. "The Sublime: In Alchemy, Aesthetics and Psychoanalysis." *Modern Philology* 74 (Feb. 1977), 289-304.

Coleridge, Samuel Taylor. *Aids to Reflection*. In *The Complete Works of Samuel Taylor Coleridge*. Ed. W.G.T. Shedd

New York: Harper & Bros., 1884.

----------, Biographia Literaria. Ed. J. Shawcross. 2 vols. London: Oxford Univ. Press, 1965.

----------, Coleridge's Shakespearean Criticism. Ed. T.M. Raysor. 2 vols. Cambridge, Mass.; Harvard Univ. Press, 1930.

----------, The Statesman's Manual. In The Complete Works of Samuel Taylor Coleridge. Ed. W.G.T. Shedd. New York: Harper & Bros., 1884.

Coplestone, Frederick Jr. Modern Philosphy: Schopenhauer to Nietzsche. Volume 7, Part II of A History of Philosophy. Garden City, N.Y.: Doubleday, Image Book, 1965.

Cox, James M. "R.W. Emerson: The Circles of the Eye." In Emerson: Prophecy, Metamorphosis, and Influence. Ed. David Levin. New York: Columbia Univ. Press, 1975.

Crews, Frederick C. The Sins of the Fathers: Hawthorne's Psychological Themes. New York: Oxford Univ. Press, 1966.

De Man, Paul. Blindness and Insight: Essays on the Rhetoric of Contemporary Criticism. New York: Oxford Univ. Press, 1971.

De Quincey, Thomas. "Literature of Knowledge and Literature of Power." The North Briton Review, August 1848. In English Romantic Works. Ed. David Perkins. New York: Harcourt, Brace & World, 1967.

Edinger, Edward. Melville's Moby-Dick: A Jungian Commentary. New York: New Directions, 1978.

Eliot, T.S. Selected Essays. New Edition. New York; Harcourt, Brace & World, 1932.

Emerson, Ralph Waldo. The Collected Works of Ralph Waldo
Emerson. Ed. Alfred R. Ferguson and Robert E. Spiller.
Cambridge, Mass.: Harvard Univ. Press, 1971 -

----------, The Early Lectures of Ralph Waldo Emerson, 1833
- 1842. Ed. Stephen Whicher, Robert E. Spiller, Wallace
Williams. 3 vols. Cambridge, Mass.: Harvard Univ. Press,
1959-1972.

----------, The Journals and Miscellaneous Notebooks of
Ralph Waldo Emerson. Ed. William H. Gilman, Alfred R.
Ferguson, Merrel R. Davis, George Clark, Merton M. Sealts,
Harrison Hayford, Ralph H. Orth, A.W. Plumstead, and Jay
Parsons. Cambridge, Mass.: Harvard Univ. Press, 1960 - .

----------, The Complete Works of Ralph Waldo Emerson. Ed.
Edward Waldo Emerson. Boston: Houghton Mifflin Co.,
1903-4.

Feidelson, Charles Jr. Symbolism and American Literature.
Chicago and London: Univ. of Chicago Press, 1953.

Foucault, Michel. The Order of Things: An Archeology of the
Human Sciences. New York: Random House, Vintage Book,
1973.

Freud, Sigmund. The Standard Edition of the Complete Psychological Works of Sigmund Freud. Ed. James Strachey.
London: The Hogarth Press, 1948-1974.

Frye, Northrop. Anatomy of Criticism: Four Essays. 1957;
rptd. New York: Atheneum, 1967.

Gelpi, Albert. "Emerson: The Paradox of Organic Form." In
Emerson: Prophecy, Metamorphosis, and Influence. Ed.
David Levin. New York: Columbia Univ. Press, 1975.

Gras, Vernon, ed. *European Literary Theory and Practice: Existential Phenomenology to Structuralism*. New York: Dell, Delta Book, 1973.

Green, André. "The Unbinding Process." *New Literary History* 12 (Autumn 1980), 11-39.

Griffin, Susan. *Woman and Nature: The Roaring Inside Her*. New York: Harper & Row, 1980.

Harris, Kenneth Marc. *Carlyle and Emerson: Their Long Debate*. Cambridge, Mass.: Harvard Univ. Press, 1978.

Harris, William T. *The Genius and Character of Emerson*. Ed. Frank Sanborn. Boston and New York: Houghton Mifflin & Co., 1898. Excerpt rptd. in *Emerson's Nature -- Origin, Growth, Meaning*. Ed. Merton M. Sealts and Alfred R. Ferguson. New York: Dodd, Mead & Co., 1969.

Hartman, Geoffrey H. "Romanticism and Antiself-Consciousness." *Centennial Review* 6, No.4 (Fall 1962), 553-65. Rptd. in *Romanticism: Points of View*. Ed. R.F. Gleckner and G.E. Enscoe. Englewood Cliffs, N.J.: Prentice-Hall, 1970.

Hawthorne, Nathaniel. *The Centenary Edition of the Works of Nathaniel Hawthorne*. Ed. William Charvat, Roy Harvey Pearce, Claude M. Simpson. Columbus, Ohio: Ohio State Univ. Press, 1962 -

Hegel, G.W.F. *The Phenomenology of Mind*. Trans. J.B. Baillie. New York: Harper & Row, 1967.

Heidegger, Martin. *Basic Writings*. Ed. David F. Krell. New York: Harper & Row, 1977.

----------, *Poetry, Language, Thought*. Trans. Albert Hofstadter. New York: Harper & Row, 1971.

Hennelly, Mark. "Hawthorne's Opus Alchymicum: 'Ethan Brand.'" ESQ 22, No.2 (1976), 96-106.

Hillman, James. Re-Visioning Psychology. New York: Harper & Row, 1975.

Hoffman, Daniel. Form and Fable in American Fiction. New York: Norton, 1973.

Hull, Raymona E. "Hawhtorne and the Magic Elixir of Life: The Failure of a Gothic Theme." ESQ 18, No.2 (1972), 97-107.

Husserl, Edmund. Ideas: General Introduction to Pure Phenomenology. Trans. W.R. Boyce Gibson. New York: Collier, 1962.

James, Henry. The Art of the Novel: Critical Prefaces by Henry James. Ed. Richard P. Blackmur. New York: Charles Scribner's Sons, 1934.

Johnson, Edward. Johnson's Wonder-Working Providence, 1628-1651. Ed. J. Franklin Jameson. New York: Barnes & Noble, 1967.

Jung, Carl Gustav. The Collected Works of C.G. Jung. Ed. Sir Herbert Read et. al. Trans. R.F.C. Hull. Princeton Univ. Press: Bollingen Series XX, 1957-1979.

----------, The Portable Jung. Ed. Joseph Campbell. New York: Viking Press, 1971.

----------, Two Essays on Analytical Psychology. Trans. R.F.C. Hull. New York: Meridian, 1956.

Kaufmann, Walter. Nietzsche: Philosopher, Psychologist, Antichrist. Princeton, N.J.: Princeton Univ. Press, 1974.

Lacan, Jacques. Écrits: A Selection. Trans. Alan Sheridan. New York: Norton, 1977.

----------, "Of Structure as an Inmixing of an Otherness Prerequisite to Any Subject Whatever." In The Languages of Criticism and the Sciences of Man: The Structuralist Controversy. Ed. Richard Macksey and Eugenio Donato. Baltimore: Johns Hopkins Univ. Press, 1970.

Langbaum, Robert. The Mysteries of Identity. New York: Oxford Univ. Press, 1977.

Lévi-Strauss, Claude. Structural Anthropology. Trans. Claire Jacobson and Brooke Grundfest Schoepf. Garden City, N.Y.: Doubleday, Anchor Book, 1967.

Lewis, R.W.B. The American Adam: Innocence, Tragedy and Tradition in the Nineteenth Century. Chicago: Univ. of Chicago Press, 1959.

Lovejoy, Arthur O. The Great Chain of Being: A Study of the History of an Idea. 1933, rptd. Cambridge, Mass.: Harvard Univ. Press, 1976.

Magliola, Robert. Phenomenology and Literature: An Introduction. West Lafayette, Ind.: Purdue Univ. Press, 1977.

Matthiessen, F.O. American Renaissance: Art and Expression in the Age of Emerson and Whitman. London and New York: Oxford Univ. Press, 1941.

May, Rollo. Power and Innocence: A Search for the Sources of Violence. New York: Norton, 1972.

Melville, Herman. Pierre; or the Ambiguities. Vol. 7 of The Writings of Herman Melville. Ed. Harrison Hayford, Hershel Parker, G. Thomas Tanselle. Evanston and Chicago:

Northwestern Univ. Press and The Newberry Library, 1971.

Merleau-Ponty, Maurice. Sense and Non-Sense. Trans. Herbert L. Dreyfus and Patricia A. Dreyfus. Evanston, Ill.: Northwestern Univ. Press, 1964.

Miller, J. Hillis. "The Critic as Host." In Deconstruction and Criticism. Ed. Harold Bloom, Paul De Man, Jacques Derrida, Geoffrey Hartman, J. Hillis Miller. New York: Continuum, 1979.

Miller, Perry. Nature's Nation. Cambridge, Mass.: Harvard Univ. Press, 1967.

----------, The New England Mind. 1939; rptd. Boston: Beacon Press, 1961.

----------, ed. The Transcendentalists: An Anthology. Cambridge, Mass.: Harvard Univ. Press, 1950.

Milton, John. Complete Poems and Major Prose. Ed. Merritt Y. Hughes. Indianapolis: Bobbs-Merrill, Odyssey Press, 1957.

Murray, Henry A., ed. Herman Melville, Pierre; or the Ambiguities. New York: Hendricks House, 1949.

Neumann, Erich. The Origins and History of Consciousness. Trans. R.F.C. Hull. Princeton Univ. Press: Bollingen Series XLII, 1970.

Nietzsche, Friedrich. The Birth of Tragedy & The Case of Wagner. Ed. and trans. Walter Kaufmann. New York: Random House, Vintage Book, 1967.

----------, On the Genealogy of Morals & Ecce Homo. Ed. Walter Kaufmann. Trans. Kaufmann and R.J. Hollingdale. New York: Random House, Vintage Book, 1967.

----------, The Portable Nietzsche. Ed. and trans. Walter Kaufmann. New York: Viking Press, 1954.

----------, Selected Letters of Friedrich Nietzsche. Ed. and trans. Christopher Middleton. Chicago: Univ. of Chicago Press, 1969.

----------, The Will To Power. Ed. Walter Kaufmann. Trans. Kaufmann and R.J. Hollingdale. New York: Random House, Vintage Book, 1968.

Otto, Walter F. Dionysius: Myth and Cult. Trans. Robert B. Palmer. Bloomington: Indian Univ. Press, 1973.

Paul, Sherman. Emerson's Angle of Vision. Cambridge, Mass.: Harvard Univ. Press, 1952.

Perkins, David, ed. English Romantic Works. New York: Harcourt, Brace & World, 1967.

Porte, Joel. "Emerson, Thoreau, and the Double-Consciousness." New England Quarterly 41 (March 1968), 40-50.

----------, Representative Man: Ralph Waldo Emerson In His Time. New York: Oxford Univ. Press, 1979.

----------, The Romance in America. Middletown, Conn.: Wesleyan Univ. Press, 1969.

Pound, Ezra. The Cantos of Ezra Pound. New York: New Directions, 1973.

Reed, Sampson. Observations on the Growth of the Mind. 1826; rptd. New York: Arno Press, 1972.

Richardson, Robert D. Jr. Myth and Literature in the American Renaissance. Bloomington: Indiana Univ. Press, 1978.

Ricoeur, Paul. Freud and Philosophy: An Essay on Interpretation. Trans. Denis Savage. New Haven: Yale Univ. Press, 1970.

----------, The Philosophy of Paul Ricoeur: An Anthology of His Work. Ed. Charles E. Reagan and David Stewart. Boston: Beacon Press, 1978.

----------, The Symbolism of Evil. Trans. Emerson Buchanon. Boston: Beacon Press, 1969.

Schiller, Friedrich von. Naive and Sentimental Poetry; On The Sublime. Trans. Julius A. Elias. New York: Frederick Ungar, 1966.

Schlegel, Friedrich. Dialogue on Poetry and Literary Aphorisms. Ed. and trans. Ernst Behler and Roman Struc. Univ. Park and London: Penn. State Univ. Press, 1968.

Sealts, Merton M. Jr. and Ferguson, Alfred. Emerson's Nature-- Origin, Growth, Meaning. New York: Dodd, Mead & Co., 1969.

Shea, Daniel B. "Emerson and the American Metamorphosis." In Emerson: Prophecy, Metamorphosis, and Influence. Ed. David Levin. New York: Columbia Univ. Press, 1975.

Sheats, Paul D. The Making of Wordsworth's Poetry, 1785-1798. Cambridge, Mass.: Harvard Univ. Press, 1973.

Skene, Reg. The Cuchulain Plays of W.B. Yeats. New York: Columbia Univ. Press, 1974.

Stevens, Wallace. The Collected Poems of Wallace Stevens. New York: Alfred A. Knopf, 1965.

Stowe, Harriet Beecher. Uncle Tom's Cabin. New York: New American Library, Signet Classic, 1966.

Tatar, Maria. Spellbound: Studies on Mesmerism and Literature. Princeton, N.J.: Princeton Univ. Press, 1978.

Thoreau, Henry David. The Portable Thoreau. Ed. Carl Bode. New York: Viking Press, 1964.

Tillich, Paul. *The Courage To Be.* New Haven: Yale Univ. Press, 1952.

----------, *Love, Power, and Justice: Ontological Analyses and Ethical Applications.* New York and London: Oxford Univ. Press, 1954.

Trilling, Lionel. *Sincerity and Authenticity.* Cambridge, Mass.: Harvard Univ. Press, 1971.

The Upanishads. Trans. Juan Mascaró. New York: Penguin, 1965.

Van Leer, David M. "Aylmer's Library: Transcendental Alchemy in Hawthorne's 'The Birthmark.'" *ESQ* 22, No.4 (1976), 211-220.

Whyte, Lancelot Law. *The Unconscious Before Freud.* London: Tavistock Pub., 1962.

Wigglesworth, Michael. *The Diary of Michael Wigglesworth 1653-1657: The Conscience of a Puritan.* Ed. Edmund S. Morgan. Gloucester, Mass.: Peter Smith. 1970.

Yeats, William Butler. *Essays and Introductions.* New York: Collier Books, 1968.

For Product Safety Concerns and Information please contact our EU representative GPSR@taylorandfrancis.com
Taylor & Francis Verlag GmbH, Kaufingerstraße 24, 80331 München, Germany

www.ingramcontent.com/pod-product-compliance
Lightning Source LLC
Chambersburg PA
CBHW070237230426
43664CB00014B/2334